T0348380

RESEARCH IN ACCOUNTING REGULATION

RESEARCH IN ACCOUNTING REGULATION

Series Editor: Gary J. Previts

Recent Volumes:

RESEARCH IN ACCOUNTING REGULATION

EDITED BY

GARY J. PREVITS

Case Western Reserve University,
Cleveland, USA

ASSOCIATE EDITOR

THOMAS R. ROBINSON

University of Miami, Coral Gables, USA

ASSISTANT EDITOR

NANDINI CHANDAR

School of Management, Rutgers University, USA

2002

JAI
An Imprint of Elsevier Science

Amsterdam – London – New York – Oxford – Paris – Shannon – Tokyo

ELSEVIER SCIENCE Ltd
The Boulevard, Langford Lane
Kidlington, Oxford OX5 1GB, UK

First edition 2002

Library of Congress Cataloging in Publication Data
A catalog record from the Library of Congress has been applied for.

British Library Cataloguing in Publication Data
A catalogue record from the British Library has been applied for.

ISBN: 0-7623-0841-9
ISSN: 1052-0457 (Series)

⊗The paper used in this publication meets the requirements of ANSI/NISO Z39.48-1992 (Permanence of Paper).
Transferred to digital printing 2005
Printed and bound by Antony Rowe Ltd, Eastbourne

CONTENTS

PART II: RESEARCH REPORTS

PART III: PERSPECTIVES

PART IV: BOOK REVIEWS

EDITORIAL BOARD

ix

LIST OF CONTRIBUTORS

Lawrence J. Abbott	Fogelman College of Business and Economics, University of Memphis, USA
Ashton C. Bishop	James Madison University, USA
Kevin Carduff	Weatherhead School of Management, Case Western Reserve University, USA
Jeffrey R. Casterella	Colorado State University, USA
Orhan Celik	University of Ankara, Turkey
Charles P. Cullinan	Bryant College, USA
Timothy J. Fogarty	Weatherhead School of Management, Case Western Reserve University, USA
Julia Grant	Weatherhead School of Management, Case Western Reserve University, USA
Aim-orn Jaikengkit	Weatherhead School of Management, Case Western Reserve University, USA
Barry L. Lewis	University of Colorado at Boulder, USA
Garen Markarian	Weatherhead School of Management, Case Western Reserve University, USA
Jimmy W. Martin	University of Montevallo, USA
Albert L. Nagy	Boler School of Business, John Carroll University, USA

Nancy B. Nichols	James Madison University, USA
Larry Parker	Weatherhead School of Management, Case Western Reserve University, USA
Susan Parker	Santa Clara University, USA
Gary John Previts	Weatherhead School of Management, Case Western Reserve University, USA
Reed Roig	Weatherhead School of Management, Case Western Reserve University, USA
Mark Segal	Mitchell College of Business, University of South Alabama, USA
Donna L. Street	James Madison University, USA
Lynn E. Turner	U.S. Securities and Exchange, Commission, USA
Frank R. Urbancic	Mitchell College of Business, USA
David R. Vruwink	Kansas State University, USA
Wanda A. Wallace	College of William and Mary, USA
Paul Walker	University of Virginia, USA

INVITED REFEREES

Aaron Ames
Ernst & Young, LLP, Canada

Kristen L. Anderson
Georgetown University

Robert Bricker
Case Western Reserve University

Dale Buckmaster
University of Delaware

Salvador Carmona
*Juan Carlos III University,
Madrid*

Orhan Celik
University of Ankara

A. Rick Elam
University of Mississippi

Tonya K. Flesher
University of Mississippi

Ross Fuerman
Northeastern University

Sabam Hutajulu
Case Western Reserve University

Terrence B. O'Keefe
University of Queensland

Jimmy W. Martin
University of Montevallo

David Pearson
Public Oversight Board

Reed Roig
Case Western Reserve University

Jay Rothberg
American Institute of CPAs

Mark Segal
University of South Alabama

Tom Tyson
St. John Fisher College

Steve Young
*Financial Accounting Standards
Board*

PART I:
MAIN PAPERS

SEGMENT DISCLOSURES UNDER SFAS 131: IMPACT ON THE BANKING INDUSTRY

Nancy B. Nichols, Ashton C. Bishop and Donna L. Street

ABSTRACT

This research reviews the 1997 and 1998 annual reports of the U.S.'s largest banks to determine whether SFAS 131 adequately addressed user concerns about segment disclosures and the extent to which the anticipated benefits set forth in SFAS 131 materialized. The findings reveal that segment reporting in the banking industry has improved. For example, the number of segments reported and the consistency of segment information with the introductory annual report material and MD&A increased significantly in 1998 as compared to 1997. The findings also reveal that 28 of the nation's largest banks provided reportable operating segment disclosures in 1998 although the same banks previously provided no segmental data in the footnotes of their financial statements. Thus, the SEC's recent focus on segmental reporting combined with the release of SFAS 131 have all but ended many banks' tendency to provide no segmental data in the notes to their financial statements.

On a less positive note, the banking industry continues to utilize the board, vague geographic groupings for which SFAS 14 was criticized. Few banks provided reportable segment data or enterprise wide information

Research in Accounting Regulation, Volume 15, pages 3–37.
ISBN: 0-7623-0841-9

based on meaningful geographic groups. The findings also reveal the lack of comparability resulting from the FASB's decision not to define segment profit or loss. Additionally, the findings suggest that the FASB and/or AICPA should provide guidance regarding the format banks should utilize to report segment revenues.

INTRODUCTION

Research addressing segment reporting under Statement of Financial Accounting Standard (SFAS) 14 highlighted a number of problem areas. These included too much scope for managerial discretion in regard to segment identification and the lack of consistency of reportable segments with a company's organization structure and internal reporting system (Solomons, 1968; Gray & Radebaugh, 1984). Based on an examination of segment reporting in the banking industry, Tyson and Jacobs (1987) concluded that as a result of preparer discretion comparability was adversely affected and because of the manner in which the disclosures were made there were indications that understandability and decision usefulness were unfavorably affected. In another study of the banking industry, Phillips and Brezovec (1998) reported that most financial institutions concluded that under SFAS 14 they operated in one industry segment; therefore, few provided reportable segment disclosures in the notes to their financial statements.

The potential for improving segment reporting was discussed in the report *Improving Business Reporting – A Customer Focus*, by the American Institute of Certified Public Accountants (AICPA) Special Committee on Financial Reporting (1994). Indeed the AICPA Committee listed improvements in business segment information as its first recommendation for improving business reporting. The Committee's list of the most important improvements needed in segment reporting included:

- Greater number of segments for some enterprises.
- More information about segments.
- Segmentation that corresponds to internal management reports.
- Consistency of segment information with other parts of an annual report.

Regarding the first concern, the AICPA Special Committee stated "[users] believe that many companies define industry segments too broadly for business reporting and thus report on too few industry segments" (p. 69).

The Association for Investment Management Research (AIMR) also expressed concerns about segment reporting under SFAS 14. In a position paper, the AIMR stated:

> FAS 14 requires disclosure of line-of-business information classified by "industry segment." Its definition of segment is necessarily imprecise, recognizing that there are numerous practical problems in applying that definition to different business entities operating under disparate circumstances. That weakness in FAS 14 has been exploited by many enterprises to suit their own financial reporting purposes. As a result, we have seen one of the ten largest firms in the country report all its operations as being in a single, very broadly defined industry segment (AIMR, 1993, p. 60).

The AIMR and other financial statement users also argued that segment information is more useful if it is enhanced by explanatory information provided elsewhere in the annual report (FASB, 1996). They stated that the business review section and the chairman's letter in the annual report frequently discuss the company's operations on a basis that is not consistent with the segment footnote information and MD&A which is required by SEC rules to correspond to the SFAS 14 information. The AIMR further argued that disaggregation based on the internal organization structure should facilitate consistent discussion of segment data and results throughout a company's annual report.

To address the concerns of financial statement users, the Financial Accounting Standards Board (FASB) issued SFAS 131, *Reporting Disaggregated Information about a Business Enterprise*, in 1997. SFAS 131 became effective for fiscal years beginning on or after January 1, 1998. The new accounting standard requires companies to report disaggregated information about reportable segments based on management's organization of the enterprise. Reportable segments may be based on lines of business (LOB), geographic location, or a combination of line of business and geographic location (mixed). For each reportable segment, an enterprise must provide information about:

- *segment profit/loss and certain revenues and expenses included in segment profit/loss* (to include revenues, interest revenue, interest expense, depreciation/depletion/amortization, amount of non-cash items other than depreciation/amortization that are included in the determination of segment profit/loss, unusual items, equity in the net income of investees accounted for by the equity method, income tax expense/benefit, and extraordinary items), and
- *segment assets* (to include assets, expenditures for additions to segment assets, and the amount of investment in equity method investees included in segment assets).

The FASB (1997) noted an enterprise may not be divided into components with similar products/services or geographic areas for managerial purposes and many users would prefer disaggregation on one of those bases. Instead of requiring an alternative to segmentation based on management structure, the Board elected to require enterprise wide disclosures of additional information about products/

services and geographic operations if the basic reportable operating segment disclosures do not provide this information. For each reportable operating segment that has not been determined based on differences in products/services, SFAS 131 requires disclosure of revenues derived from transactions with external customers from each product/service or each group of similar product/service. Similarly, for each operating segment that has not been determined based on geography, the enterprise must disclose revenues and long-lived assets for each geographic region.

SFAS 131 represents a significant modification in US segment reporting guidelines. SFAS 14 defined reportable industry segments based on related products and services and also required limited disclosures for geographic regions and major customers. Alternatively, SFAS 131 requires companies to base reportable operating segments on the organization's internal structure, which is not necessarily by industry. In addition, SFAS 131 requires limited enterprise wide disclosures for: (1) related products and services, (2) geographic regions, and (3) major customers. Figure 1 compares the disclosure requirements of SFAS 14 and SFAS 131. Utilizing the 1998 segment reporting of JP Morgan, Figure 2 provides an illustration of SFAS 131's two-tier disclosure approach whereby companies provide reportable segment data and/or enterprise wide data.

In its Basis for Conclusions, FASB (1997) states that the Board believes the primary benefits of SFAS 131 include:

- Some enterprises will report a greater number of segments.
- Most enterprises will report more items of information about each segment.
- Enterprises will report segments that correspond to internal management reports.
- Enterprises will report segment information that will be consistent with other parts of their annual report.

For the banking industry, the current research addresses the extent to which user concerns were addressed by SFAS 131 and if the above benefits materialized.

RESEARCH QUESTIONS

To provide information about the application of SFAS 131 in the banking industry and to determine whether SFAS 131 addressed user concerns regarding segment reporting under SFAS 14, the current study addresses the following research questions:

1. In practice, what types of reportable segments are disclosed by banks under SFAS 131 (LOB, geographic, mixed)?

SFAS 131	SFAS 14
Reportable Operating Segments	**Reportable Industry Segments**
Determined by organizational structure using management approach (can be based on LOB or geographic region or a combination of LOB and geographic region)	Determined by grouping products and services by industry line
Required Disclosures include information about:	Required Disclosures include:
(1) Segment profit/loss (including revenues, interest revenue, interest expense, depreciation/depletion/ and amortization, unusual items, equity in the net income of investees accounted for by the equity method, extraordinary items, and significant noncash items) (2) Segment assets (including amount of investment in equity method investees and capital expenditures)	(1) Revenues (2) Operating profit or loss (3) Identifiable assets (4) Other Related Information (including depreciation/depletion/amortization, capital expenditures, equity in income and investment in equity method investees, effect of change in accounting principle)
Enterprise Wide Disclosures	**Foreign operations**
All companies, including those with one reportable operating segment, must disclose data about:	For each foreign operation disclose: (1) Revenues (2) Profitability information (3) Identifiable Assets

(1) Products and services
   (a) revenues from external customers
(2) Geographic Areas
   (a) revenues from external customers attributed to the country of domicile and attributed to all countries in total. If revenues from any individual country are material, those revenues are disclosed separately.
   (b) long-lived assets located in the country of domicile and located in all other countries. If assets in any individual country are material, those assets are disclosed separately.
(3 Major Customers
   (a) fact that revenues from any one customer account for more than 10% of total, total revenues from each such customer, and identity of the segment(s) reporting the revenues.
	Major Customers
	
	Disclose fact that revenues from any one customer account for more than 10% of total, total revenues from each such customer, and identity of the segment(s) reporting the revenues.

Fig. 1. Comparison of SFAS 131 and SFAS 14 Disclosure Requirements.
LOB: Line of business

NANCY B. NICHOLS, ASHTON C. BISHOP AND DONNA L. STREET

LOB BASED REPORTABLE OPERATING SEGMENTS

Disclosures Provided	Investment Banking	Equities	Foreign Exchange	Interest Rate Markets	Credit Markets	Credit Portfolio	Global Finance	Asset Management and Servicing	Equity Investment	Proprietary Investing and Trading
Net interest revenues	XX	XX	XX	XX	XX	XX	XX	XX	XX	XX
Non-interest revenues	XX	XX	XX	XX	XX	XX	XX	XX	XX	XX
Total revenues	XX	XX	XX	XX	XX	XX	XX	XX	XX	XX
Total expenses	XX	XX	XX	XX	XX	XX	XX	XX	XX	XX
Pretax income	XX	XX	XX	XX	XX	XX	XX	XX	XX	XX
Non-cash amounts incl. in pretax income	XX	XX	XX	XX	XX	XX	XX	XX	XX	XX
Assets	XX	XX	XX	XX	XX	XX	XX	XX	XX	XX

ENTERPRISE WIDE SEGMENT DATA

Product/Services Enterprise Wide Segment Data

Disclosures	Global Finance	Asset Management and Servicing	Proprietary Investments
Net interest revenues	XX	XX	XX
Trading revenue	XX	XX	
Investment banking revenue	XX	XX	XX
Investment management revenue	XX	XX	XX
Fees and commissions	XX	XX	XX
Investment securities revenue	XX	XX	XX
Other revenue	XX	XX	XX
Total non-interest revenue	XX	XX	
Total revenues	XX	XX	XX

Geographic Region Enterprise Wide Segment Data			
Disclosure	Europe	Asia-Pacific	Latin America
Total Assets	XX	XX	XX
Total Revenues	XX	XX	XX
Total expenses	XX	XX	XX
Pretax income	XX	XX	XX
Income tax expense	XX	XX	XX
Net income	XX	XX	XX

Fig. 2. Illustration of SFAS 131's Two-Tiered Approach: Reportable Operating Segments and Enterprise Wide Disclosures for JP Morgan.

2. Has SFAS 131 resulted in the reporting of a greater number of LOB segments by banks? In particular, has the number of banks claiming to operate in only one LOB declined?
3. Under SFAS 131, what specific items do banks disclose for LOB based reportable segments, and to what extent do these include voluntary disclosures? Are banks reporting more items of information about each segment than they did under SFAS 14?
4. Under SFAS 131, what types of enterprise wide data are banks reporting?
5. For the banking industry, has SFAS 131 improved the consistency of segment information with other parts of the annual report?
6. Under SFAS 131, what comments do members of the banking industry provide in their footnote disclosures regarding the "forced" allocations associated with segment reporting? Do some members of the industry continue to question the reliability of segment disclosures as they did under SFAS 14?

Research Question 1: Types of SFAS 131 Reportable Operating Segments Disclosed by Banks

SFAS 131 allows companies to base reportable segments on LOB, geographic region, or a mix of LOB and geographic region based on organizational structure. The research will reveal how SFAS 131 is applied in practice by the banking industry and thereby will provide valuable information on how the nation's largest banks are managed.

Research Question 2: SFAS 131 Impact on Number of LOB Segments

Expectations were that SFAS 131 would have a significant impact on the number of segments reported in the banking industry. The Bank Holding Act of 1956, as amended, defines permissible activities that are a natural incident to banking (AICPA, 1984). Traditionally, banks tended to believe these permissible activities consisted of services closely related to banking and thus they constituted a single industry segment. Hence, under SFAS 14, the majority of the nation's largest banks claimed to operate in one LOB (see Phillips & Brezovec, 1998). Alternatively, a few banks with significant permissible activities such as mortgage banking, consumer finance, and title insurance disclosed separately financial information related to such activities (AICPA, 1984).

While the aggregation criteria of SFAS 131 leave some room for subjectivity, they nonetheless represent a formidable hurdle for aggregation as all the aggregation criteria must be met in order to report two or more material segments on a combined (aggregated) basis.[1] Hence, expectations would be that the number of banks aggregating permissible activities and claiming to operate in one LOB under SFAS 131 would be drastically reduced.

Research Question 3: Items of Information Supplied for
Reportable Segments Under SFAS 131

Cates and Lewin (1999) argue the SFAS 131 guidelines for reporting segment revenues do not adequately address the unique nature of the banking industry. While SFAS 131 does require separate disclosure of net interest income for all companies, there is no requirement to distinguish externally generated from internally generated revenue. This is because in a typical industry for which the accounting standard was written, finance is seen as supporting sales. Alternatively, in banking the majority of net interest income is indeed revenue from bona fide sales. Cates and Lewin argue this creates a problem of interpretation for the banking industry that SFAS 131 does not address.

Cates and Lewin (1999) further contend banking is the only customer-focused industry whose official financials neither define nor summarize total revenue. Based on a 1983 SEC bank reporting mandate, the AICPA Audit and Accounting Guide for Banks and Savings Institutions refers to the following categories related to banking revenues: interest income, interest expense, net interest income, provision for loan losses, net interest income after provision for loan losses, non-interest income, and non-interest expense. These groupings provided by the AICPA do not summarize the two basic streams of bank revenue: net interest income (arising from spread management) and non-interest income (primarily from managing or servicing product volumes, both on and off the balance sheet). Additionally, there is no consensus regarding the most appropriate measure of net interest income (before or after loss provision). The SEC's 1983 rules (which bind the AICPA) do not specify which categorization is preferable. However, informally, total revenue in the banking industry is the sum of net interest income and non-interest income, exclusive of loss provision. This informal distinction enjoys widespread acceptance among bank executives and financial analysts at credit rating agencies and brokerage firms. In addressing Research Question No. 3, this research will reveal how, in the absence of official guidance from the FASB or the AICPA, the largest banks in the US satisfy the SFAS 131 requirements that revenues, interest income, and interest expense be disclosed.

When the FASB voted on SFAS 131, then Vice-Chairman Leisenring dissented because the statement does not define segment profit or loss and does not require that whatever measure of profit or loss is reported be consistent with the attribution of assets to reportable segments. By not defining segment profit or loss, SFAS 131 allows any measure of performance to be displayed as segment profit or loss as long as that measure is reviewed by the chief operating decision-maker. Street, Nichols and Gray (2000) reveal that segmental reporting outside the finance industry illustrates the lack of comparability resulting from FASB's decision not to define segment profit or loss. In addressing Research Question No. 3, the current research will reveal whether this lack of comparability in regard to reporting a measure of segment profit or loss is also characteristic of the banking industry.

Research Question 4: Enterprise Wide Segment Data Disclosures Under SFAS 131

The research will reveal whether banks utilized meaningful geographic groupings under SFAS 131 or if they have continued to utilize the broad, vague geographic groupings that were associated with SFAS 14. SFAS 14 did not provide a precise definition of geographic segments leaving the question of segment identification subject to managerial discretion. According to the statement:

> Foreign geographical areas are individual countries or groups of countries as may be determined to be appropriate in an enterprise's particular circumstances. Factors to be considered include proximity, economic affinity, similarities in business environments and the nature, scale and degree of interrelationship of the enterprise's operations in the various countries (FASB, 1976, para. 34).

In response to SFAS 14's somewhat general guidelines, companies tended to aggregate on a continental or multi-continental basis. In a study of geographic disclosures by U.S. and U.K. firms, Gray and Radebaugh (1984) provided illustrations of geographic segments identified by US multinationals. These included:

- U.S./Other Western Hemisphere/Europe and Middle East/Africa/Pacific.
- U.S./Western Hemisphere/Eastern Hemisphere.
- U.S./Europe/Western Hemisphere/Africa, Asia, and Pacific.
- U.S./Europe and Africa/Canada and Latin America/Asia and Pacific.
- U.S./Other Western Hemisphere/Europe/ Eastern Hemisphere.
- U.S./Europe, Africa and Middle East/Americas and Far East.

Gray and Radebaugh argued that this tendency toward a high level of aggregation was unlikely to be informative given the different economic and political environments and risk factors involved.

Tyson and Jacobs (1987) also addressed the aggregation problem and reported that, in a study of the banking industry, one company grouped as one segment all of its operations in Asia, the Middle East, and North Africa combined. Three companies displayed two segments, Asia and Middle East/Africa. Two additional companies reported two segments utilizing the categories Asia – Pacific and Other. Tyson and Jacobs also noted that groupings by region overlapped between firms (i.e. one firm provided disclosures for Asia, Middle East and North Africa combined, while others reported separately for Asia and the Middle East). The authors argued that the different choices made by preparers in the banking industry did not enhance comparability. They concluded that while SFAS 14 may have been applied correctly by the sample companies, the results were not comparable between homogeneous firms in the same industry.

Research Question 5: Impact of SFAS 131 on Consistency of Segment Information with Other Parts of the Annual Report

As noted previously, prior research revealed inconsistencies between SFAS 14 data and other sections of the annual report (FASB, 1997). For example, segment disclosures are considered inconsistent when additional segment information is included in the introductory annual report information (i.e. letter to share-holder's, etc.) or MD&A but not in the segment footnote. The AIMR and other users argue that segment information is more useful if it is consistent with explanatory information provided elsewhere in the annual report. They noted that under SFAS 14 the business review section and the chairman's letter in an annual report often discussed the enterprise's operations on a basis differ-ence from that of the segment information in the notes to the financial statements. Additionally, numerous examples abound of MD&A discussion that was inconsistent with SFAS 14 disclosures (see Street, Nichols & Gray, 2000) despite SEC requirements that the MD&A correspond to SFAS 14 (now SFAS 131) disclosures. The results will reveal if, as anticipated by FASB and finan-cial statement users, segmentation based on the internal organization structure facilitates consistent discussion of segment financial results throughout the annual report for the banking industry.

Research Question 6: Comments Regarding Reliability of SFAS 131 Disclosures

Tyson and Jacobs (1987) reported that comments regarding SFAS 14 geographic disclosures included in the footnotes of banks suggested a serious concern over reliability. Examples of such disclosures included:

- Allocations of certain income and expense items are necessarily based on *assumptions* and *subjective* criteria.
- It is difficult to *estimate* the amount of assets . . . attributable to international activities. Such amounts are based on internal allocations which are necessarily *subjective*.
- ". . . Thus, *subjective* judgements . . . were used to derive operating results."[2]

The current research will reveal whether such assertions questioning the reliability of segment disclosures continue under SFAS 131. This is a key concern as one of the primary qualitative characteristics of financial information according to Statement of Financial Accounting Concepts No. 2 is reliability.

SAMPLE SELECTION AND METHODOLOGY

Annual reports for 1997 and 1998 were attained for the 41 US domiciled banks included in the Business Week Global 1000 and/or the Fortune 500. A member of the research team analyzed each annual report, and a data sheet based on the research questions was completed. To promote accuracy of the data, each annual report was re-examined by a second researcher. Table 1 provides descriptive statistics for the banks included in the sample.[3] A list of the banks is included in the Appendix.

FINDINGS AND DISCUSSION

Research Question 1: Types of SFAS 131 Reportable Operating Segments Disclosed by Banks

SFAS 131 allows companies to base reportable segments on LOB, geographic region, or a mix of LOB and geographic region. As illustrated in Table 2, the majority (36) of banks are managed, and hence determine reportable segments, based on LOB. More discussion of these LOB based reportable segments is provided in the following sections.

Only one bank, Golden West Financial, claimed to operate in a single reportable segment during 1998. Additionally, only Regions Bank determined reportable segments based solely on geographic location. Interestingly, all of Regions' geographic segments were based in the US (Central; North; Northeast; South; Southwest; and West). In other industries, geographic based reportable segments tend to represent non-domestic operations (see Nichols, Street & Gray, 2000).

Three banks determined reportable segments based on a mix of LOB and geographic location.[4] SunTrust's reportable segments included two LOB

Table 1. Sample Descriptive Statistics.

(in millions)	Mean	Median	Minimum	Maximum	Standard Deviation
Total Revenue 1997	9,052	3,175	1,215	72,306	13,841
Total Revenue 1998	9,758	3,501	1,331	73,431	14,540
Interest Income 1997	6,475	2,716	582	42,101	9,025
Interest Income 1998	6,861	2,892	769	6,239	9,551
Non-interest Income 1997	2,637	935	81	30,205	5,074
Non-interest Income 1998	2,960	1,249	138	30,192	5,166
Total Assets 1997	100,566	39,590	4,449	697,384	145,531
Total Assets 1998	106,258	47,082	7,231	668,641	147,212
Foreign Revenues 1997*	2,040	1,348	437	5,142	1,502
Foreign Revenues 1998*	1,797	1,126	221	4,322	1,533
Foreign Assets 1997*	35,214	16,937	3,260	130,851	40,443
Foreign Assets 1998*	48,323	32,918	4,372	112,915	41,965

* For firms with foreign revenues and/or assets.

(Crestar and Other)[5] and three US based geographic regions (Florida, Georgia, and Tennessee). Again, a member of the banking industry, SunTrust, has geographic reportable segments based on domestic regions; whereas, non-domestic geographic groupings are the norm in other industries.

Bank Boston's reportable segments included three LOB (Wholesale Bank; Regional Bank; and Other Businesses)[6] and two geographic regions (Argentina and Brazil). Bank Boston's geographic reportable segments are noteworthy, as both are country specific. Outside the banking industry, country specific segment information tends to be provided only at the enterprise wide level (see Nichols, Street & Gray, 2000).

Table 2. Types of Reportable Segments Reported in 1998 Under SFAS 131.

Type of Segment	Number of Companies
LOB	36
GEO	1
Mixed	3
One	1
Total	41

Notes:

LOB – Reportable segments based on lines of business.

GEO – Reportable segments based on geographic areas.

Mixed – Reportable segments based on a combination of lines of business and geographic areas.

One – Company had only one reportable segment.

Seven LOB were reported by Banker's Trust (Investment Banking; Trading & Sales; Emerging Market's Group; Private Client Services Group; Global Institutional Services; Australia/New Zealand/International Funds Management; and Other Business Segments). Banker's Trust's Emerging Markets Group LOB was split into three reportable geographic regions (Latin America; Middle East and Africa; and Asia) for a total of nine reportable segments.

In several instances within the banking industry, categorization of reportable segments as geographic or LOB is not obvious from the segment name provided by the bank. Such categorizations for this research are based on careful consideration of the segment descriptions provided in the footnotes. Examples include Bankers Trust's Global Institutional Services and Australia/New Zealand/International Funds Management segments. The Australia/New Zealand/International Funds Management reportable segment provides funds management, corporate finance, and financial markets services to local and international clients, and trades for its own account in related markets and is hence a LOB. The Global Institutional Services reportable segment provides asset management services, corporate trust and agency services, cash management services and trade finance services to financial institutions, corporations and governments and their agencies around the world. The segment's asset management services include: custody, investment management, securities lending, brokerage, retirement administration, performance and risk measurement. The segment also provides trustee, depository and trade services to include global payments and collections, cash concentration and investments and trade finance products. Again, the description denotes a LOB.

Research Question 2: SFAS 131 Impact on Number of LOB Segments

Fewer Banks Claim to Operate in One LOB

The research findings indicate SFAS 131 was effective in increasing the number of LOB segments reported by most banks, particularly those that provided no segment data in their footnotes under SFAS 14. Under SFAS 14, 30 banks provided no segment data in their 1997 footnotes. Illustrating the impact of SFAS 131's organizational structure approach to defining reportable segments, only one of these banks, Golden West Financial, disclosed no reportable segments in 1998 (see Table 3). Suggesting that its claim to operate in one LOB provides an accurate illustration of Golden West's operations, the 1997 and 1998 introductory annual report material and MD&A were both consistent with the bank's claim to operate in one LOB.

Under SFAS 131, 28 of the 29 remaining banks that provided no segment data in their 1997 footnotes disclosed reportable segments based on LOB in

Table 3.   Impact of SFAS 131. Change in Number of Reportable Segments from 1997 to 1998.

No Change	3
Increased from 1 segment in 1997	29
Increase in Number	2
Decrease in Number	1
Same Number, Different Segments	1
Involved in major merger in 1998 that altered reportable segments	4*
One in both years	1
Total	41
Average Number of Segments – 1997	1.5
Average Number of Segments – 1998	4.6**

* BankAmerica, Citigroup, Sun Trust, First Star.
** Average increase in number of segments significant at $p = 0.0000$ ($t = 8.13$).

1998.[7] These included several of the U.S.'s largest banks. In 1997, Banc One Corporation (the 3rd largest bank in the U.S., ranked 59th in the 1998 U.S. Global 1000) disclosed no segment data in its footnotes. In 1998, Banc One provided reportable segment data for five LOB (Commercial Banking; Credit Card; Retail Banking; Finance One; and Other Activities). While providing no segment data in its 1997 footnotes, First Union (the 5th largest bank in the U.S., ranked 41st in the U.S. Global 1000) disclosed information for four LOB in 1998 (Consumer Bank; Capital Management; Commercial Bank; and Capital Markets). Omission of segment data in the 1997 footnotes by these two banks was inconsistent with both their introductory annual report material and MD&A. Alternatively, the 1998 introductory annual report material and MD&A were consistent with Banc One's five reportable LOB and First Unions' four reportable LOB. Overall, the research findings indicate SFAS 131 was effective in reducing the number of large banks that inappropriately report as single LOB firms.

Overall Increase in the Number of Reportable Segments
Table 3 compares the number of reportable segments disclosed in 1998 to the number of LOB reported in 1997.[8] SFAS 131 had a marked impact on the number of reportable segments disclosed. Along with the 29 banks that moved from providing no segment data in their 1997 footnotes to supplying reportable segment footnote data, two additional banks increased the number of reportable segments they disclosed in 1998. For example, Fifth Third Bancorp supplied data for five LOB (Retail Banking; Commercial Banking; Investment Advisory Services; Data Processing; and Other) in 1997. In 1998, Fifth Third Bancorp

disclosed data for six reportable segments based on LOB (Retail Banking; Commercial Banking; Investment Advisory Services; Data Processing; Acquired Entities; and Other). Overall, 31 of the 37 (84%) banks that had not been involved in a major merger (that altered segment composition) had an increase in the number of reportable segments that may be linked to adoption of SFAS 131.[9] For the 37 banks not involved in a major merger, the average number of reportable segments disclosed in 1998 was 4.6 compared to an average of 1.5 LOB reported during 1997. A t-test indicates this increase is significant at $p = 0.0000$ ($t = 8.13$).[10] Hence, the FASB was correct in anticipating that one of the primary benefits of SFAS 131 would be that some companies would report a greater number of segments.

For three banks, the number of reportable segments disclosed in 1998 was the same as the number of LOB disclosed in 1997. In both 1997 and 1998, First Tennessee National Bank provided information for four LOB (Regional Banking Group; Mortgage Banking; Capital Markets; and Transaction Markets). In both years, Chase Manhattan disclosed three LOB segments (Global Bank; National Consumer Services; and Chase Technology Solutions). For both Chase Manhattan and First Tennessee, the number of LOB segments disclosed in both 1997 and 1998 parallel the information in MD&A and the annual report taken as a whole.

While Bankers Trust disclosed the same number of segments in both 1997 and 1998, the composition of the segments changed. In 1997, Bankers Trust supplied only geographic segment data in the footnotes to the financial statements. However, the footnote on international operations referred to the MD&A where segment information based on "how management views the operations of the corporation" was provided. The 1997 MD&A of Bankers Trust provided information on several broad organizational units. These were organized around five LOB (Investment Banking; Risk Management Services; Trading and Sales; Private Client Services Group; and Global Institutional Services). Three additional units represent geographical regions (Australia/New Zealand; Asia; and Latin American). Bankers Trust also reported a segment labeled Other for a total of nine. In 1998, Bankers Trust also provided data for nine segments but the composition changed moderately (see description above).

The number of reported LOB decreased for only one bank. In 1997, Wells Fargo disclosed segment data for seven LOB (Retail Distribution Group; Business Banking Group; Investment Group; Real Estate Group; Whole Products Group; Consumer Lending; and Other). Wells Fargo decreased the number of reportable LOB segments to four (Community Banking; Wholesale Banking; Mortgage Banking; and Norwest Banking) in

1998. The introductory annual report material and MD&A were consistent with the segment information supplied by Wells Fargo in both 1997 and 1998.

Research Question 3: Items of Information Supplied for Reportable Segments Under SFAS 131

For 1998, Table 4 summarizes the specific items of reportable segment data provided by banks. As a general purpose accounting standard, SFAS 131

Table 4. Number of Companies Disclosing Specific Items.

	Basis of Reportable Segments		
Item Disclosed:	LOB	Mixed	GEO
Revenue Disclosures:			
Net interest income (net of interest expense)	33	3	1
Non-interest income	21	2	1
Intersegment revenue	7	1	0
Other income	10	0	0
Expense Disclosures:			
Interest Expense	10	1	0
Provision for loan losses	23	3	1
Income tax expense	29	3	1
Non-interest expense	23	2	1
Restructuring/merger costs	6	0	0
Profit Measure Disclosures:			
Net income	29	3	1
Income before taxes	19	2	0
Other profit measure*	6	0	0
Other Disclosures:			
Total assets	35	3	1
Average loans	9	0	0
Depreciation/Amortization	9	1	0
Capital expenditures	7	1	0
Average deposits	11	0	0
Average equity	6	0	0
Ratio disclosures	12	0	0
Total Firms	36	3	1

* Other profit measures include one each: income before tax and capital charge, cash operating earnings, operating profit, tangible net income, profit or loss, and income before non-recurring items.

requires the disclosure of revenues, interest income, interest expense, income tax expense/benefit, and a measure of segment profit or loss, with no specific guidance provided for the banking industry. In compliance with SFAS 131, all the sample banks disclosed a measure of segment revenue and a measure of segment profit/loss.

In regard to segment revenues, all but three banks labeled the primary source of revenue as "net interest income." Northern Trust and Washington Mutual deviated somewhat from the norm and reported "net interest income after a provision for credit losses." Citigroup disclosed "total revenue net of interest expense" as a primary source of revenue. Sixty-eight percent (27) of the banks additionally reported provision for loan losses, and 28% (11) disclosed interest expense.

In addition to reporting a measure(s) of interest income, 60% (24) reported non-interest income. Other sources of revenue supplied on a reoccurring basis by the banks included inter-segment revenue (20%, 8 banks), and other income (25%, 10 banks). These results indicate the banking industry is fairly consistent in its presentation of segment revenues under SFAS 131. However, in line with Cates and Lewin (1999), guidance from the FASB and/or AICPA in regard to the application of SFAS 131 in the banking industry could assist in eliminating the few inconsistencies identified by the research findings.

As required by SFAS 131, 83% (33) disclosed income tax expense. Non-interest expense was disclosed by 65% (26) of the banks. SFAS 131 also requires the disclosure of unusual items as defined by APB Opinion No. 30. In response, 15% (6) of the banks disclosed costs associated with restructuring or merger activity.

Given the flexibility SFAS 131 allows in regard to the measurement of operating profit, several categorizations were used by the banks. The majority (83%, 33 banks) reported segmental net income. The method for determining segmental net income was generally not disclosed. Others utilized categorizations such as income before taxes, income before tax and capital charge, cash operating earnings, operating profit, tangible net income, profit or loss, and income before recurring items. The findings, which are consistent with other industries (see Street, Nichols & Gray, 2000) illustrate the lack of comparability resulting from FASB's decision not to define segment profit or loss.

SFAS 131 requires the disclosure of a measure of segment assets. In response, 98% (39) reported total or average segment assets. The remaining bank, First Union alternatively disclosed average loans as a measure of segment assets. An additional eight banks disclosed average loans for a total of 23%.

SFAS 131 requires the disclosure of segmental depreciation/amortization/ depletion and capital expenditures. In response, 25% (10) of the banks disclosed depreciation/amortization/depletion expense, and 20% (8) reported capital expenditures. While a correlation would normally be expected between the number of companies that disclose segment assets and those that disclose segment depreciation/amortization/depletion and capital expenditures, this is not the case for the banking industry. Financial assets (i.e. loans, investments in securities, etc) account for a large proportion of a bank's total assets; alternatively, in other industries, fixed assets (such as property, plant, and equipment) represent a large portion of company's total assets.

As illustrated in Table 4, voluntary disclosures provided by the banks were somewhat limited and included:

- Average deposits (28%, 11 banks).
- Average equity (15%, 6 banks).
- Select ratios (30%, 12 banks).

Street, Nichols and Gray (2000) report that outside the financial industry the disclosure of segment liabilities for U.S. Global 1000 companies is all but non-existent. Thus, the voluntary disclosure of average deposits by some banks should be welcome by analysts since deposits are often the institution's most significant liability and interest expense on deposits the most significant expense. In the Exposure Draft (ED) preceding SFAS 131, FASB (1996) proposed disclosure of segment liabilities and stated (see Basis for Conclusions) that disclosure of segment assets and liabilities together with interest revenue and interest expense included in segment profit/loss would provide information about the financing activities of the segment. The Board dropped the segment liability disclosure requirement prior to issuing SFAS 131. As the new version of International Accounting Standard (IAS) 14 (*Segment Reporting*) requires disclosure of segment liabilities beginning with 1999 financial statements (IASC 1997), our results may reflect the intent of some U.S. domiciled banks to provide disclosures that are in line with their international competitors that utilize IASs.

Table 5.   Number of Companies Providing Enterprise-Wide Segment Disclosures in 1998.

Type of Disclosure	Number of Firms
Product Information	7
Geographic Disclosures	11
Major Customer	1
Total Firms in Sample	41

*Research Question 4: Enterprise Wide Segment Data Disclosures
Under SFAS 131*

As reflected in Fig. 1, SFAS 131 requires the disclosure of enterprise wide data for: (1) products and services, (2) geographic regions, and (3) major customers. Enterprise wide data is required even for companies with one reportable operating segment. Table 5 reports the number of banks that disclosed enterprise wide information.

Product Based Enterprise Wide Data
While none of the banks that are managed by geographic region or a mix of LOB and geographic region supplied enterprise-wide product data, seven managed by LOB reported enterprise wide product information. These included Bank One, Chase Manhattan, First Union, Marshall and Illsley, JP Morgan, State Street, and Wells Fargo. For example, Wells Fargo provided detailed reportable segment data for four LOB (Community Banking, Wholesale Banking, Mortgage Banking, and Norwest Financial). Additionally, for its mortgage banking activities, which include Norwest Mortgage Banking and certain mortgage banking activities in other reportable segments, Wells Fargo provided product enterprise wide data. The enterprise data disclosed the components of mortgage banking non-interest income (i.e. origination and other closing fees; servicing fees, net of amortization; net gains/losses on sales of servicing rights; net gains on sales of mortgages; and other).

   In its segment reporting footnote, Chase Manhattan disclosed detailed reportable segment data for three LOB (Global Bank, National Consumer Service, and Global Services). The footnote then refers to certain pages in the MD&A for a further discussion concerning Chase's segments including a description of products and services. These pages of the MD&A provide enterprise wide product information for certain reportable segments. While SFAS 131 only requires disclosure of product revenues, Chase discloses operating revenues, cash operating earnings, and the cash efficiency ratio for seven products/services (Global Markets, Global Investment Banking, Corporate Lending, Chase Capital Partners, Global Private Bank, Middle Markets, and Chase Texas) within the Global Bank reportable segment and four products/services (Chase Card-member Services, Regional Consumer Banking, Chase Home Finance, and Diversified Consumer Services) within the National Consumer Services reportable segment.

Geographic Based Enterprise Wide Data
Eleven banks supplied enterprise wide geographic information (see Tables 5 and 6). These included nine banks managed by LOB: BankAmerica, Bank

of New York, Chase Manhattan, Citigroup, JP Morgan, Northern Trust, Popular, Republic NY, and State Street. For Bank Boston and Banker's Trust, the geographic enterprise wide information was in addition to the detailed reportable segment data supplied for geographic regions included in reportable segments based on a mix of LOB and geographic region. In 1998, Bank Boston supplied reportable segment data for a mix of three LOBs (Wholesale Bank; Regional Bank; and Other Businesses) and two geographic regions (Argentina and Brazil). Additionally, Bank Boston supplied enterprise wide data for Domestic, Argentina, Brazil, and Other. In 1998, Banker's Trust provided detailed reportable segment data for seven LOB (Investment Banking; Trading & Sales; Emerging Market's Group; Private Client Services Group; Global Institutional Services; Australia/New Zealand/International Funds Management; and Other Business Segments). Banker's Trust's Emerging Markets Group LOB was split into three reportable geographic regions (Latin America; Middle East and Africa; and Asia) for a total of nine reportable segments. Additionally, Banker's Trust provided enterprise wide data for Domestic, Asia, Australia/New Zealand, Western Hemisphere, Europe, United Kingdom, and Middle East/Africa.

As required by SFAS 131, all 11 banks providing enterprise wide geographic information disclosed information on segment revenues that included separate information for the country of domicile. With the exception of Citigroup, Bank Boston, and Republic NY, these banks also disclosed assets by geographic region. It is not surprising that Bank Boston did not disclose geographic asset data as a considerable amount of geographic information was provided via mixed reportable segments. Citigroup's only reference to geographic segment data was provided in a footnote to the LOB reportable segment data, where Citigroup disclosed only domestic revenues. In respect to Republic Bank, several items of geographic information, including segment assets, were disclosed in 1997. Hence, it appears that segment assets by geographic region would also be a required disclosure under SFAS 131 in 1998.

Table 6 reveals that several of the banks provided enterprise wide geographic data that exceeded the SFAS 131 requirements. For example, six disclosed a measure of geographic segment income in 1998. Eight had provided a similar measure in 1997 under SFAS 14. While analysts will likely be disappointed with this loss of information within the banking industry, the loss is less extensive than that which occurred in other industries (See Street, Nichols & Gray, 2000). Additionally, several banks voluntarily disclosed a measure of income and/or income tax expense (Bank of New York, Banker's Trust, JP Morgan, State Street, Chase Manhattan, and Northern Trust). The voluntary disclosures provided by State Street were quite extensive (see Table 6, Panel B).

Table 6. Comparison of SFAS 14 and SFAS 131 Geographic Disclosures.

Bank	1998 Geographic Segments	1998 vs. 1997	1998 Disclosures	1998 vs. 1997
Panel A				
Bank America	Domestic Asia Europe, Middle East, and Africa Latin America and Caribbean	Not comparable due to merger	Total Revenue Total Assets	Not comparable due to merger
Citigroup	U.S. International	Not comparable due to merger	Revenues net of interest expense	Not comparable due to merger
Panel B				
Bank of New York	Domestic Europe Asia Other Foreign	Same	Total Revenue Total Assets Net Income Income before Tax	Same
Banker's Trust	Domestic Asia Australia/New Zealand Western Hemisphere Europe United Kingdom Middle East and Africa	Same	Total Revenue Total Assets Net Income Income before Tax	Same
JP Morgan	U.S. Canada and Caribbean Europe (includes Middle East and Africa) Asia-Pacific Latin America (includes Mexico, Central America and South America)	Same	Total Revenue Total Assets Net Income Pretax Income Income Tax Expense Total Expenses	Same

Republic New York	U.S. United Kingdom Europe Canada Far East and Australia Caribbean, Central and South America Middle East and Africa	Same	Total Revenue	Same	Total Revenue Total Assets Net Income Income before Tax
State Street	U.S. Other	Same	Total Revenue Total Assets Net Income Fee Revenue Interest Revenue Interest Expense Net Interest Provision Loan losses Operating Expense Income Before Tax Income Tax Interest Bearing Deposits Loans and Other Assets	Same	Same
Panel C **Chase Manhattan**	Domestic Europe/Middle East and Africa Asia and Pacific Latin America and Caribbean Other	From 6 to 5 Combined Europe with Middle East and Africa	Total Revenue Total Assets Net Income Income before Tax Total Expenses	Same	Same

Table 6. Continued.

Bank	1998 Geographic Segments	1998 vs. 1997	1998 Disclosures	1998 vs. 1997
Northern Trust	Domestic International	From 4 to 2 Combined Europe; North America; Latin America; and Asia- Pacific to form International	Total Revenue Total Assets Net Income Income before Tax	Total Revenue Net Income Income beforeTax Time deposits with banks Loans Customer's acceptance liability
Panel D Popular, Inc	U.S. Puerto Rico Other	Had no 1997 geographic disclosures	Total Revenue Total Assets Loan deposits	None
Bank Boston	Domestic Argentina Brazil Other	Split Latin America into Argentina and Brazil. Combined Europe; Asia/Pacific; and Other into Other	Total Revenue (With Mixed reportable segments)	Total Revenue Total Assets Net Income Income before Tax Total Expenses

Table 7. Comparison of Number of Geographic Locations Disclosed.
SFAS 14 Versus SFAS 131. For Companies with Enterprise-Wide
Geographic Disclosures in 1998.

No change	5
Increase in Number	1
Decrease in Number	3
Same Number, different segments	0
Total	9
Average locations 1997	4.6
Average locations 1998	4.3

Total firms equal 9 (2 firms involved in major mergers in 1998)

As reflected in Tables 6 and 7, overall SFAS 131 had a minimal impact on geographic segment reporting in the banking industry. For Bank America and Citigroup comparisons to 1997 are not meaningful due to significant merger activity that altered segments (see Table 6, Panel A). For most of the other banks, the geographic groupings remained the same or the number of geographic segments declined. Five banks (see Table 6, Panel B) reported the same geographic segments that again represented the broad, vague groupings for which analysts and other financial statement users had criticized SFAS 14. For example, Banker's Trust continued to utilize geographic groupings such as Western Hemisphere and Middle East and Africa. Three banks (see Table 6, Panels C and D) decreased the number of geographic segments reported. For example, Northern Trust followed the SFAS 131 option of reporting only Domestic and Other as no single country accounted for 10% or more of sales or assets.

Only two banks appear to have improved their geographic groupings for 1998 (See Table 6, Panel D). Popular, which had no geographic data in 1997, supplied 1998 data for the US, Puerto Rico, and Other in 1998. In 1998, State Street split its Latin America segment into two country specific segments (Argentina and Brazil) as SFAS 131 requires separate reporting for any country accounting for 10% of sales or assets.

In summary, SFAS 131 had a minimal impact on the geographic data provided by the banking industry. SFAS 131 requires that companies supply enterprise wide data for any country accounting for at least 10% of sales or assets. However, as noted above, Banker's Trust and Republic NY supplied identical by-country information for 1997 and 1998, while the by-country information for Popular and Bank Boston appears to be the only response to SFAS 131's 10% rule. Additionally, most banks continued to utilize the broad geographic groupings for which SFAS 14 was criticized. For example, JP Morgan included the Middle East and Africa in a single segment labeled Europe. Citigroup, Northern Trust, and State Street took advantage of the U.S./Other option provided by SFAS 131. The geographic disclosures across banks vary greatly, from detailed country specific information such as BankBoston to U.S./Other such as Citigroup. Hence, much of the enterprise wide geographic information provided by the banking industry may be of limited usefulness to analysts and other financial statement users.

Major Customer Enterprise Wide Data
Like SFAS 14, Statement 131 requires companies to report revenues from a single customer that accounts for 10% or more of revenue and the segments from which sales to each major customer were made. We did not anticipate any major customer disclosures due to Federal Deposit Insurance Corporation restrictions regarding aggregate lending limitations to a single customer. In 1998, Synovus was the only bank in our sample that disclosed major customer data. For its subsidiary Total System Services, Inc. (TSYS), Synovus noted that a significant amount of revenues are derived from long-term contracts with significant customers, including certain major customers. For the year ended December 31, 1998, BankAmerica Corporation accounted for 21% of TSYS' total revenues. As a result, the loss of BankAmerica Corporation, or other major or significant customers, could have a material adverse effect on TSYS' financial condition and results of operations.

Research Question 5: Impact of SFAS 131 on Consistency of Segment Information with Other Parts of the Annual Report

Banks Report Information that is More Consistent With the Introductory Annual Report Information
Excluding the banks involved in a significant merger that altered segment composition for 1998, 37 banks provided reportable segment data in 1998. In 1997, 21 of these 37 (57%) reported segment data that was inconsistent with the annual report introductory material (i.e. letter to shareholder's, etc.) (see Table 8). For example, segment disclosures were rated as inconsistent where additional segment information was included in the introductory annual report information but not in the segment footnote. In 1998, the situation under SFAS 131 improved when the level of inconsistency reduced to one (3%). A t-test indicates the increase in consistency is significant at $p = 0.0000$ ($t = 6.87$).

Table 8. Consistency of LOB Disclosures with Introductory Annual Report Information* and MD&A SFAS 14 Versus SFAS 131.

	Annual Report		MD&A	
	1997	1998	1997	1998
LOB Based Reportable Segments				
Consistent	12	32	14	31
Not Consistent	20	1	19	2
No Information	1	0	0	0
Total	33	33	33	33
MIXED Reportable Segments				
Consistent	1	2	1	2
Not Consistent	1	0	1	0
No Information	0	0	0	0
Total	2	2	2	2
GEO Based Reportable Segments				
Consistent	1	1	0	1
Not Consistent	0	0	1	0
No Information	0	0	0	0
Total	1	1	1	1
One Reportable Segment				
Consistent	1	1	1	1
Not Consistent	0	0	0	0
No Information	0	0	0	0
Total	1	1	1	1
Total Sample				
Consistent*	15	36	16	35
Not Consistent	21	1	21	2
No Information	1	0	0	0
Total	37	37	37	37

- * Level of consistency between introductory annual report information and segment reporting significantly increased ($p = 0.0000$, $t = 6.87$).
- Level of consistency between MD&A and segment reporting significantly increased ($p = 0.0000$, $t = 6.16$).
- Introductory annual report information includes items other than the MD&A and audited statements including the shareholder's letter, business at-a-glance, operations review, etc.
- Total number of firms equals 37 (41 sample firms less 4 firms involved in major mergers that altered reportable segments).

Banks Report Information that is More Consistent With the Management Discussion & Analysis

In 1997, 21 of the 37 banks (57%) reported segment information that was inconsistent with the MD&A (see Table 8). Segment disclosures were rated as inconsistent where additional segment information was included in MD&A but not in the segment footnote. The situation improved considerably in 1998 when inconsistencies between the reportable segments and MD&A was reduced to only two (5%) banks. A *t*-test indicates the increase in consistency is significant at $p = 0.0000$ ($t = 6.16$). The improvement in consistency between segment reporting and the banks' MD&A may be linked to the increased number of segments reported under the management approach as reflected in Table 3, particularly for those banks that provided no segment data in their 1997 footnotes.

As noted previously, 29 banks provided reportable segment data in the 1998 footnotes that had provided no segment data in their 1997 footnotes. For 21 of the 29 (72%) the 1997 MD&A was inconsistent with the omission of segment data from the footnotes. For example, in 1997 Keycorp's introductory annual report material and MD&A discussed "four primary lines of business" (Key Corporate Capital, Key Capital Partners, Key Consumer Finance, and Key Community Bank). While a figure in the MD&A provided some segmental data for these LOB, there was no segment footnote. Consistent with the introductory annual report material and the MD&A, the 1998 footnotes include SFAS 131 disclosures for Keycorp's four LOB based reportable segments.

Providian's 1997 introductory annual report material discussed various LOB such as the unsecured spread business, the "unbanked" business, and home loan business. The 1997 MD&A indicated that Providian was a leading provider of consumer lending products including unsecured credit cards, revolving lines of credit, home loans, secured credit cards and fee-based products. But, no segment data was included in the footnotes (or in the MD&A). Alternatively, in line with Providian's introductory annual report material and MD&A, the 1998 footnotes include SFAS 131 data for the reportable operating segments Credit Card, Home Loan, and Other.

These findings raise questions regarding the location of segment data within the annual report. Under SFAS 14, segment disclosures were to be reported either:

- Within the body of the financial statements.
- Entirely in the footnotes.
- Or, in a separate schedule that is included as an integral part of the financial statements.

Table 9. Method of Disclosing Segment Information.
Comparison of 1997 to 1998.

Method of Disclosure	1997	1998
No disclosure	12	1
Footnote	5	30
Footnote reference to disclosure elsewhere in annual report	2	6
Not referenced in footnote but information provided elsewhere in annual report	18	0
Total	37	37

Total number of firms equals 37 (41 sample firms less 4 firms involved in major mergers that altered reportable segments).

However, in 1997, 18 banks that provided some segment data within the MD&A provided no SFAS 14 data via any of the above options. Hence, some, if not all, of these banks may not have been in compliance with SFAS 14 (see Table 9). Under SFAS 131, this reporting behavior ceased. Most of the banks (30) reported segment data in a footnote. The remaining six provided a reference in the footnotes indicating the page number where the segment data was located within the annual report and stated that this information was an integral part of the financial statements. Hence, the issuance of SFAS 131 and the SEC's current stance on segment reporting provided a strong incentive for banks to more clearly display their segment data.

Research Question 6: Comments Regarding Reliability of SFAS 131 Disclosures

Table 10 summarizes comments made by 10 banks regarding the reliability and/or comparability of SFAS 131 disclosures. Consistent with the findings of Tyson and Jacobs (1987), a few members of the banking industry continue to question the reliability of segment disclosures. For example, Banker's Trust states, "certain estimates and judgements have been made to apportion revenue and expense items" and Wells Fargo states, "the process is dynamic and somewhat subjective." However, comments that may lead financial statements users to question the reliability of segment disclosures appear to be less prevalent under SFAS 131. Alternatively, several banks take aim at the SFAC 2 qualitative characteristic of comparability.

As illustrated by Table 10, eight banks indicate that the segment reporting based on management structure does not provide information that is comparable

Table 10. Footnote Comments Regarding Reliability and Comparability of SFAS 131 Data.

Company Name	Discussion Regarding Use of Estimates
Panel A: Reliability and Comparability Concerns	
Banker's Trust	"Because the Corporation's business is diverse in nature and its operations are integrated, certain **estimates and judgments** have been made to apportion revenue and expense items. The internal management accounting process, unlike financial accounting in accordance with generally accepted accounting principles, is based on the way management views its business and is **not necessarily comparable** with similar information disclosed by other financial institutions."
State Street	"The operating results of these lines of business are **not necessarily comparable** with other companies."
	"Revenue and expenses are directly charged or allocated to the lines of business through **algorithm-based** management information systems."
Well's Fargo	"The results are determined based on the Company's management accounting process, which assigns balance sheet and income statement items to each responsible operating segment. This process is dynamic and **somewhat subjective**. Unlike financial accounting, there is no comprehensive, authoritative body of guidance for management accounting equivalent to generally accepted accounting principles. The management accounting process measures the performance of the operating segments based on the management structure of the Company and is **not necessarily comparable** with similar information for any other financial institution."
Panel B: Comparability Concerns	
Fifth Third Bancorp	"The measurement of the performance of the operating segments is based on the management structure of the Bancorp and is **not necessarily comparable** with similar information for any other financial institution. The information presented is also not necessarily indicative of the segment's financial condition and results of operations if they were independent entities."
UnionBanCal Corp	"The information presented does not necessarily represent the business units' financial condition and results of operations as if they were independent entities. Unlike financial accounting, there is no authoritative body of guidance for management accounting equivalent to generally accepted accounting principles. Consequently, reported results are **not necessarily comparable** with those presented by other companies."

Table 10. Continued.

Company Name	Discussion Regarding Use of Estimates
Washington Mutual	"Since SFAS No. 131 requires no segmentation or methodology standardization, the organizational structure of the company and the allocation methodologies it employs result in business line financial results that are **not necessarily comparable** across companies. As such, Washington Mutual's business line performance **may not be directly comparable** with similar information from other financial institutions."
Northern Trust Corp	"Allocations of capital and certain corporate expenses **may not be representative** of levels that would be required if the segments were independent entities."
AM South	"AmSouth's segments are **not necessarily comparable** with similar information for any other financial institution."
KeyCorp	"Further, unlike financial accounting, there is no authoritative guidance for management accounting similar to generally accepted accounting principles. Consequently, reported results are **not necessarily comparable** with those presented by other companies."
Huntington	"This is a dynamic process that mirrors Huntington's organizational and management structure. Accordingly, the results are **not necessarily comparable** with similar information published by other financial institutions that may define business segments differently."

to other financial institutions. For example, Huntington states that determination of segment data is a dynamic process that mirrors the bank's organizational and management structure. As a result, the segment results are not necessarily comparable with similar information published by other financial institutions that may define business segments differently.

In an appendix to SFAS 131, FASB (1997) acknowledges that comparability of accounting information is important. According to SFAC 2 "Comparability between enterprises and consistency in the application of methods over time increases the informational value of comparisons of relative economic opportunities or performance. The significance of information . . . depends . . . on the user's ability to relate it to some benchmark." However, SFAC 2 also notes that "Improving comparability may destroy or weaken relevance or reliability, if, to secure comparability between two measures, one of them has to be obtained by a method yielding less relevant or reliable information."

In regard to SFAS 131, the FASB concluded that both relevance and comparability may not be achievable in all cases, and in such instances, relevance should be the overriding concern. Hence, the FASB down-played the concerns of respondents to the Board's Exposure Draft that indicated segments based on the structure of an enterprise's internal organization may not be comparable between enterprises that engage in similar activities and may not be comparable from year to year for an individual enterprise. Alternatively, the Board was influenced by the majority of respondents to the Exposure Draft that indicated that defining segments based on the organizational structure would result in improved information. These users of financial information argued that not only would enterprises be likely to report more detailed information but that knowledge of the structure of an enterprise's internal organization is valuable in itself because it highlights the risks and opportunities that management believes are important. Additionally, an argument can be made that banks could present enterprise wide data for similar products/services and/or geographic areas in order to achieve industry comparability.

CONCLUSIONS

This research reviewed the 1997 and 1998 annual reports of the U.S.'s largest banks to determine whether SFAS 131 adequately addressed user concerns about segment disclosures and the extent to which the anticipated benefits set forth in SFAS 131 materialized. In particular, the research addressed:

- the extent to which banks reported a greater number of segments in 1998, with special reference to banks that provided no segment footnote data in 1997,
- the extent to which banks reported more items of information about each reportable segment,
- the extent to which banks moved toward more useful geographic groupings as opposed to the broad, vague groupings utilized under SFAS 14, and
- whether the consistency of segment information with other parts of the annual report improved under SFAS 131.

Taken overall, under SFAS 131 segment reporting in the banking industry has improved. The number of segments reported and the consistency of segment information increased significantly in 1998 as compared to 1997. Further, it is noteworthy that, as the SEC continues to challenge segment disclosures, most notably for companies that disclose only one operating segment (see Ernst & Young, 2000), 28 of the nation's largest banks provided reportable operating segment disclosures in 1998 although the same banks previously provided no segment data in their footnotes. Apparently, the SEC's recent focus on segmental reporting combined with the release of SFAS 131 has all but ended many banks' tendency to claim one LOB.

Our findings also reveal that consistency between the segment data supplied in the footnotes with the introductory annual report material and the MD&A increased significantly for the banking industry. However, a couple of the nation's largest banks continue to report segment information on a basis inconsistent with their introductory annual report information and MD&A. This finding is surprising given that SEC comment letters in regard to segmental reporting tend to follow a particular pattern that begins with the SEC challenging inconsistencies in information provided in other sections of the 10-K as compared to the financial statement footnotes.

On a less positive note, the findings reveal that the banking industry continues to utilize the broad, vague geographic groupings for which SFAS 14 was often criticized. Very few of the banks provided reportable segment data or enterprise wide information based on meaningful geographic groups. While a few banks provided country specific geographic groupings, most utilized broad groupings such as Western Hemisphere and Far East/Asia. Additionally, the findings suggest that the FASB and/or AICPA should provide guidance regarding the format banks should utilize to report segment revenues as a few banks deviated from the industry norm. The findings also illustrate the lack of comparability resulting from the FASB's decision not to define segment profit or loss.

In concluding, our findings suggest SFAS 131 has supplied analysts and other users of financial statements from the banking industry with several of the benefits anticipated by the FASB (1997). However, the results indicate there is opportunity for improvement particularly in regard to standardizing the definitions for segment revenues and profitability measures and in the nature of geographic groupings utilized in enterprise wide segment data.

NOTES

1. SFAS 131 allows operating segments to be combined for reporting purposes, even though they may be individually material, if: (1) aggregation is consistent with the objective and basic principles of SFAS 131, (2) the operating segments have similar economic characteristics, and (3) the segments have similar basic characteristics in each of the following areas:

- The number of the products or services.
- The nature of the production processes.
- The type or class of customer for their products or services.
- The methods used to distribute their products or provide their services.
- If applicable, the nature of the regulatory environment (for example, banking, insurance).

2. Emphasis added.

3. We also evaluated the sample by separating the banks based on international versus national operations and by separating the banks based on size. There were no significant differences between the groups. Therefore, the combined findings are reported.

4. The ability to report mixed LOB and geographic segments is a new feature of SFAS 131.

5. SunTrust Banks' "Other" segment includes the company's credit card bank and non-bank subsidiaries.

6. Bank Boston's "Other Businesses" segment includes all other businesses that are not encompassed in the four major LOB.

7. The remaining bank that provided no segment footnote data in 1997, Regions Bank, based reportable segments on geographic region in 1998.

8. Recall that in 1998, reportable segments for four banks were based on a mix of LOB and geographic region and for one bank was based on geographic region.

9. The number of reportable segments disclosed for these four banks (BankAmerica, Citigroup, First Star, and Sun Trust) increased during 1998; however, the increase in segments is at least partially attributable to the merger and hence is not fully attributed to the adoption of SFAS 131. Accordingly, the four banks are deleted from all analysis addressing the impacted of SFAS 131 on the number of segments disclosed in 1998 as compared to 1997.

10. The non-parametric Wilcoxon Signed Rank Test provides similar results at $p = 0.0000$ (= 4.824).

REFERENCES

American Institute of Certified Public Accountants (AICPA) (1984). *Industry Audit Guide: Audits of Banks* (prepared by AICPA Banking Committee).

American Institute of Certified Public Accountants (AICPA) (1994). *Improving Business Reporting – A Customer Focus.* Report of the AICPA Special Committee on Financial Reporting,

Association for Investment Management and Research, Financial Accounting Policy Committee (AIMR) (1993). *Financial Reporting in the 1990s and Beyond: A Position Paper of the Association for Investment Management and Research.* Prepared by Peter H. Knutson. Charlottsville, VA: AIMR.

Cates. D. C., & Lewin, W. (1999). SFAS No. 131 and the Future of Bank Financial Reporting. *Bank Accounting and Finance, 7.*

Ernst & Young (2000). *Developments to Date – FASB: Segment Disclosures* (web: http://eydomino.txcast.com/aabs/E).

Financial Accounting Standards Board (FASB) (1976). *Statement of Financial Accounting Standards No. 14: Financial Reporting for Segments of a Business Enterprise.* Stamford, CT. FASB.

Financial Accounting Standards Board (FASB) (1996). *Proposed Statement of Financial Accounting Standards: Reporting Disaggregated Information about a Business Enterprise.* Stamford, CT. FASB.

Financial Accounting Standards Board (FASB) (1997). *Statement of Financial Accounting Standards No. 131: Disclosures about Segments of an Enterprise and Related Information.* Stamford, CT. FASB.

Gray, S. J., & Radebaugh, L. H. (1984). International Segment Disclosures by U.S. and U.K. Multinational Enterprises: A Descriptive Study. *Journal of Accounting Research,* (Spring), 351–360.

IASC (1997). IAS 14, Segment Reporting, London, IASC.

Nichols, N. B., Street, D. L., & Gray, S. J. (2000). Geographic Segmental Disclosures in the United States: Reporting Practices Enter a New Era. *Journal of International Accounting, Auditing, and Taxation*, forthcoming 2000.

Phillips. L., & Brezovec, R. L. (1998). The FASB's New Segment Disclosure Rules: What They Mean for Banks (http://www.aabscast.com/tsi/bafsummer98).

Solomons, D. (1968). Accounting Problems and Some Proposed Solutions. Public Reporting by Conglomerates. A. Rappaport, P. A. Firmin & S. A. Zeff (Eds). Englewood Cliffs, NJ: Prentice-Hall.

Street, D. L., Nichols, N. B., & Gray, S. J. (2000). Segment Disclosures Under SFAS 131: Has Business Segment Reporting Improved? *Accounting Horizons*, forthcoming.

Tyson, T. N., & Jacobs, F. A. (1987). Segment Reporting in the Banking Industry: Does It Meet the Criteria of the Conceptual Framework? *Accounting Horizons*, (December), 35–41.

APPENDIX

LIST OF BANKS

AM South Bancorporation
BankAmerica Corporation
BankBoston Corporation
Bank of New York Company, Inc.
Bank One Corporation
Bankers Trust Corporation
BB&T Corporation
Chase Manhattan Corporation
Citigroup, Inc.
Comerica, Inc.
Fifth Third Bancorp
First Security Corporation
First Tennessee National Corporation
First Union Corporation
Firstar Corporation
Fleet Financial Group
Golden West Financial Corporation
Huntington Bancshares, Inc.
JP Morgan & Co., Inc.
KeyCorp
Marshall & Ilsley Corporation

Mellon Bank Corporation
Mercantile Bancorporation
National City Corporation
Northern Trust Corporation
PNC Bank Corp.
Popular, Inc.
Providian Financial Corporation
Regions Financial Corporation
Republic New York Corporation
South Trust Corporation
State Street Corporation
Summit Bancorp
SunTrust Banks, Inc.
Synovus Financial Corporation
Union Planters Corporation
UnionBanCal Corporation
US Bancorp
Wachovia Corporation
Washington Mutual, Inc.
Wells Fargo & Co.

DELAY IN ACCOUNTING HARMONIZATION: EVIDENCE ON AUDITOR SELECTION AND COST-OF-CAPITAL EFFECTS, 1986–1990

Wanda A. Wallace

ABSTRACT

As entities compete for capital, they can choose a variety of bonding and monitoring mechanisms that improve the quality of information and hence are expected to lower the cost of capital, one component of which is effective interest cost. Lending contracts have long included language requiring audited financial statements, at times being specific as to the auditing firm. The Big 5 auditors are world firms, which represent that their use of world-wide auditing standards enhance the consistency of audit quality around the globe. In 1991, the Financial Accounting Standards Board (FASB) changed its mission to incorporate international harmonization. Arguably, until such date, debate was active as to whether this was even a preferred course of action. This study focuses on the time frame from 1986 to 1990, to assess whether use of the Big 5 was a temporary solution to disparate national accounting practices across borders. Although the Big 5 are not the largest of firms in many countries, they do have trademark recognition in global markets. Banking markets are increasingly global, and the Big 5 have been viewed as "deep pockets,"

Research in Accounting Regulation, Volume 15, pages 39–68.
ISBN: 0-7623-0841-9

creating insurance or stewardship incentives for their selection. This research poses the question of whether Big 5 auditor association, as well as the event of a change toward one of these Big 5 CPA firms, are associated with the five-year average effective interest rate incurred, once leverage, size, profitability, and effective tax rate are controlled. Evidence is consistent with lower interest cost being incurred by those entities in six countries – Italy, Spain, Australia, Germany, France, and the United Kingdom (as well as a hold-out sample from Canada) – that have selected Big 5 auditors. Preliminary evidence is also provided that differences in countries even for the brief time frame analyzed have declined over time, consistent with the evolution toward more unity of information reporting and/or increased globalization of markets. An interpretation is that delay in accounting harmonization created an apparent reward to those selecting global auditors. The latter provided a substitute for the evolving international accounting regulatory infrastructure.

INTRODUCTION

When creditors evaluate borrowers, a number of characteristics of that borrower are expected to influence the effective interest rate. Among these traits are those information items provided to the creditor to assess the creditworthiness and risk profile of the prospective borrower. Reputation models commonly require that the parties trying to signal their reputation incur a sunk cost. The presence of such costs means that the parties must be anticipating rents in the future in order to recover that sunk cost investment and earn a return from signalling. The selection of a Big 5 auditor (historically referred to as the Big 8, then Big 6 within the time frame of study – Big 5 is used in this study and is intended to refer back to the respective components of the current firms) can be a reputation signal in international debt markets. This research provides initial evidence that Big 5 auditor selection is associated with lower effective interest costs in global markets during the time frame corresponding with a period of debate as to whether accounting harmonization was desirable and feasible. Not until 1991 did the Financial Accounting Standards Board (FASB) revise its mission to incorporate international harmonization. Choi and Levich (1991) document the debate among international participants and lack of consensus pre-1991 regarding harmonization. Likewise, Goeltz (1992) argued harmonization of accounting practices was unnecessary, Grinyer and Russell (1992) pointed out national impediments existed to international harmonization, and Samuels and Oliga (1982) argued it was potentially harmful. Yet, by 1992/1993, harmonization had been achieved in the European Community in such areas as foreign currency translation and inventory valuation (Herrmann & Thomas, 1995). Hence, the time frame from 1986 to 1990 can be viewed as a period of "delay" in the regulatory infrastructure essential to international accounting harmonization. The evidence is consistent with a market solution in the short run. Specifically, use of a global auditor reduced perceived information costs to creditors of international disharmony in reporting practices.

The research questions include: (1) cross-sectionally, are companies audited by Big 5 auditors from 1986 to 1990 incurring lower interest costs than those who are not audited by the Big 5; (2) when a company changes from other than a Big 5 auditor to a Big 5 auditor between 1986 and 1990, are its interest costs observed to decrease; and (3) given the active debate regarding international harmonization in this period preceding FASB's change in mission, (a) is the evidence consistent with a reward to use of a world firm as a potential substitute for harmonized accounting, and (b) does this element of reward appear to become more consistent across borders as harmonization shifts toward a 'foregone conclusion.' Companies in Italy, Spain, Australia, Germany, France, the United Kingdom, and Canada (as a hold out sample) are analyzed. Specifically, five-year average effective interest rates (for 1990, Worldscope computes the arithmetic average from 1986 to 1990) are modeled for Big 5 auditees relative to non Big-5 auditees, once leverage, size, profitability, and effective tax rate are controlled. Moreover, the **event** of changes to a Big 5 auditor are tracked within this 1986 to 1990 time frame to assess whether observed lower interest costs occur at the point of change.

The global nature of debt markets suggests the importance of comparison among various countries with accounting practices not yet harmonized, when assessing possible implications of global auditor choice for borrowing costs. Prior research reports that countries' real interest rate is highly correlated with the estimated world real interest rate (Gagnon & Unferth, 1995), further implying the global nature of debt markets. This theoretical framework and empirical evidence provide a foundation for the pooled methodology applied here.

The information role of the audit might be represented as an assurance role, whereby the Big 5 auditor provides greater assurance of fair reporting, reduces information asymmetries, and improves the estimates or perceptions of the firm's quality of earnings – particularly in the absence of international harmonization – leading to lowered effective interest rates on debt. Concurrently, if the Big 5 auditor is perceived to provide greater insurance protection to debtholders to recover any losses given the Big 5's "deep pockets," then such protection (considered by some as a sort of warranty) would also be expected to influence effective interest rates (Wallace, 1980; Menon & Williams, 1994).

This research does not separate out the assurance from the insurance factors of demand, but proxies these with the single attribute of Big 5 auditor selection. Yet, the use of various countries with differential need for insurance protection due to differing litigation environments (Taylor & Simon, 1999) is seen as a vehicle to increase the likelihood of the interaction of both factors being reflected in the research design. As an example of the rich variation across countries is Germany, which is unique in that a statutory cap on auditor liability has been in effect since 1931 (see Gietzmann & Quick, 1998).

RELEVANT LITERATURE

In describing the economics of information generation, Fama and Laffer (1971, p. 291) observe that the producer of information "should generate information to the point where its marginal value (to him) in all its uses is equal to its marginal cost." They recognize that information improving a firm's operating decisions in general would also be risk reducing and have potential value for trading purposes. In cost-benefit terms, an optimal choice of audit quality, as well as the mix of auditing versus other monitoring mechanisms (Cravens & Wallace, 2001, p. 13), can be derived. In global markets, information systems are increasingly disaggregated, subject to varying institutional, cultural, and behavioral influence that affect both the raw data and the translation of such statistics into performance measures and financial statements.

Accounting Systems

The advantage of the mix of countries represented in the total data set is that it crosses the accounting system clusters defined by Nobes and Parker (1985), and permits assessment of auditing effects in the presence of such variability. Nobes (1992) describes a classification framework for financial reporting and measurement practices. Included among the sample companies are those operating within three of the seven classifications:

- U.K.-type accounting systems: Australia and United Kingdom.
- Tax or plan-based continental systems: France, Italy, Spain.
- Law-based continental systems: Germany.

If the phenomenon of lower interest costs is demonstrable for this heterogeneous group of countries, the ability to generalize the findings is enhanced, as is the likelihood that institutional arrangements (such as common covenants in a particular country) are not driving the results.

International Markets

The 1980s witnessed a change from the 1975 scope of transactions in United States securities by foreign investors and transactions in foreign securities by United States investors: from an aggregate estimate of $66 billion to the 1989 statistic of more than 80 times, or $5.4 trillion (Roussey, 1992, p. 4, cited as provided by the Office of Economic Analysis of the United States Securities and Exchange Commission). The pressure for movement toward harmonization with such large pools of international capital is unmistakable by the early nineties. Note that given the nature of global markets, Eurodollar financing, and the flexibility with which multinationals seek financing across borders, the effective interest rates are expected to be more comparable among countries than other accounting numbers.

The six countries in this study have substantial trading relationships (Celik, 2001), which may influence the relative homogeneity of certain information reporting in globally integrated markets. As an example, as of 1989/1990, West Germany was cited as one of the top five importers for five other countries in the sample, while France, the United Kingdom, and Spain have four of the sample countries cited, and Italy has three (GateWaze, 1990).

There were 1,276 European cross-border acquisitions valued at $56.6 billion in 1989 (Barrett, 1990), and investments in terms of dollars by U.S. enterprises in foreign manufacturing activities are reported to have increased more than 100% relative to 1980 (*Journal of Accountancy*, 1990). Managers in such settings face significant asymmetries of information (Myers & Majluf, 1984; Choi & Levich, 1991). One tool available to entities grappling with such challenges is to contract with a world-firm provider of auditing services, thereby achieving a more consistent information quality for both decision making internally and for third-party users. This may be characterized as a sort of substitution for an infrastructure of accounting harmonization that took the following decade to evolve, with 2001 marking the appointment of an International Accounting Standards Board.

Auditor Selection

While all businesses will try to reduce their own cost of borrowing (Myers & Majluf, 1984; Healy & Palepu, 1993), the better entrepreneurs can be expected to ask for terms that help to differentiate themselves, including exposing the poor-performing entrepreneurs who are seeking capital in competitive markets. Those terms might include selection of a world auditor that would be capable of imposing some consistency on information quality over time and signal auditee companies' comfort with careful scrutiny of their financial representations. Embedded in the auditor selection phenomenon may be lending institutions' stipulations that audit reports be issued by a Big 5 firm – cost of capital would be expected to be enhanced by improved information whether demand is generated by the creditor or borrower. Domestic auditing standards can vary in terms of the requirements held to achieve certification and perform an audit (Tang, 2000), as well as the steps required by the auditor regarding such primary aspects of the audit as planning materiality (Price & Wallace, 2001). If one believes domestic auditing standards in various countries lead to differential quality and less ability to compare information for both internal decision making and monitoring, then selection of a world-firm auditor would be expected to make creditors' evaluation more effective.

Beattie and Fearnley (1995) identify eight uncorrelated audit firm dimensions of importance to companies selecting their auditor, with the top four being reputation/quality, acceptability of third parties, value for money, and ability to provide non-audit services. This study proxies for these four dimensions by using Big 5 auditor – empirically supported by Beattie and Fearnley (1995, p. 238), as well as by quality, credibility, and specialist knowledge arguments by Dopuch and Simunic (1980 and 1982) and Simunic and Stein (1986). Table 1 cites additional literature relevant to the expectation that selection of a Big 5 auditor implies a lower effective interest rate. The conceptual and empirical research studies described in terms of their major findings suggest relevant control variables to isolate the association between effective interest and auditor selection.

MODEL

Conceptually, interest rate parity can be expected among countries due to global debt markets and the economic and financial conceptual framework in which smaller countries can be expected to have their rates more or less "pegged" to the world rate. As Gagnon and Unferth (1995, p. 845) observe,

> It is a generally accepted proposition in international economic theory that mobility of goods and capital across national borders leads to equalization of the real interest rate in different countries. In practice the existence of non-traded goods, barriers and adjustment lags for traded goods, and transactions costs and risks in financial markets, create the potential for significant deviations in real interest rates across countries, at least temporarily." [They continue by noting that] "existing empirical literature generally has rejected a strict interpretation of real interest rate parity across countries."

However, they point out that significant positive correlations have been observed (e.g. Cumby & Mishkin, 1986, p. 20) and that in their study they move away from the previous literature's focus on bilateral comparisons and focus on raw data, avoiding imposing assumptions such as expected inflation on the data set.

Their evidence suggests "the deviations of a country's ex post real interest rate from the world real interest rate (plus a constant risk premium for some countries) are close to white noise." (p. 853) They note that the U.S. distinction is likely tied to the smaller role of trade, since a link in trade is an essential part of real interest rate equalization. Since the focus of this study is the individual company, it is useful to control for the overall bond market within each country and capture the *differences* from such general market rates and the experience of individual companies. The trading relations previously cited enhance the expected comparability of effective interest rates.

The dependent variable is specifically measured as effective interest per company less the bond rate for the country in which the company is domiciled. In "a well-functioning international credit market, there can't be any cross-country real interest rate differentials." (Beaudry, 1997, p. 812) Diwan (1989, p. 126) explains that foreign banks act competitively in setting the interest rate that they charge on their foreign loans. The idea of using countries' average rate as an adjustment to individual companies' cost is supported by Ohanian and Stockman (1997).

Big 5 Auditor Selection

This study analyzes whether a company's auditor is a Big 5 firm, as well as the incidence of a change to or from a Big 5 Auditor in the particular year modeled. The world firm status of Big 5 auditors provides coherency in audit quality across borders for international market participants. The historical Big 8 have gradually merged into the current Big 5 auditing firms, which provide the structure used in this research for coding: Arthur Young and Ernst and Whinney merged in 1989 to form Ernst & Young; Deloitte, Haskins, and Sells and Touche Ross merged in 1989 to form Deloitte & Touche. Most recently, Price Waterhouse and Coopers & Lybrand have merged into PriceWaterhouseCoopers. Arthur Andersen has remained distinct, recently changing its name to Andersen, and Peat Marwick Main is now referred to as KPMG Peat Marwick. If a company is audited by a Big 5 auditor for the entire period from 1985 to 1990, a 1 is recorded; otherwise a zero is reflected. If a firm changes to a Big 5 firm in the time frame, a one is entered to represent change to Big 5; otherwise a zero is recorded. If a company changes from a Big 5 auditor to a non-Big 5 firm, a one is entered; otherwise a zero is recorded. Changes among Big 5 firms were not tracked. Each of the Big 5 firms is represented in the data set.

Table 1. Literature Relevant to Expectation that Selection of a Big 5 Auditor Implies Lower Effective Interest Incurred.

Past Literature	Major Findings	Implications for This Research
Akerlof, 1970 Spence, 1973 Ross, 1977, 1979 Wallace, 1980 Antle, 1982, 1984 Baiman et al., 1987	Auditing function facilitates markets in the presence of incentive problems; private markets have mandated audits	International lending markets are facilitated by auditor self-selection of trademark firms with a world-wide audit approach
Healy & Lys, 1986	Investors' information costs of assessing audit quality are lower for Big Eight firm than non-Big Eight firm	Savings in information costs should reduce effective interest
Klein & Leffler, 1971	Investments in reputation represent a bond by auditing firms to assure clients they will receive the contracted-for audit quality	World-wide audit approach of Big 5 is a bonding mechanism
Healy & Palepu, 1993	Means of mitigating information gaps between managers and owners are discussed; a call is made for research on how voluntary disclosure affects a firm's cost of capital	Part of voluntary signaling is the selection of auditor
Kinney & Martin, 1994	The quality of information is improved through the audit process, as demonstrated empirically	Audits reduce measurement error in information used in monitoring
DeAngelo, 1981 Palmrose, 1986 Francis & Simon, 1987 Francis & Wilson, 1988 Eichenseher, Hagigi, & Shields, 1989 Raman & Wilson, 1992 Ettredge & Greenberg, 1990	Trademark and reputation effects on markets are observable in —initial public offerings (Simunic & Stein, 1987; Balvers et al., 1988; Beatty, 1989; Feltham et al., 1991; Menon & Williams, 1991; Datar et al., 1991; Jang & Lin 1993 – focusing on trading volume; Clarkson & Simunic, 1994; Hogan, 1997) —bankruptcy (Menon & Williams, 1994) —bond market settings (Wallace, 1981; Wilson & Howard, 1984)	Global markets, Eurodollar financing, and flexibility of multinationals in seeking financing across borders create an expectation of comparable effective interest rates which permit consideration of reputation costs in international markets

Wallace, 1980, 1987 Chow et al., 1988 Schwartz & Menon, 1985 Melumad & Thoman, 1990	Insurance theory posits that stewardship considerations of agents and "deep pocket" advantages (i.e. potential loss recovery) of larger firms would combine to create demand for Big 5 auditors	The Big 5 auditors' "deep pockets" and presence in the markets that face litigation exposure under U.S. law may be valued potential loss recovery to lenders in the international market, reducing interest costs
Moore & Ronen, 1990 Elliott & Jacobson, 1994	Information theory contends positive reputation, signaling, and homogeneity of service quality can help to address asymmetry of information concerns by capital providers [Evidence on the interplay of information and cost of capital is provided in Dhaliwal 1978 and Conover and Wallace 1995]	World firm audit organizations can be expected to have more homogeneous service quality which, in turn, would be valued by creditors as a source of reducing asymmetry of information
Craswell, Francis, & Taylor, 1995	Big 5 brand name premium over non-Big 5 auditors averages around 30%; audit fee literature is reviewed and the agency cost basis for expecting quality-differentiated audits is described, as is the cost-benefit framework for determining optimal audit quality choice from among monitoring mechanisms	Self-selection of auditors is influenced by many cost-benefit parameters, one of which can be expected to be reduced interest cost
Diamond, 1989	Cites borrowers' reputation as encompassing public information, track record, interest rate path and implicitly credit rating, and acknowledges the tool of precommitment to some degree by writing contracts dependent on publicly observed variables as a monitoring mechanism to facilitate contracting	Creditors set interest rate as a function of borrowers' reputation, one attribute of which is the auditor of record and associated effects on information provided for monitoring contracts
Myers, 1977	Incentive problems in debt markets are noted to be most severe in early periods for entities with short track records with respect to repayment of debt; reputation is a function of project selection, often assessed using public information	The use of Big 5 auditors may be of greater value to entities with less of a track record, proxied by size or profitability metrics

Methodology

Smieliauskas (1996) points out the inconsistency of archival findings on individual countries' experiences to date and observes that "the more satisfactory way of dealing with these issues would be through a more systematic analysis of pooled data from the various countries, perhaps pooled cross-sectional time series analysis." (p. 141). While he was discussing litigation risk and audit pricing, the problem of reconciling different studies one-country-at-a-time at different points in time is a more pervasive issue. This study follows the pooled approach that he recommends to this problem. This research design is further supported by the evidence previously cited on interest rate parity.

The power of the tests performed is enhanced through focusing on average ratios over five years which provides a more normalized depiction of the phenomenon of interest (the measure is less exposed to single year interest fluctuations and anomalies such as inverted short-term and long-term interest rates). Power is also gained by modeling the auditor change **event** whereby interest rates in the year following change are compared with the year prior to the change, controlling for the year of change, the domicile, and changes in that same time frame of both size and profitability.

Control Variables

A set of control variables is implied by prior research. However, most of that literature has focused on a single country at a time (e.g. Woo & Koh, 2001), which means the theoretical interrelationships may not map to a pooled analysis. The intentional focus on a time frame pre-harmonization increases the measurement error in ratios' comparability. With this caveat, the models estimated include four dimensions: effective tax rate, leverage, size, and profitability.

Effective Tax Rate
The tax deductibility of debt relative to equity may influence choices of capital sources, meaning that the differential tax rates among countries, as well as among the companies within the country, needs to be controlled. As an example of differences that arise between two of the countries in the data set, consider the following:

> It should be noted that in countries where the integrated system of taxation is generally applicable, there is a lower tax rate on distributed income. A clear example of this would be Germany, where the tax rate has varied from 34% to 50% by being distributed as opposed to retained . . .. In the international environment, it is even more important, since U.S. parent corporations have used a technique of bringing profits out of a subsidiary company by having

a very high debt to equity ratio at the subsidiary level . . . the payment of interest was very likely deductible in the U.S., and not subject to U.S. withholding tax (O'Connor, 1992, p. 69).

The same research reports the prevalence of tax controversies as to capital vs. ordinary expenditures, debt vs. equity classifications, and transfer pricing in the United Kingdom. These types of considerations are the motivation for including the effective tax rate as a control variable. Higher tax rates are a two-edged sword: if interest is tax deductible, then higher rates may encourage higher interest, but since higher tax rates take a greater share of profitability, affecting an entity's ability to borrow, the directional relation to effective interest is ambiguous.

Leverage

Increased leverage is expected, ceteris paribus, to increase effective interest rates because of the higher risk in such settings (Simunic & Stein, 1996) and less debt protection should defaults occur (Chen & Wei, 1993). Begley and Feltham (1999, p. 243) explain that the higher leverage may reflect the "stronger incentives for management (acting on behalf of equity-holders) to engage in opportunistic behaviour when the debtholders provide a larger proportion of the firm's capital." They cite evidence that has found firms with higher leverage likewise have more restrictive debt covenants (Begley, 1990, 1994). Beneish and Press (1993) model incremental interest[1] as a function of leverage and profitability (measured as return on assets), as well as return on common stock and violation of debt agreements. They report that "the distinctive feature in all regressions . . . is that only leverage is significantly correlated with incremental interest costs." (Beneish & Press, 1993, p. 247). This suggests that there is no need to track the separate element of violation of debt agreements, as leverage should be a sufficient control variable.

Though the literature provides a straightforward directional implication, a pooled data set internationally is expected to have certain distinctive ratios (O'Connor, 1992; *Finance & Treasury*, 1994) relating to debt structure. Moreover, the literature has suggested that the use of favorable financial leverage is beneficial to stockholders, suggesting a preferable range of leverage, below which profitability is foregone, and above which risk is incurred. With these considerations, a pooled analysis faces ambiguity as to the likely association with interest cost.

Size of borrowers is expected to influence the scale of lending activities, participation in global debt markets, and implied risk. The relation of size to interest costs is ambiguous, due to interactive effects of leverage and age of the company, as well as the nature of markets. For example, surviving, older firms in concentrated markets pay higher nominal rates than surviving older firms in competitive markets. Finally, the natural response of older firms who have few investment opportunities [and] are faced with higher interest rates is to use less external finance. This would explain why older firms in concentrated markets rely on internal [as] opposed to institutional finance (Petersen & Rajan, 1995, p. 440).

Myers (1977) argues absence of a track record increases interest costs.

Profitability
Finally, a key risk measure described in lending decisions relates to profitability and rates of return relative to costs of capital. In this study, profitability is considered in three forms: operating income/last year's total capital, multiplied by 100, return on assets (ROA), and return on investment capital – Beneish and Press (1993) analyzed both ROA and return on common stock. Ceteris paribus, profitability is expected to lower the effective interest rate for a company. Yet, the ratios' variation due to disparate definitions of capital structure components increases the likelihood that the profitability ratios incorporating bases of total capital, total assets, and investment capital will likewise capture variability associated with leverage. This is considered advantageous in a period of disharmony of accounting systems and implies some ambiguity in sign.

Empirical Specification

In order to capture each of these effects, the empirical specification of the model, with hypothesized signs, is:

[(Interest Expense on Debt/(Short-Term Debt + Current Portion of Long-Term Debt + Long-Term Debt))*100] per company – Bond Yield for that country in which the company is domiciled = $a_0 \pm b_1$ [(Assets/Owners' Equity)*100] $\pm b_2$ Net Sales or Revenues/Number of Employees in Millions $\pm b_3$ [(operating income/last year's total capital)*100] $\pm b_4$ return on investment capital (ROIC) $\pm b_5$ return on assets (ROA) $\pm b_6$ [(income taxes/pretax income)*100] $\pm b_{7-11}$ Indicator Variable is 1 if that country, 0 if not – since six countries, a total of five indicator variables capture the variation, with the sixth country captured in the constant term – $\pm b_{12}$ Indicator Variable is 1 if a Big 5 Audit for the entire 1985 to 1990 time frame, 0 otherwise $\pm b_{13}$ Indicator Variable is 1 if a change to a Big 5 Auditor occurs, 0 otherwise $+ \pm b_{14}$ Indicator Variable is 1 if a change from a Big 5 Auditor occurs, 0 otherwise $+ \varepsilon$

The mixed sign indicated for the country indicator variables is due to the diversity of the countries, their different proportions in the data set, and an expectation that Germany will have a relative positive sign due to the primary role of debt capital rather than equity sources in that particular country during the time frame under study.

The control variables are expected to be interrelated. Table 2 provides correlation matrices for the 1988 observations and five-year averages (i.e. 1984 to 1988) to demonstrate that intercorrelations are reasonably moderate other than between ROA and ROIC. In the reduced modeling of events of auditor change, these two variables are removed, with only operating income to total capital controlled. Multicollinearity's presence, which is common in economic and financial modeling, need not be harmful (Belsey, Kuh, & Welsch, 1980), and can be tested since when multicollinearity is harmful, either the removal or addition of observations or independent variables can be expected to lead to large changes in the sign and magnitude of the coefficients. Such is not the case here; the relative stability of the models estimated – likely enhanced by use of natural logarithms and differencing – suggests that multicollinearity is not harmful in this setting.

Note that other risk measures could be considered, such as book value to market value ratios, beta values, going concern opinions[2] and loan defaults; however, in this research, the leverage, size, and profitability ratios are intended to proxy for such diverse risk components. Features of particular debt (such as fixed or floating rates, convertible, subordinated, or redeemable features and maturity) are not individually measured but are proxied by the effective interest rate incurred by the company.

This research pursues different specifications with respect to time periods and estimation methods. In particular, regression in 'changes' form is estimated, reducing the likelihood of correlated omitted variable problems (Skinner, 1996).

DATA BASE

Disclosure International "Worldscope Global" data base is the source for the companies analyzed. These databases are in CD-ROM form.[3] The "Worldscope Global" database constantly adds companies for which international company information is available as to financial data items. Due to the combined text and numerical format, which often omits line items for particular companies and does not consistently align years, considerable file alignment effort was expended to create a parallel data set among countries for analysis in the time frame of interest.

Five-year averages (i.e. the average of four years preceding each year with the current year) for 1986 through 1990 of the variables described in Table 2 were derived from this data set, to control for leverage, size, profitability, and

Table 2.   Descriptive Statistics.

Country	Frequency	Percent	INDUSTRY MIX OF ENTITIES CHANGING TO BIG 5 IN	1988	(1989)
Italy	11	3.6	Banks	13.0%	(7.4%)
Spain	3	1.0	Other Financial	3.2%	(4.4%)
Australia	18	5.8	Insurance	–.–	(5.9%)
Germany	74	23.9	Transportation	3.2%	(1.5%)
France	49	15.9	Utilities	9.7%	(1.5%)
United Kingdom	154	49.8	Industrial	70.9%	(79.3%)
Total	309	100.0			

AUDITOR CHANGES

24 changes to Big 5 in 1990 out of 309 entities: 7.8%	24 changes from Big 5 in 1990 out of 309 entities: 7.8%
18 changes to Big 5 in 1989 out of 309 entities: 5.8%	5 changes from Big 5 in 1989 out of 309 entities: 1.6%
11 changes to Big 5 in 1988 out of 309 entities: 3.6%	2 changes from Big 5 in 1988 out of 309 entities: 0.6%

Variable Name	Variable Definition: Natural Logarithm of (antilog of means 1990; 1989; 1988)	1990 mean (std. dev.) N 1989 mean (std. dev.) N 1988 mean (std. dev.) N
ln (Financial Leverage)	(Assets/Owners' Equity) * 100 (antilogs: 2.25; 2.27; 2.29)	0.81 (0.71) 694 0.82 (0.65) 622 0.83 (0.70) 506
ln (size and efficiency)	Net Sales or Revenues/Number of Employees in millions (antilogs: 0.31; 0.29; 0.28)	−1.17 (2.03) 863 −1.25 (2.02) 863 −1.26 (2.02) 773
ln (profitability – operating income to total capital) (OPITC)	(Operating Income/Last Year's Total Capital) * 100 (antilogs: 13.87; 14.01; 14.15)	2.63 (0.96) 852 2.64 (0.90) 788 2.65 (0.86) 682
ln (effective tax rate)	(Income Taxes/Pretax Income) * 100 (antilogs: 34.81; 35.52; 37.34)	3.55 (0.40) 583 3.57 (0.44) 591 3.62 (0.47) 530
ln (profitability – ROA)	Return on Assets (antilogs: 6.17; 5.87; 5.16)	1.82 (0.78) 930 1.77 (0.78) 838 1.64 (0.80) 710
ln (profitability – ROIC)	Return on Investment Capital (antilogs: 11.36; 11.02; 10.28)	2.43 (0.73) 926 2.40 (0.74) 839 2.33 (0.69) 708
ln (effective interest rate: [interest expense on debt/ (short-term debt + current portion of long-term debt + long-term debt)*100] − bond yield)	Effective Interest Rate – Bond Yield For Respective Country (antilogs: 5.47; 7.69; 10.07)	1.70 (1.67) 710 2.04 (1.62) 782 2.31 (1.48) 773

tax effects within the model of effective interest rate. The antilogs are reported in the middle column of Table 2, corresponding to each year's reported average in the far right column, in order to facilitate interpretation. All companies on the database for the countries reflected in Table 2 were included in the study; indeed, a data set of 959 entities was assembled which included Singapore, Belgium, Austria, Switzerland, Finland, and the Netherlands. However, missing data reduced the companies available for modeling to the six countries in Table 2 and a total of 309 entities.[4] The use of ratios rather than "level" variables was viewed as most appropriate, given the diverse countries being compared and the nature of currency fluctuations among countries.[5] The mix of industries is described for the entities analyzed that changed to Big 5 auditors. Prior literature does not imply a need to control for industry; this information is provided for descriptive purposes only.

The analysis reflected in Table 3 adjusts for the bond yield of the respective countries in the corresponding year; this information was retrieved from graphics available on the worldwide web entitled World Economic Window, Bonaparte Inc., then accessible via the address <http://nmg.clever.net/wew/curves/>. Those years were not available for Australia, but bond yield information was obtained from the *International Financial Statistics Yearbook* (International Monetary Fund (IMF), 1995). A sample of the data from the web was compared with measures reported by the IMF and found to correspond. The bond rates are intended to represent the risk-free rate in the entity's home country. The government instruments' maturity is matched to the appropriate year and time horizon of the data set.

ANALYSIS AND RESULTS

Ordinary least squares (OLS) models were estimated for each of the three years with data available for analysis, as reported in Table 3. Without transformation to natural logarithms, the residuals of the regression models lack normality, although the findings are qualitatively similar to those reported herein. The natural logarithmic approach produces well-behaved residuals, compliant with the underlying assumptions of regression analysis. The largest (in absolute value) standardized residual in each model is -3.97 for 1990, -3.61 for 1989, and 4.27 for 1988. The use of logarithms assists in controlling for the nonlinear effect of size expected in modeling financial phenomena – a likely source of the nonnormality. In addition, the double log transformation causes the estimated coefficients on the explanatory variables to be elasticity estimates whereby a percentage change in the explanatory variable causes a percentage change in the dependent variable. This form can be theoretically tied to points and pricing practices in debt markets, providing a practice-based linkage for the statistical model estimated. For example, a 5% improvement in ROA is observed to reduce effective interest by an average of 13 to 20%.

Table 3 reports a significant role for leverage, with a negative sign. This likely stems, as reflected in Table 2, from the sample hovering at about 55% debt (i.e. 100/45 or 2.2 financial leverage), within the range of favorable leverage without excessive risk. The profitability measure ROIC has a significant positive sign, behaving more like a leverage construct. ROA is significantly negative, suggesting greater profitability is associated with lower interest costs. Since the ROIC represents in part the invested capital relative to debt, the capital structure is being concurrently measured. The penalty for leverage may not be perceptible within the pooled international sample beyond the relatively higher levels observed in Germany and captured by that indicator variable (significant in 1988 and 1989). In contrast to domestic research, ratio proxies for international settings during accounting disharmony have increased noise tied to such definitional differences as debt vs equity (Wallace & Walsh, 1995).

The size variable lacks significance except in 1988 (reaching a 0.10 two-tailed level, when it takes on a positive sign, implying higher interest for larger entities). The relative dominance of the financial leverage variable may mean the size variable is only a secondary consideration. (This appears to be borne out in the Table 4 results, discussed later, where size increases in significance in the absence of the leverage variable.) The effective tax rate has no statistically significant sign at a 0.05 level.

As Table 3 reports, the selection of a Big 5 auditor is associated with a lower effective interest rate in each of the three models, as hypothesized, with a one-tail significance level of 0.01, 0.10, and 0.03 respectively.[6] The incidence of changes to and from Big 5 in each year is measured by an indicator variable and using a one-tailed approach implies a 0.03 level of significance for a higher interest cost association in 1990 for entities changing to Big 5 – contrary to expectations – and a 0.02 significance level for a higher interest cost association in 1988 for changing from a Big 5 auditor – in line with expectations. The general lack of significance of the six coefficients relating to changes, as well as the unexpected sign, is likely to be a joint effect of the low incidence of such changes (see Table 2) and the necessity for a longer window post-change to be considered to assess the effective interest associations over time. Indeed, one could postulate that it is the higher interest to date that prompts a change to a Big 5 auditor, anticipating rewards longer term. It may also be argued that entities which change from Big 5 auditors are willing to incur higher interest costs as a possible result of such a change. This is an implication of signalling theory, as described earlier. For these reasons, the change variables

Table 3. Regression Modeling of Effective Interest.

Independent Variables sign hypothesized	Dependent Variable: ln(1990 effective interest-bond yield) coefficient (t-value)	Dependent Variable: ln(1989 effective interest-bond yield) coefficient (t-value)	Dependent Variable: ln(1988 effective interest-bond yield) coefficient (t-value)
Constant	-0.14 (-0.13)	-2.21 (-2.49)***	0.11 (0.12)
ln(Financial Leverage)	-3.21 (-9.90)***	-2.22 (-8.67)***	-2.20 (-8.25)***
ln(size)	0.12 (1.24)	-0.05 (-0.56)	0.12 (1.67)*
ln(profitability – operating income to total capital)	-0.04 (-0.35)	-0.11 (-0.93)	-0.07 (-0.61)
ln(profitability – ROA)	-4.17 (-11.79)***	-2.81 (-9.99)***	-2.61 (-9.27)***
ln(profitability – ROIC)	5.35 (12.71)***	4.17 (11.34)***	3.68 (10.78)***
ln(effective tax rate) •	-0.29 (-1.22)	0.15 (0.79)	-0.07 (-0.37)
Italy	-0.92 (-1.04)	0.49 (0.68)	-1.30 (-1.96)**
Spain	0.25 (0.17)	–	-3.68 (-3.93)***
Australia	-0.21 (-0.48)	0.48 (1.26)	-0.32 (-1.12)

Table 3. Continued.

Independent Variables sign hypothesized	Dependent Variable: ln(1990 effective interest-bond yield) coefficient (t-value)	Dependent Variable: ln(1989 effective interest-bond yield) coefficient (t-value)	Dependent Variable: ln(1988 effective interest-bond yield) coefficient (t-value)
France	-0.13	0.56	0.06
	(-0.38)	(1.90)*	(0.21)
Germany	0.12	0.83	0.71
+	(0.43)	(3.35)***	(3.12)***
Big 5 Auditor	0.37	-0.19	-0.27
−	(-2.26)***	(-1.29)*	(-1.88)**
Change to Big 5	0.52	0.23	0.13
−	(1.91)**	(0.91)	(0.55)
Change from Big 5	0.18	0.12	0.44
+	(0.65)	(0.52)	(2.11)**
R-Square (Adjusted R-Square) [F-stat (df) prob.]	0.353 (0.328) [14.475 (14,372) 0.0000]	0.331 (0.308) [14.74 (13,388) 0.0000]	0.41 (0.39) [16.89 (14,338) 0.0000]

* 0.10 level of significance (two-tailed, unless a hypothesized sign is indicated).
** 0.05 level of significance (two-tailed, unless a hypothesized sign is indicated).
*** 0.01 level of significance (two-tailed, unless a hypothesized sign is indicated).

in Table 3 must be interpreted with caution. Table 4 increases both sample size and power of testing to investigate the change to Big 5 auditor event.

Note that Table 3 provides preliminary evidence of growing harmonization. In 1988, three of the five countries were statistically significant, while in 1989, two of the five countries were significant, and by 1990, none of the five countries were significantly different. This disappearance of significant differences among the countries is consistent with a trend toward more unity of information reporting and convergence to an international standard. It is similarly consistent with increased globalization of debt markets and convergence of interest rates across borders.

Change in Auditor Event

The sample can be enlarged and the window widened by giving up some of the control variables in the models, i.e. by focusing on a more parsimonious model and by combining into a single analysis the 1987, 1988, 1989, and 1990 information on the event of an auditor change. By reducing the model to only considering the change in size and profitability measures, it is possible to secure a sample size of over 500 companies for analysis. The model, as reported in Table 4 looks at the change in the effective interest rate relative to the change in the smaller set of core variables, and even reduces the model further to control only one profitability measure and thereby enlarge the sample by another 10%. The two models permit a check on the stability of the relationships. Since the entities' changes could be from 1987 to 1988, 1988 to 1989, or 1989 to 1990, two indicator variables are used to capture these three categories – 1988 and 1989 changes, relative to the 1990 changes that are captured automatically by the constant term. Note that only changes **to** Big 5 are addressed in this analysis.

The models are consistent in their reported significance levels, with none of the indicator variables for countries being significant at the conventional 0.05 level and with the change variable being significant at a 0.002 or better level for all four models estimated. The residuals are well behaved and all but two observations were below three standardized residuals. When the dependent variable is not transformed to a natural logarithm, a significantly negative sign results for the change to Big 5, since the difference compares post change to pre change, the quantity will be negative whenever effective interest rate is reduced, and the quantity becomes more negative as an entity is observed to change to a Big 5 auditor. As an example, if the effective interest rate were 20% pre-change and 15% post-change, the dependent variable would be – 5%; the CHG8890 event indicator variable explains that about 70% of the decline is associated with a change to a Big 5 auditor. Since any change in general

Table 4. Multivariate Comparison of Change in 5-year Average Effective Interest Rate.

Dependent Variables	DIFEIR = effective interest post change – effective interest pre-change 507 cases	DIFEIR 548 cases	LNDIFEIR = ln(abs(difeir)) 507 cases	LNDIFEIR 548 cases
LNDIFSAL = ln(abs(difsal)) coefficient DIFSAL = sales/employees post change – sales/employees pre-change (t-value)	−8.71 (−1.55)	−7.05 (−1.36)	10.32 (1.84)*	8.61 (1.67)*
LNDIFOPI=ln(abs(difopi)) DIFOPI = operating income to total capital post change – operating income to invested capital pre-change	−3.51 (−0.75)	−3.44 (−0.842)	3.30 (0.703)	3.31 (0.814)
LNDIFROA = ln(abs(difroa)) DIFROA = ROA post change – ROA pre change	−7.15 (−1.14)	–.– –.–	6.21 (0.997)	–.– –.–
LNDIFROC = ln(abs(difroc)) DIFROC = ROC post change – ROC pre change	5.81 (0.96)	–.– –.–	−5.09 (−0.846)	–.– –.–
C88 = 1 if change to Big 5 firm in 1988; 0 otherwise	81.53 (2.31)**	75.12 (2.28)**	−84.66 (−2.41)**	−77.91 (−2.373)**
C89 = 1 if change to Big 5 firm in 1989; 0 otherwise	74.57 (2.35)**	70.11 (2.40)**	−77.56 (−2.46)**	−72.64 −2.49**
U.K.: 1 if country; 0 otherwise (Australia has no indicator variable and remains in constant term)	−11.49 (−0.475)	−8.81 (−0.382)	13.75 (0.570)	11.11 (0.483)
ITALY: 1 if country; 0 otherwise	49.83 (0.968)	45.01 (0.934)	−61.83 (−1.21)	−55.98 (−1.17)
SPAIN: 1 if country; 0 otherwise	−9.83 (−0.212)	12.70 (−0.292)	16.56 (0.359)	19.06 (0.44)
FRANCE: 1 if country; 0 otherwise	13.61 (0.512)	13.48 (0.535)	−14.28 (−0.540)	−13.94 (−0.56)
GERMANY: 1 if country; 0 otherwise	−31.91 (−1.23)	−21.46 (−0.908)	35.68 (1.39)	25.69 (1.09)
CHG8890 = 1 if change to Big 5 auditor in 1988, 1989, or 1990; 0 otherwise (thereby permitting measurement of a longer window) Expected Sign: −	−71.29 (−3.15)***	−67.29 (−3.23)***	70.28 (3.12)***	66.22 (3.19)***

Table 4. Continued.

Dependent Variables	DIFEIR = effective interest post change – effective interest pre-change 507 cases	DIFEIR 548 cases	LNDIFEIR = ln(abs(difeir)) 507 cases	LNDIFEIR 548 cases
CONSTANT	−36.85	−27.30	44.50	34.87
	(−1.07)	(−0.850)	(1.29)	(1.09)
R-Square	0.04	0.03	0.05	0.04
[F-Statistic] df	[1.72]	[1.87]	[1.96]	[2.18]
(signif.)	12,494	10,537	12,494	10,537
	(0.0588)*	(0.0463)**	(0.0259)**	(0.0176)**

Note: The absolute value of each variable was taken before it was converted to natural logarithms; therefore, the signs of the coefficients for the lndifeir models must be obtained through reference to the models using difeir as the dependent variable.

* 0.10 level of significance (two-tailed, unless a hypothesized sign is indicated).
** 0.05 level of significance (two-tailed, unless a hypothesized sign is indicated).
*** 0.01 level of significance (two-tailed, unless a hypothesized sign is indicated).

market interest rates should be consistent among the data set companies, be they changing entities or the control group entities, the aggregate models in Table 4 do not adjust for the changes in market-wide interest rates, except in the sense that the 1988 and 1989 change companies are flagged with an indicator variable.

CONCLUDING REMARKS AND LIMITATIONS

This research documents a possible interplay of international debt markets and selections of the Big 5 audit firms. Preliminary evidence is also available concerning entities changing to and from Big 5 auditors. Cross-sectional pooled results support an average lower effective interest rate by companies audited by the Big 5 from 1986 to 1990, but has too few by-year audit changes to adequately address such events. Use of a reduced model form and focus on the event of change facilitated estimation of a multivariate model of effective interest rate change in adjacent years of an observed change to a Big 5 auditor and quantifies a statistically significant reduction in effective interest rate relative to those entities not changing.

Future work should pursue longitudinal study of key events associated with audit-related information signals and the cost of borrowing, as well as other sources of capital.[7] Clearly, a joint selection process exists in auditing, whereby the auditor accepts the client and the client chooses the auditor. As a result, it is difficult to attribute cause and effect, directionally, without more in-depth control for the manner of auditor selection, including attention to auditing fees associated with obtaining the assurance and insurance attributes hypothesized for Big 5 audit firms. Yet, a systematic association does exist between those companies which are audited by a Big 5 auditor in 1990, 1989, or 1988 in six countries and lower effective interest rates. The hold-out sample comparison of Canada further corroborates the resiliency of empirical specifications estimated, as does the persistence of the findings in both levels and change analyses. The methodology that focuses on the event of auditor changes in the pooled analysis reported in Table 4 increases the power of the tests, quantifying that 70% of observed declines in effective interest costs from 1986 to 1990 is attributable to entities changing to Big 5 auditors.

Future inquiry would no doubt benefit from directing attention to intricacies within specific industries, particular debt and equity markets, and varying ownership structures, providing further insight as to the magnitude of the cost of capital savings reasonably expected from audit-associated selections by individual companies. A determinant of interest is credit rating, and it may be that the creditworthiness of an issuer changed coincidentally with the change in auditors and/or that the change in auditor enhanced the rating which in turn affected the interest incurred. Such precision of chronology and interacting variables has not been controlled and awaits further research to be addressed. This study has the limitation of focusing on a relatively short time frame, 1986 to 1990, and being subject to archival database constraints.

As capital markets have increased in their complexity with derivatives, hedging, debt-equity swaps, floating swaps, and plans for a common market currency, means of relating effective interest, reported financial numbers, and market-based measures likewise increase in complexity. Some might argue that the movement toward Big 5 auditing affiliations relate to more sophisticated derivatives strategies or enhanced global tax strategies aided in some manner by the professional service firm's consulting activities. Tax effects and foreign currency translation are seen as explanations for some companies' apparent high interest rates, although some of these differences would be expected to be mitigated through access to international markets. Differential tax treatment of capital gains on currency, deductibility of stated interest, and similar considerations produce sources of measurement error in analyzing effective interest. These observations suggest that there is substantial opportunity to finesse measures of cost of capital and comparison among countries through more detailed analysis of focused samples. The results reported herein are encouraging, since statistically significant and fairly consistent reductions of five-year effective interest rates are demonstrated, despite the multiple sources of measurement error pervasive in economic and accounting-based numbers[8] associated with international settings. The evidence of a convergence among countries over time is also suggestive of a move toward an international standard, plausibly reflective of more unity of information reporting. Of course, this may also relate to increased globalization of debt markets.

The regulatory infrastructure is now tentatively in place to a point that international standards harmonization is fully feasible, if not a reality. However, it has been long in the making, and the markets have had to use substitutes along the way toward globalization of markets, in the absence of such harmonization. This article is consistent with an explanation of one such substitute, in the 1986 to 1990 time frame, when harmonization's desirability was still actively debated, being the selection of a Big 5 auditor by companies in a diverse set of countries. Such borrowers have incurred systematically lower effective interest costs as they changed toward world-firm auditors.

NOTES

1. Beneish and Press (1993) measure basis points over prime to evaluate debt costs but report that of 61 firms studied, changes in borrowing rates could be identified for only 48 firms because of limitations in the availability of contracts and the extent of interest rate disclosures in financial statements. Interest rate changes were drawn from contracts for 43 of the 48 firms and from Management Discussion and Analysis (MDAs) and debt footnotes for the remaining five firms (p. 244).

2. The incidence of other than a clean or unqualified audit report for the total data base is 7.3% for Italy, 15.9% for Spain, 14.1% for Australia, 5.1% for Germany, 8.8% for France, and 6.7% for the United Kingdom. Note that the other types of reports include qualified, not containing an audit report in the abbreviated version, consolidated statement not audited but parent company audited, and partial audit (not all statements audited).

3. To verify the computation of each ratio used, as well as provide a "walk-through" of the validity of the database, I compared a company in Sweden: BPA Byggproduktion AB, a public industrial construction company, to the original annual report from that company and was able to tie each figure to the source document computationally. Note that the universe of companies contained on the database has risen from 4,000 in 1987 to 27,000 in 1999, covering 53 countries and 95% of the total value of the world's markets (Worldscope 2000, p. 24). The base year was 1980 but the company itself states "statistically significant company and data item representation is best represented from January 1985 forward" (Worldscope, 2000, p. 4) which is the start point for the period analyzed herein. See Worldscope (1999) for a discussion of companies inclusion criteria for the database.

4. The differing counts in Tables 2 and 3 stem from missing data; the maximum number of observations available for the initial population is reported in the descriptive statistics, while only those entities with data on each of the control variables, as well as effective interest, are able to be analyzed within the models.

5. The ratios will be influenced by underlying differences in accounting treatment; for example, Germany and Italy use historical cost less accumulated depreciation for valuation, whereas France allows revaluation, with gains taxable. Accumulated depreciation may be straight-line or declining balance for France and Germany, whereas Italy uses straight-line rates. Further details are provided from such resources as the Price Waterhouse series *Doing Business in___* which are available for Germany (1992), Italy (1993), and France (1994), as well as publications by the American Institute of Public Accountants such as the series entitled *The Accounting Profession in___* available for France (1988) and Italy (1991), among other countries. Nonetheless, these ratios provide reasonable proxies for the control variables for this inquiry.

6. As a hold-out sample test of the stability of relationships estimated, Compustat's listing of companies in Canada provided a sample of 82 entities (out of a total population of 756 entities) with complete information to estimate the model:

	regression coefficient	t-value (2-tail sig. except for Big 5)
natural logarithm of interest rate =	−2.37 constant	−1.76 (0.08)
	0.18 natural logarithm of size	1.10 (0.28)
	−0.64 natural logarithm of profitability–operating income	−9.67 (0.00)
	−0.59 natural logarithm of effective tax rate	−2.21 (0.03)
	0.66 natural logarithm of ROA	1.81 (0.07)
	0.11 natural logarithm of ROIC	0.30 (0.76)
	−0.33 Big 5 auditor	−1.31 (0.098) one-tail

The R-square is 0.62, with adjusted R-square value of 0.59, F-value of 20.32, significant at 0.0000 and standardized residuals ranging from −3.75 to 2.69; Durbin-Watson is 1.71. Of the entities, 50.7% are Big-6 audited entities, with unqualified auditor reports (eight cases have missing information on report type). This model does not adjust for the bond yield level in Canada or the level of financial leverage, yet produces coefficients with consistent signs (save the differing weights and dominance within the set of profitability measures–operating income, ROA, and ROIC) and even similar magnitude of coefficient for size and Big 5 auditor (relative to similar 1990 data displayed in Table 3). Using a one-tailed interpretation, the significance level of the Big 5 negative coefficient, representing a reduction in the effective interest cost is 0.09785.

Further corroborative evidence is available from a model estimated for the larger set of countries by only including an indicator variable per country and a single profitability measure that had the least missing information from the data set, focusing only on the cross-sectional variable of presence or absence of a Big 5 auditor (without attention to the natural logarithmic transformation):

Effective Interest Rate Averaged For Five Years Ended 1990 =

	regression coefficient	t-value (2-tail sig.)
Big 5 Auditor where 1 = Yes and 0 = No	−1.011	−1.987 (0.047)
Operating Profit Margin Averaged For Five Years Ended 1990	−0.146	−5.08 (0.000)
Indicator Variables Used Per Country, i.e. 1 = Yes and 0 = No		

	regression coefficient	t-value (2-tail sig.)
Malaysia	2.151	0.759 (0.448)
Sweden	2.169	0.924 (0.355)
Netherlands	1.943	0.822 (0.411)
Finland	−2.413	0.981 (0.327)
France	0.270	0.125 (0.900)
Germany	2.665	1.226 (0.221)
United Kingdom	2.471	1.218 (0.224)
Japan	1.726	0.864 (0.388)
(Constant)	14.433	7.148 (0.000)

F-statistic 4.358 $_{10,571}$ Significant at 0.000.

This model shows the persistence across other countries and different model forms of the results reported herein. The absence of any statistically significant indicator variables by country, as well as the positive sign for Germany, are both consistent with expectations and suggest that by 1990, less variability among the countries was observed.

7. Current literature proposes varied approaches to measuring firms' cost of equity capital, including use of a constant discount rate, industry-based discount rates, and various one-factor and three-factor models. Moreover, valuation models have been analytically derived (e.g. Ohlson, 1995) which are helpful in comparing market and book values of companies, explicating associated assumptions. Arguably, book values and market values of debt instruments are more aligned than are asset measures, suggesting the usefulness of reported effective interest rate measures when analyzing the debt component of capital costs.

8. Examples of the challenge in reconciling economic and accounting-based numbers, aside from international complications, are discussed in Fisher (1988), Salamon (1988), and Salamon and Kopel (1993). Some encouragement regarding ratio comparisons is provided in Kwong et al. (1995) and Wallace and Walsh (1995).

ACKNOWLEDGMENTS

The support of the KPMG Peat Marwick Foundation's Research Opportunities in Auditing Program is gratefully acknowledged. A number of research assistants at both Texas A & M University and College of William and Mary have assisted me in this inquiry; in particular, I appreciate the assistance of Scott Summers, now on the faculty at Brigham Young University, and Mark Ruback, Brandon Steele, Greg Dawson, and John Walsh, alumni of the MBA program at the College of William and Mary. The comments received on earlier versions of this article by reviewers and colleagues, as well as those received at a College of William and Mary workshop were most helpful. I also appreciate information provided by the Editor and Orhan Celik, a Visiting Scholar at Case Western Reserve University from the University of Ankara.

REFERENCES

Akerlof, G. (1970). The Market for "Lemons": Quality Uncertainty and the Market Mechanism. *Quarterly Journal of Economics*, (August), 488–500.

Antle, R. (1982). The Auditor as an Economic Agent. *Journal of Accounting Research*, *20*(2), 503–527.

Antle, R. (1984). Auditor Independence. *Journal of Accounting Research* (Volume 22): 1–20.

Baiman, S., Evans III, J., & Noel, J. (1987). Optimal Contracts With a Utility Maximizing Auditor. *Journal of Accounting Research*, *25*(2), 217–244.

Balvers, R. J., McDonald, B., & Miller, R. E. (1988). Underpricing of New Issues and the Choice of Auditor as a Signal of Investment Banker Reputation. *The Accounting Review*, *63*(4)(October), 605–622.

Barrett, G. R. (1990). What 1992 means to small and mid-sized businesses. *Journal of Accountancy*, (July), 63–69.

Beattie, V., & Fearnley, S. (1995). The Importance of Audit Firm Characteristics and the Drivers of Auditor Change in UK Listed Companies. *Accounting and Business Research*, *25*(100)(Autumn), 227–239.

Beatty, R. (1989). Auditor Reputation and the Pricing of Initial Public Offerings. *The Accounting Review*, *64*(4)(October), 693–709.

Beaudry, P. (1997). Comment on Short-Run Independence of Monetary Policy Under Pegged Exchange Rates. *Journal of Money, Credit, and Banking*, *29*(4)(November, Pt. 2), 811–814.

Begley, J. (1990). The use of debt covenants to control agency problems. Dissertation, University of Rochester.

Begley, J. (1994). Restrictive covenants included in public debt agreements: An empirical investigation. Working Paper, University of British Columbia.

Begley, J., & Feltham, G. A. (1999). An Empirical examination of the relation between debt contracts and management incentives. *Journal of Accounting and Economics*, *27*(2)(April), 229–259.

Belsey, D. S., Kuh, E., & Welsch, R. E. (1980). *Regression Diagnostics: Identifying Influential Data and Sources of Collinearity*. New York, NY: Wiley.

Beneish, M. D., & Press, E. (1993). Costs of Technical Violation of Accounting-Based Covenants. *The Accounting Review*, *68*(2)(April), 233–257.

Celik, O.(2001). Investment and Trade Data: U.S. and Principal Partner Economic Relationships. Weatherhead School of Management Accountancy Working Paper 29-4-01, Case Western Reserve University, Cleveland, Ohio (Visiting Scholar from University of Ankara).

Chen, K., & Wei, K. (1993). Creditors' decisions to waive violations of accounting-based debt covenants. *The Accounting Review*, *68*(April), 218–232.

Choi, F. D. S., & Levich, R. M. (1991). Behavioral effects of international accounting diversity. *Accounting Horizons*, (June), 1–13.

Chow, C., Kramer, L., & Wallace, W. A. (1988). The Environment of Auditing. In: A. R. Abdel-Khalik & I. Solomon (Eds), *Research Opportunities in Auditing: The Second Decade* (pp. 155–183). Sarasota, Florida: American Accounting Association.

Clarkson, P. M., & Simunic, D. A. (1994). The association between audit quality, retained ownership, and firm-specific risk in U.S. vs. Canadian IPO markets. *Journal of Accounting and Economics*, *45*(September), 1045–1067.

Conover, T. L., & Wallace, W. A. (1995). Equity Market Benefits to Disclosure of Geographic Segment Information: An Argument for Decreased Uncertainty. *Journal of International Accounting, Auditing, and Taxation*, *4*(2), 101–112.

Conover, T. L., & Wallace, W. A. (1994). Two Roads Diverge. *Financial Executive*, (May–June), 6.

Craswell, A. T., Francis, J. R., & Taylor, S. L. (1995). Auditor Brand Name Reputations and Industry Specializations. *Journal of Accounting and Economics*, *20*(3)(December), 297–322.

Cravens, K. S., & Wallace, W. A. (2001). A Framework for Determining the Influence of the Corporate Board of Directors in Accounting Studies. *Corporate Governance: An International Review*, *9*(1)(January), 2–24.

Cumby, R. E., & Mishkin, F. S. (1986). The international linkage of real interest rates: The European-U.S. connection. *Journal of International Money and Finance*, *5*(January), 5–23.

Datar, S. M., Feltham, G. A., & Hughes, J. S. (1991). The role of audits and audit quality in valuing new issues. *Journal of Accounting and Economics*, *14*(March), 3–49.

DeAngelo, L. E. (1981). Auditor Size and Audit Quality. *Journal of Accounting and Economics*, *3*(2), 183–199.

Dhaliwal, D. (1978). The Impact of Disclosure Regulations on the Cost of Capital. *Economic Consequences of Financial Accounting Standards: Selected Papers* (pp. 73–100). Stamford, Connecticut: Financial Accounting Standards Board.

Diamond, D. W. (1989). Reputation Acquisition in Debt Markets. *Journal of Political Economy*, *XCVII*, 828–861.

Diwan, I. (1989). Foreign debt, crowding out and capital flight. *Journal of International Money and Finance*, *8*, 121–136.

Dopuch, N., & Simunic, D. (1980). The Nature of Competition in the Auditing Profession: A Descriptive and Normative View. In: J. W. Buckley & J. F. Weston (Eds), *Regulation and the Accounting Profession*. Lifetime Learning Publications.

Dopuch, N., & Simunic, D. (1982). Competition in Auditing: An Assessment. *Fourth Symposium on Auditing Research*, University of Illinois.

Eichenseher, J. W., Hagigi, M., & Shields, D. (1989). Market Reaction To Auditor Changes By OTC Companies. *Auditing: A Journal of Practice and Theory*, *9*(1), 29–440.

Elliott, R. K., & Jacobson, P. (1994). Costs and Benefits of Disclosing Information. Report prepared for the AICPA Special Committee on Financial Reporting.

Ettredge, M., & Greenberg, R. (1990). Determinants of Fee Cutting on Initial Audit Engagements. *Journal of Accounting Research*, *28*(1)(Spring), 198–210.

Fama, E. F., & Laffer, A. B. (1971). Information and Capital Markets. *The Journal of Business*, *44*(3)(July), 289–298.

Feltham, G. A., Hughes, J. S., & Simunic, D. (1991). Empirical assessment of the impact of auditor quality on the valuation of new issues. *Journal of Accounting and Economics*, *14*(December), 375–399.

Finance & Treasury (1994). *Financial Reporting: The Grass is Always Greener* (April 25), 5–7.

Fisher, F. M. (1988). Accounting Data and the Economic Performance of Firms. *Journal of Accounting and Public Policy*, *7*(4), 253–260.

Francis, J. R., & Simon, D. (1987). A Test of Audit Pricing in the Small-Client Segment of the U.S. Audit Market. *The Accounting Review*, *62* (1)(January), 145–157.

Francis, J. R., & Wilson, E. R. (1988). Auditor Changes: A Joint Test of Theories Relating to Agency Costs and Auditor Differentiation. *The Accounting Review*, *63*(4)(October), 663–682.

GateWaze, Inc. (1990). World Trader Information Base.

Gagnon, J. E., & Unferth, M. D. (1995). Is there a world real interest rate? *Journal of International Money and Finance*, *14*(6), 845–855.

Gietzmann, M. B., & Quick, R. (1998), Capping Auditor Liability: The German Experience. *Accounting, Organizations and Society*, (January), 81–103.

Goeltz, R. K. (1991). Commentary: International Accounting Harmonization: The Impossible (and Unnecessary?) Dream. *Accounting Horizons*, (March), 85–88.

Grinyer, J. R., & Russell, A. (1992). National Impediments to International Harmonization: Evidence of Lobbying in the U.K. *Journal of International Accounting, Auditing & Taxation 1*(1), 13–31.

Guenther, D. A. (1994). The Relation Between Tax Rates and Pre-Tax Returns Direct Evidence From the 1981 and 1986 Tax Rate Reductions. *Journal of Accounting & Economics, 18*, 379–393.

Healy, P., & Lys, T. (1986). Auditor Changes Following Big Eight Mergers with Non-Big Eight Audit Firms. *Journal of Accounting and Public Policy, 5*, 251–265.

Healy, P. M., & Palepu, K. G. (1993). The Effect of Firms' Financial Disclosure Strategies on Stock Prices. *Accounting Horizons, 7*(1)(March), 1–11.

Herrmann, D., & Thomas, W. (1995). Harmonisation of Accounting Measurement Practices in the European Community. *Accounting and Business Research, 25*(100)(Autumn), 253–265.

Hogan, C. E. (1997). Costs and Benefits of Audit Quality in the IPO Market: A Self-Selection Analysis. *The Accounting Review, 72*(1)(January), 67–86.

International Monetary Fund (1995). *International Financial Statistics Yearbook* (International Monetary Fund).

Jang, H. J., & Lin, C. (1993). Audit Quality and Trading Volume Reaction: A Study of Initial Public Offering of Stocks. *Journal of Accounting and Public Policy, 12*(Fall), 263–287.

Journal of Accountancy (1990). Editorial: U.S. Companies increase overseas investments. (December). 22.

Kinney, Jr., W. R., & Martin, R. D. (1994). Does Auditing Reduce Bias in Financial Reporting? A Review of Audit-Related Adjustment Studies. *Auditing: A Journal of Practice & Theory, 13*(1)(Spring), 149–156.

Klein, B., & Leffler, K. (1981). The Role of Market Forces in Assuring Contractual Performance. *Journal of Political Economy*, (August).

Kwong, M. F. C., Munro, J. W., & Peasnell, K. V. (1995). Commonalities Between Added Value Ratios and Traditional Return on Capital Employed. *Accounting and Business Research, 26*(1)(Winter), 51–67.

Melumad, N. D., & Thoman, L. (1990). On Auditors and the Courts in an Adverse Selection Setting. *Journal of Accounting Research, 28*(1)(Spring), 77–120.

Menon, K., & Williams, D. D. (1994). The Insurance Hypothesis and Market Prices. *The Accounting Review, 69*(2)(April), 327–342.

Menon, K., & Williams, D. (1991). Auditor Credibility and Initial Public Offerings. *The Accounting Review, 66*(2)(April), 313–332.

Monsen, N., & Wallace, W. A. (1994). Norsk Hydro's Communication to International Capital Markets: A Blend of Accounting Principles. Collected Abstracts of the *American Accounting Association's Annual Meeting* (August), 93–94. [Published in the Scandinavian *Journal of Management, 13*(1), 1997, 95–112].

Monsen, N., & Wallace, W. A. (1995). Evolving financial reporting practices: the dilemma of conflicting standards in the Nordic Countries. *Contemporary Accounting Research*, (11), 973–997.

Moore, G., & Ronen, J. (1990). External Audit and Asymmetric Information. *Auditing: A Journal of Practice and Theory, 9*(Suppl.), 234–252.

Moulin, D. J., & Solomon, M. B. (1989). Practical Means of Promoting Common International Standards. *The CPA Journal*, (December), 38–48.

Myers, S. (1977). Determinants of Corporate Borrowing. *Journal of Financial Economics, 4*, 147–176.

Myers, S. C. (1984). The Capital Structure Puzzle. *The Journal of Finance, XXXIX*(3)(July), 575–592.

Myers, S., & Majluf, N. (1984). Corporate Financing and Investment Decisions when Firms have Information that Investors do not have. *Journal of Financial Economics*, *14*(2), 187–221.

Nobes, C. W., & Parker, R. H. (1985). *Comparative International Accounting* (2nd ed.). Oxford: Phillips Allan Publishers Ltd.

Nobes, C. W. (1992). *International Classification of Financial Reporting* (2nd ed.). London and New York: Routledge.

O'Connor, W. F. (1992). A Comparative Analysis of the Major Areas of Tax Controversy in Developed Countries. *Journal of International Accounting, Auditing & Taxation*, *1*(1), 61–79.

Ohanian, L. E., & Stockman, A. C. (1997). Short-Run Independence of Monetary Policy Under Pegged Exchange Rates and Effects of Money on Exchange Rates and Interest Rates. *Journal of Money, Credit, and Banking*, *29*(4)(November, Pt. 2), 783–806.

Ohlson, J. (1995). Earnings, Book Values and Dividends in Security Valuation. *Contemporary Accounting Research*, (11), 661–687.

Palmrose, Z. (1986). Audit Fees and Auditor Size: Further Evidence. *Journal of Accounting Research*, *24*(1)(Spring), 97–110.

Petersen, M. A., & Rajan, R. G. (1995). The Effect of Credit Market Competition on Lending Relationships. *The Quarterly Journal of Economics*, (May), 407–443.

Price, R., & W. A. Wallace. (2001). *Shades of Materiality*. Research Monograph, 24. Vancouver, BC, Canada: CGA-Canada Research Foundation.

Raman, K. K., & Wilson, E. R. (1992). An Empirical Investigation of the Market for "Single Audit" Services. *Journal of Accounting and Public Policy*, *11*, 271–295.

Ross, S. (1977). The Determination of Financial Structure: The Incentive-Signaling Approach. *Bell Journal of Economics*, *8*, 23–40.

Ross, S. (1979). Disclosure Regulations in Financial Markets: Implications of Modern Finance Theory and Signaling Theory. *Key Issues in Financial Regulation*, 177–201.

Roussey, R. S. (1992). Developing International Accounting and Auditing Standards for World Markets. *Journal of International Accounting Auditing & Taxation*, *1*(1), 1–11.

Salamon, G. L. (1988). On the Validity of Accounting Rates of Return in Cross-sectional Analysis: Theory, Evidence, and Implications. *Journal of Accounting and Public Policy*, *7*(4)(Winter), 267–292.

Salamon, G. L., & Kopel, R. (1993). Accounting Method Related Misspecification in Cross-Sectional Capital Market Research Designs. *Journal of Accounting and Public Policy*, *12*(3)(Fall), 217–238.

Samuel, J. M., & Oliga, J. C. (1982). Accounting Standards in Developing Countries. *International Journal of Accounting*, (Fall), 69–88.

Schwartz, K., & Menon, K. (1985). Auditor Switches by Failing Firms. *The Accounting Review*, (April), 248–261.

Simunic, D., & Stein, M. (1986). On the Economics of Product Differentiation in Auditing. In: *Proceedings of the 1986 Touche Ross/University of Kansas Symposium on Auditing Problems* (pp. 69–99).

Simunic, D., & Stein, M. (1987). *Product Differentiation in Auditing: Auditor Choice in the Market for Unseasoned New Issues*. Vancouver, British Columbia: The Canadian Certified General Accountants' Research Foundation.

Simunic, D., & Stein, M. T. (1996). The Impact of Litigation Risk on Audit Pricing: A Review of the Economics and the Evidence. *Auditing: A Journal of Practice and Theory*, *15*(Suppl.), 119–134.

Skinner, D. J. (1996). Are Disclosures About Bank Derivatives and Employee Stock Options 'Value-Relevant'? *Journal of Accounting and Economics*, *22*, 393–405.

Smieliauskas, W. (1996). Discussion Of The Impact of Litigation Risk on Audit Pricing: A Review of the Economics and the Evidence. *Auditing: A Journal of Practice and Theory*, *15*(Suppl.), 139–144.

Spence, M. (1973). Job Market Signaling. *Quarterly Journal of Economics*, *87*, 355–374.

Tang, Y. (2000). Bumpy Road Leading to Internationalization: A Review of Accounting Development in China. *Accounting Horizons*, (March), 93–102.

Taylor, M. H., & Simon, D. T. (1999). Determinants of Audit Fees: The Importance of Litigation, Disclosure, and Regulatory Burdens in Audit Engagements in 20 Countries. *The International Journal of Accounting*, *34*(3), 375–380.

Wallace, W. A. (1980). *The Economic Role of the Audit in Free and Regulated Markets. The Touche Ross & Co. Aid to Accounting Education Program*. Reprint by South-Western Publishing, in *Auditing Monographs*. Available on the web at (http://raw.rutgers.edu/raw/wallace/homepage.html).

Wallace, W. A. (1981). The Association Between Municipal Market Measures and Selected Financial Reporting Practices. *Journal of Accounting Research*, *19*(2), 502–520.

Wallace, W. A. (1987). The Economic Role of the Audit in Free and Regulated Markets: A Review. *Research in Accounting Regulation*, *1*, 7–34.

Wallace, W. A., & Walsh, J. (1995). Apples-To-Apples Profits Abroad. *Financial Executive*, (May/June), 28–31.

Wells, S. C., Thompson, J. H., & Phelps, R. A. (1995). Accounting Differences: U.S. Enterprises and International Competition for Capital. *Accounting Horizons*, *9*(2)(June), 29–39.

Wilson, E. R., & Howard, T. P. (1984). The Association Between Municipal Market Measures and Selected Financial Reporting Practices: Additional Evidence. *Journal of Accounting Research*, *22*(1), 207–224.

Woo, E., & Koh, H. C. (2001). Factors Associated With Auditor Changes: A Singapore Study. *Accounting and Business Research*, *31*(2)(Spring), 133–144.

Worldscope (1999). *Capital Markets Guide*. Primark – Client Services 1–800–228–3220.

Worldscope (2000). *Worldscope Data Definitions Guide*. Primark.

VOLUNTARY DISCLOSURE OF VALUE DRIVER INFORMATION: A CONTENT ANALYSIS OF GLOBAL M&A AND OTHER CROSS-BOUNDARY DISCLOSURES OF THE FORD MOTOR COMPANY 1995–2000

Orhan Celik, Garen Markarian and Gary John Previts

ABSTRACT

The interest of financial executives, regulators and standard setters to provide investors with 'key performance indicators' may be served by articulating "value drivers" as a step in the process toward such indicators. Value Drivers serve as a collecting focus, identifying content items from which patterns of information are observed. Such patterns improve understanding of useful non-financial as well as financial performance measures. Universal and particular value drivers are developed as orientation guides to determine whether information reported is relevant to important management objectives. In this study particular value drivers are established for automotive (OEM) and merger and acquisition activity. These are developed in a global, cross boundary, context that represents the geographic, social and political environment of management.

Research in Accounting Regulation, Volume 15, pages 69–94.
ISBN: 0-7623-0841-9

I. INTRODUCTION

Global M&A activity is leading to the rapid disintegration of traditional political boundaries between countries, and reshaping the economic landscape with respect to industrial hegemony (Anderson et al., 2000). In 1998, M&A transactions aggregated more than $2.5 trillion (as compared with just $100 billion in 1987), and had increased to $1.5 trillion for the first two quarters of 1999 alone, providing strong evidence that M&A has become the strategic centerpiece of many companies' growth strategy (KPMG, 2000). Additionally, 70% of cross-border acquisitions are horizontal, indicating that there are generally companies from the same line of business that are combining to generate strategic gains (Braid, 1999). Many factors have influenced this trend, including competitive pressures from low cost producers, and competition on a product quality basis (Tan et al., 2000). The pattern of global M&A activity can also be attributed to firms' motivations to create wealth by internalizing ownership-specific advantages in foreign locations – advantages derived from financial, technological, informational, and organizational characteristics (Dunning, 1993).

A global M&A strategy focuses on seeking target markets, and involves detailed planning of logistics, tactics, and policy. The benefits realized from achieving a global presence include reduction in transportation costs, access to low cost factors of production, proximity to local markets, avoidance of tariff and non-tariff boundaries, and greater economies of scale (Marquardt, 1999). Other benefits include shorter lead times, on-time delivery, increased innovation and flexibility for both processes and products, and greater responsiveness to the determinants of international competition (Lockamy et al., 1995; Matlay et al., 2000).

We assert that this recent trend in cross-boundary M&A activity, gaining tremendous popularity within the past ten years, should be accompanied by significant changes in the model of business reporting. In today's business environment, M&A activity is a significant trend. Many companies are becoming larger through M&A activities. For that reason, M&A activity is a growth strategy that has fundamental impacts and changes on companies' operations. Such changes are needed to provide users of financial information with the benefits of timely and relevant disclosure necessary for evaluating cross boundary investment decisions. Quality of disclosure is deemed a factor for a lower cost of capital for operating firms (Botosan, 1997). More informative disclosure is associated with both a higher analyst following (Bricker et al., 1999), and more accurate forecasting (Lang & Lundholm, 1996). Finally, expanded disclosure is associated with increases in stock returns, institutional ownership, analyst following, and stock liquidity, while simultaneously controlling for risk, growth and firm size (Healy et al., 1999). Effective business reporting is a cornerstone on which a global capital market system is built, and it contributes to the efficient allocation of resources, a crucial element for a healthy global economy. Effective business reporting indirectly enhances productivity, encourages innovation, and provides an efficient and liquid market for both buying and selling securities, and obtaining and granting credit. Without information suited to users' needs, stakeholders cannot judge the opportunities and risks of alternative investment opportunities (AICPA, 1993).

This paper presents a study of Ford Motor Company disclosures to analyze the adequacy of that firm's financial reporting model in light of the global scale of its operations. The paper is divided into six sections. Following the introduction, we identify a cross-boundary view of M&A activity that transcends culture, tradition, and politics. The third section explains why Ford Motor Company is a suitable test subject for purposes of a cross-boundary study. The fourth section discusses the information needs of Ford's investors, creditors, and other stakeholders, and outlines the value drivers deemed significant to twenty-first century corporate communication policy. The fifth section is the research design, followed by an analysis of Ford's 10-Ks and Annual Reports for the period 1995 through 2000 in terms of the quality of disclosure, giving special attention to global value drivers. The final section summarizes our findings and suggests implications for future policy and research.

II. THE CROSS-BOUNDARY MODEL OF OVERSEAS EXPANSION: BETTER, CHEAPER, FASTER

Changes in the regulatory regimes of several countries have facilitated global M&A activity. During the last decade, 1,053 laws governing foreign direct investment (FDI) throughout the world were revised, and 94% of these changes have established a more favorable regulatory framework to encourage global investment. Furthermore, the number of bilateral investment treaties between nations (including an increasing number of treaties between developing countries) rose from 181 in 1980 to 1,856 in 1999. Treaties addressing double taxation have increased from 719 to 1,982 during this same period. Regulatory changes have had the most direct impact on production and trading patterns of countries. This year, worldwide sales of foreign affiliates totaled $14 trillion (up from $3 trillion in 1980), with global exports accounting for less than half of this amount (OECD, 2000). These numbers demonstrate the increased importance of overseas production activity vis-à-vis exporting functions. The regulatory changes, which usually have decreasing direction between countries, increase companies' international activities. In addition, regulatory authorities of countries have important cooperation activities to establish common regulations for each country.

The liberalization of capital markets, brought about by regulatory changes and the proliferation of new methods of financing M&As, have made the transactions much easier to accomplish. Moreover, the notion that there is a global market for firms that can be bought and sold has become culturally and politically acceptable. Host countries are more willing to permit, and even embrace, this form of global investment because of the benefits associated with the inflow of foreign capital. For example, global M&A activity is often followed by successive investments by foreign acquirers. It usually involves the introduction of new and better technologies, or superior organizational and managerial practices. If the investments prove successful, it generally leads to increases in the level of employment over time (KPMG, 2000). An example of cross-boundary activity is General Motors' production of the Pontiac Le Mans. This car model was designed in Germany by GM's Opel subsidiary, while components and sub-assemblies were obtained in Australia, the United States, Canada, Japan, South Korea, and France. Final assembly was completed in South Korea, and the car was ultimately marketed in the United States and Canada (KPMG, 2000).

At least three patterns of overseas expansion exist in practice: the multinational model, the international model, and the global model. Each model developed in a different historical context and each has its own unique characteristics. The *multinational model* developed in conjunction with the mercantile and colonial activities prior to the twentieth century. Seeking opportunities overseas, companies established positions in untapped, off-shore markets, managing them as independent businesses. This model was based on a decentralized structure, and relied to a great extent on interpersonal relationships and trust. The *international model* began in the post-WWII era, when U.S. firms, aided by falling transportation costs and reliable communications achieved dominance in the global economy. American-based companies, using vigorous planning and control systems, exported new technology, products, and ideas to subsidiaries operating throughout the world. The *global model* developed in a context of low transportation costs and declining protectionist views, due in major part to GATT and the renewed interest in free trade policy. Under this model, the Japanese, for example, tightly centralize management, performing R&D and manufacturing functions at home operations, while confining overseas subsidiaries to sales and service functions and providing them with little autonomy (Bartlett et al., 1989).

In the last decade of the twentieth century, a new model of global activity has developed. Due to the multitude of cross-boundary M&A transactions involving business combinations that overarch all forms of linguistic, cultural, political and economic traditions, this model is labeled the *cross-boundary model*. The current M&A drive has been due to competitive pressures to produce at a higher quality, lower cost, and faster throughput time (Celik, 1999). Quality has emerged as an essential competitive characteristic due largely to Japan's capture of a significant portion of the American automobile market by the early 1980s (Yang, 1995; Haas, 1987). Management sought effective control over quality (Juran et al., 1980), and empirical evidence demonstrated that quality is linked to firm performance (Cole, 1998).

Cost has always been considered essential to a company's competitive position, as firms must often match the cost position of rivals in order to compete (Morales, 1999). Many companies have accomplished this objective by locating their operations in geographic regions that provide access to lower-cost inputs (Porter, 1986). By becoming more competitive on a cost basis, firms are able to increase market share and profitability, and to invest in capabilities that generate a powerful, virtuous cycle of strategic competitiveness. Evidence has shown that quality control also enhances a firm's cost competitiveness (Fawcett et al., 1999).

From a foreign investor's perspective, cross-boundary M&A transactions offer time-related efficiencies as well. Comments from executives such as, "In the economy in which we live, a year has 50 days" or "Speed is our friend – time is our enemy," signify the importance of time and speed in today's business environment (OECD, 2000). Time-based controls are effective in minimizing costs and maximizing the value added to customers since longer development times, cycle times, and lead times invariably create higher costs (Vastag et al., 1994; Morales, 1999). M&A provides the fastest means of establishing a strong position in a new market, achieving market power, and delivering innovative products to the marketplace in the shortest time possible. Cross boundary M&A transactions are also the fastest method for a company to acquire tangible and intangible assets in various countries. They allow firms to rapidly acquire a portfolio of overseas assets – a key source of competitive strength in a global economy (Buxey, 2000; Belcher et al., 2000).

M&A activity, as significant growth strategy for companies, also has some unique difficulties. Especially for cross-boundary mergers, these difficulties directly effect companies' current and future performance. Cross-boundary acquisitions must stand up against cultural conflicts (Napier et al., 1993). For example, differences between a buyer's and seller's character, business culture, philosophy, and strategy raise sensitive issues that make M&A transactions unpopular in certain areas. As a remedy for such conflicts, a post-acquisition strategy implemented by the acquiring company to interact with and conform to the target company's national culture can substantially improve performance following the acquisition (Morosini, 1994).

III. FORD MOTOR COMPANY

We have chosen Ford Motor Company as our subject company for purposes of studying a cross-boundary company. The United Nations/World Investment Report ranks Ford as the world's fourth largest transnational corporation, with $44 billion in international sales and 171,276 employees outside of the United States.[1] The company has manufacturing facilities in 40 countries and sells its product in 200 countries. Ford's management consists of an international line-up of experienced executive officers, including CEO Jacques Nasser, who is of Lebanese and Australian descent; Wolfgang Ritzle, a recent addition from BMW, who is responsible for the company's Premier Automotive Group (Jaguar, Volvo, Aston Martin, Land Rover); and J.C. Mays, who came to the company from Volkswagen. This diverse management group includes several other non-U.S. executives among the top officers. The company's brands include Volvo, Jaguar, Land Rover, Mazda, Mercury, Lincoln, and Aston Martin. Its largest shareholder is foreign – Barclays PLC of Britain – and its third largest shareholder is Fayez Sarofim & Company, an American-based investor of Egyptian origin. Thus, the company represents a true blend of international brands, with factories, employees, sales, and stockholders dispersed throughout the globe.

Cross-boundary firms like Ford must use firm resources and structures to build the capabilities needed for developing a competitive edge. This requires a strategy based on value, rarity, imperfect imitatability, and strategic uniqueness (Barney, 1991). Since all firms in the automotive industry have equal access to such fundamental resources as labor and raw materials, in order to achieve a sustainable competitive advantage, the firms must create unique organizational skills and processes and build distinctive cost-competitive units (Campbell et al., 1997). In order to produce better, cheaper, and faster, Ford has followed a strategy of aggressive M&A activity to extend its market growth. The company's objective is to achieve economies of scale by acquiring diverse skills, resources, and technologies. With effective use of these economies of scale, the company seeks market dominance by building an infrastructure that allows for increased flexibility, and enables one group's expertise (e.g. Volvo) to flow to the rest of the organization. Therefore, by studying Ford, a company whose value chain extends to all four corners of the world, we can analyze a truly cross-boundary firm. Conducting a content analysis of Ford's disclosures should improve our understanding of the present content of cross-boundary company disclosure, and may assist in identifying patterns useful for establishing valuable additional disclosures useful to meet the needs of the twenty-first century corporate communication and investor needs model.

IV. STAKEHOLDERS' INFORMATION NEEDS

In order to retain capital and attract new sources, companies' business reporting must keep pace with the rapid changes affecting cross-boundary companies. Effective business reporting should, therefore, include new performance measures firms use to manage operations. As Ford's increased M&A activity in the past five to ten years makes clear, the business reporting model must be modified to reflect the company's changing environment, or else risk losing its relevance. When business reporting falls behind the pace of change in the business environment, the firm fails to provide users with the information they need (AICPA, 1993).

Given that as many as half of all mergers and acquisitions, measured in terms of shareholder value, fail to meet the performance expectations of parent companies, improved disclosure regarding M&A could assist in directing more timely and appropriate action by all parties affected. Discretionary (and, in the future, possibly mandatory) disclosure of all aspects of the firm's decision to enter a business combination, the expected synergies and efficiencies involved, and a forward-looking discussion that highlights specific objectives of the transaction should be reported.

Financial analysts, a primary user group of financial reports, also have a role in assessing the information contained in such reports while making recommendations to investors based on that information. Addressing the informational needs of financial analysts can help identify what types of disclosures other users of financial information require. The alignment of professional analysts and individual investor needs has been made more evident in the wake of the SEC's issuance of Regulation FD in late 2000. Research about analysts' needs has shown that over-reliance on accounting data yields poor predictive value regarding a company's prospects (Opdyke, 2000), indicating that the financial reporting system by itself inadequately meets the needs of investors. Therefore, analysts must often make independent inquiries of management to gain needed information (Wiegold et al., 2000). While some evidence suggests that the annual report is only moderately useful in obtaining information when compared to discussions with management (Chugh et al., 1984), a 1987 survey identified the annual report as the most frequently used source of information for analysts (SRI International, 1987), and other studies confirm that the annual report remains pre-eminent as a source of valuable information for users (Chang et al., 1985).

For purposes of this paper, we will review analysts' reports to determine what information is relevant to analysts in their decision-making process. Regulation FD, by limiting management's ability to divulge private information to preferred analysts, significantly levels the playing field for all investors – individual or institutional. As a consequence, the annual report, 10-K, and other public disclosures by companies (including press releases and public conference calls) take on added importance in the decision making process of investors. Studying analysts' reports will enable us to determine the most relevant facets of business reporting in shaping an investor's judgment.

To determine the most essential disclosures, we compiled a list of factors that drive shareholder or firm value in a cross-boundary company. These global value drivers were collected by examining analysts' reports, newspaper and magazine articles, the AICPA steering committee's report on voluntary disclosure and business information, and the findings of the FASB's business reporting research project.

We examined articles appearing in the *Wall Street Journal*, *Business Week*, the *New York Times*, and the *Financial Times* during the period 1995 through 2000 to identify the events that induced the most news coverage of Ford Motor Company, i.e. Ford's most significant activities during that time according to analysts and other followers. More than 250 articles appeared concerning Ford Motor Company alone. The news reports dealt primarily with Ford's acquisitions of Mazda (in which the company purchased a 33% controlling stake), Volvo, Land Rover, and an interest in Kia, as well as the company's failed bid for Daewoo. Other news items included Ford's practices of sharing production design and engineering expertise with subsidiaries, creating common platforms, synchronizing production cycles, and its policy of reducing both staff and the number of platforms. News coverage also centered on Ford's strategy in acquiring Volvo and gaining access to that company's safety technology, brand presence, and market share in Europe, as well as the new engineering architecture for Volvo automobiles, similar to that used for the company's Lincoln and Jaguar brands. Finally, the articles dealt with Ford's reduction of component parts duplication resulting from cross-boundary mergers and acquisitions, and the integration of non-competing product line-ups to satisfy all market segments, both of which provide evidence of the company's strong product management.

Another source we examined to determine what disclosures users require regarding global value drivers was the FASB's Business Reporting research project. The FASB task force compiled a list of the automotive industry's value drivers, including industry/economic outlook, product and market share, new products, capacity plans, cash and capital plans, work-force relationships,

strategy execution, innovativeness, etc.[2] We also considered the most important issues examined by sell-side analysts in their evaluation of equity securities
(Previts et al., 1993). Sell-side analysts examine risks and concerns, market
share, competitive position, industry and economic conditions, competitive
capabilities and products, earnings momentum, earnings variability, etc.[3] We
examined 39 analyst reports in the period 1995–2000 on the Ford Motor
Company, from brokerage houses such as Merill Lynch, HSBC, Salomon Smith
Barney, Lehman Brothers, etc., and documented the contents of those in terms
of information relevant for investment decision-making.[4] Finally, we reviewed
KPMG's recent report on M&A activity, which discussed value drivers that
facilitate successful business combinations (KPMG, 2000). KPMG's report finds
that the success of any combination depends on several factors, including
increased growth prospects, acquisition of strategic assets such as technology
and R&D, reduced SG&A costs, reduced future capital expenditures, lower
borrowing costs, enhanced gross margins, etc. Relying on these sources, we
constructed our own list of global value drivers that are essential to the success
of cross-boundary companies.[5] These value drivers should be part of the
reporting objectives met by any cross-boundary company that seeks to provide
relevant information to its stakeholders.

V. RESEARCH DESIGN

We performed a content analysis of Ford Motor Company's 10-Ks and annual
reports from the period 1995 through 1999, to determine the adequacy of the
business reporting model employed. Content analysis takes two basic forms
(Berg, 1998). *Latent content analysis* is an interpretive reading of the text that
searches for the symbolic meaning underlying presented data. *Manifest content
analysis* documents the number of times important ideas appear in a text.
Frequency of occurrence is a useful proxy for magnitude and importance.
In our study, we applied manifest content analysis to Ford's disclosures using
Non-commercial Unstructured Data Indexing Searching and Theorizing
(NUD*IST) software, the leading product in this area, distributed by Sage
Publications Software. We performed key word searches and compilations of
global value driver terms as they appear in the annual reports and 10-Ks.
10-Qs were also reviewed during announcement periods, e.g. when they
acquired Jaguar and Volvo.

After identifying the number of times each value driver was mentioned in
the annual reports and 10-Ks, we read the corresponding passages to assess the
adequacy of disclosure in relation to the reporting model presented above. We
grouped the disclosures into one of four classifications: (1) *full disclosure* of

the relevant value driver in *complete satisfaction* of users' information needs; (2) *partial disclosure* of the relevant value driver in such a manner that *adequately* addresses users' informational needs, but falls short of providing exactly what users require; (3) *partial disclosure* of the relevant value driver that *inadequately* addresses users' informational needs when compared to the relatively abundant information regarding the relevant value driver that can be found in the financial and automotive press or in financial analysts' reports; and (4) *no disclosure* concerning the relevant value driver. In our study, to determine the adequacy of value driver disclosure, we used two main stages. In the first stage, we determined the frequency of value driver disclosure. This stage is not satisfactory to understand adequacy of value driver disclosure. In the second stage we evaluated the disclosure of value drivers in the 10-K and annual report. This stage is the complementary stage to determine adequacy of disclosure. In this stage we used the classification scheme explained above by grouping the quality of value driver disclosure into four distinct groups: full disclosure, partial disclosure more than 50%, partial disclosure less than 50%, and no disclosure. For example, in the annual report the value driver "reduced SG&A costs" was evaluated in this manner in the period 1995–2000: In the years 1995, 1996, and 1997, this value driver was disclosed in a more detailed manner than in 1998 and 1999, while in 2000 this specific value driver was not mentioned at all. Also, disclosure of "reduced SG&A costs" was not satisfactory in any of the years for stakeholders to evaluate Ford's M&A activities during the period. Hence for this reason, we classify the disclosures as such (see Exhibit B), the symbol √√ (Partial disclosure more than 50%) for "reduced SG&A costs" for the years 1995–1997, √ (Partial disclosure less than 50%) for the years 1998 and 1999, and Ø (No disclosure) for the year 2000.

Our results for the year 1995–2000 (for a total of six fiscal years) are tabulated in Appendix D. Exhibit A presents disclosure of value drivers in Ford Motor 10-Ks, Exhibit B presents disclosure of value drivers in the annual report, and Exhibit C presents a comparative disclosure of value drivers in the annual report and 10-K. Other than a score for disclosure intensity, we also provide page numbers from the corresponding annual report or 10-K where the value driver is discussed.

VI. SUMMARY OF FINDINGS
(See Appendix D for a tabular presentation)

The results indicate that Ford provides more complete disclosure in the universal global value driver category, while the company provides much less disclosure in the automotive and M&A value driver categories. Moreover, the company's annual report contains greater disclosure of the global value drivers than does its 10-K, and for both the annual report and the 10-K, the frequency of disclosure increased during the period 1995 to 1999. Ford's disclosure of universal value drivers, which are relevant for companies in all industries, is adequate. This conforms to the business reporting model concept that general information affecting all industries should be disclosed by all firms. For example, Ford discusses labor costs, considered an essential component to the profitability and competitiveness of any company, extensively in both the annual report and 10-K. However, the company fails to mention such topics as labor skills or employee training programs. Ford also discusses new product innovations in great detail in the annual report, with increasing disclosure in recent years, but treats this topic less extensively in the 10-K. Automotive companies should provide disclosure of plans for the existing vehicle line-up, new model introductions, and current model upgrades, as well as technological innovations and new vehicle features. In this respect, Ford's disclosures are satisfactory. Similarly, the company discussed quality issues and policies at length over several pages in the annual reports for 1996 and 1997, while in 1998 and 1999, Ford's disclosure of quality issues occupy only part of one page. The 10-K includes no mention of quality issues. Several pages of each year's annual report is devoted to consumer satisfaction, opinions, and surveys, but these topics are mentioned only sporadically in the 10-K. Analysts' reports contain detailed information about management experience and expertise, and Ford provides full disclosure of this issue in both its annual report and 10-K. Executive compensation and incentives are adequately disclosed in the company's 10-K, but the annual report contains no disclosure of these topics. Foreign currency, hedging activities, and global tax rates are fully discussed in both the annual report and the 10-K. While the company's disclosure of e-business activities prior to 1999 is non-existent, the company discusses its e-business plans in depth in the annual report and 10-K in the following period. This information includes details regarding its online selling activities and its alliances with web portals and software manufacturers. The company makes sporadic mention of tariffs and other trade barriers in the 10-K, and overlooks the subject completely in the annual report.

As to Ford's disclosure regarding value drivers unique to the automotive industry, a discrepancy exists between what is discussed by the media and in analysts' reports, and what is reported in the company. For example, no disclosure is made regarding excess capacity in Ford plants or utilization rates in various regions. Since excess capacity, a significant problem for all automakers, has been the focus of extensive media and analyst attention, this issue deserves greater disclosure. Firm relationships with labor unions is another highly sensitive issue that receives no mention in the annual report in the period 1995–1999 although in the year 2000, we see extensive discussion about this topic. The relationships between labor unions is treated satisfactorily in all years in its 10-Ks. Product/process flexibility, the degree to which Ford vehicles have common production characteristics or make use of interchangeable parts and facilities, is not discussed in either the annual report or the 10-K. Presently, relations with suppliers are a crucial concern for automakers. Production of many components are outsourced to suppliers whose quality, timeliness, and price can have major impacts on the competitiveness of the final product (as the Firestone tire crisis made evident). With the exception of the 2000 annual report, none of Ford's annual reports or 10-Ks contain any information regarding the number of suppliers, the parts outsourced, or the nature of Ford's relationship with its suppliers. Production life cycle time is another topic that is frequently the subject of media and analyst attention. This topic came to importance when the Japanese demonstrated the ability to introduce a car to the marketplace in a much shorter time frame (only a few months) than their American counterparts. Product life cycle, therefore, drives both profitability and competitiveness; yet, Ford does not seem to focus on it in any of its reports. Ford's market power and sales growth depend on strategic distribution networks that enhance the company's presence in various geographic areas, such as Eastern Europe and Southeast Asia. Despite the vast attention this issue is given in the press, Ford does not include any disclosures about its global distribution channels and dealer networks. Ford's treatment of organizational heritage in the company's reports is well done, building upon a public relations image as the world's first mass production automaker. Ford affirms its commitment to the environment and society by giving special attention in the company's reports to environmental issues like emissions policy. The company frequently discloses sales growth on per product and per region bases. A topic of key interest for analysts is average product age, a measure of how modern the company's product line-up is. Typically, the lower the average age of a product, the greater its appeal to consumers; this topic is not discussed by the company. The financial and automotive press frequently discuss Ford's product line management, describing how Ford manages its various brands to avoid cannibalization, and determines what products to drop or extend, and what segment offerings need improvement. This topic is often ignored in Ford reports.

The M&A value drivers are given even less disclosure than the preceding two categories of value drivers. This may be due to the fact that extensive global M&A activity is a rather recent phenomenon (occurring within the last five years), and business reporting has failed to adapt sufficiently. For example, during the period from 1995 to 1998, when Mazda was part of the Ford portfolio, the company provided no disclosure regarding added growth prospects, i.e. the growth synergies obtained by opening or strengthening new markets through business combinations. In 1999, however, Ford provides partial disclosure of added growth prospects concerning its acquisition of Volvo, which suggests that disclosure practices in this area are improving. The company does not provide disclosure regarding acquisition of strategic R&D (such as Mazda's small engine technology or Volvo's renowned safety technology) in its annual reports or 10-K, nor does Ford include any information about this topic in the 10-Qs issued around the Land Rover acquisition date. Reduced SG&A costs brought about by mergers (e.g. by consolidating distribution channels and achieving economies of scale in other activities) are discussed in the annual report but not in the 10-K. Similarly, reduced capital expenditures resulting from M&A activities that eliminate duplicative processes, is briefly discussed in the annual report, but not mentioned in the 10-K. The enhanced gross margins provided by M&A activities is not discussed in the company's reports.

VII. CONCLUSION

Ford's most developed reporting seems related to traditional matching income model items. It provides general information on the company (see *universal value drivers section* of Appendix D), while specific information tailored to the characteristics of industries, and to ensuing M&A activity, is lacking. Much of the information in the financial/automotive press, and in analysts' reports, is provided by management, obtained from interviews or disclosed in press release/conferences. Prior to the issuance of Regulation FD, such information may not have had a place in company reports or in other public media. To get the complete picture of Ford, one must consider many different sources. Information regarding company specific information such as capacity information, M&A activity and ensuing synergies and economies of scale, is not well addressed in traditional outlets. It is surprising that much of the detailed analysis found in analyst reports and the popular press (information that may aid in investment decision-making) never gets disclosed in corporate reports. If the percentage of defect free assemblies or the efficiency and quality of Ford's suppliers is disclosed in the press, then such type of information is considered relevant by market participants; hence, it should be disclosed in the annual report. Both the 10-K and annual report contain similar information, yet the annual report's "Company Presentation" (usually the first quartile or third of an annual report) makes a lasting impression. Also, the annual report contains a much lengthier discussion of M&A activity in the "Company Presentation" section where the various brands, such as Volvo and Jaguar, are discussed; this information is not to be found in the 10-K. Thus, compared to the 10-k, the annual report contains a superior level of discussion and detailed regarding M&A activity; however, it is still deficient in satisfying what is considered proper disclosure by market participants. Cross-boundary M&A activity is significant growth strategy of Ford Motor Company; conversely, Ford Motor Company's performance is closely related with cross-boundary M&A activity. If Ford Motor Company's M&A activities are successful and display satisfactory performances, its market value will increase. As a measurement of M&A performance, the disclosure of value drivers is important for both institutional investors and individual investor. We also examined 10-Qs, specifically in those periods preceding and following the acquisitions of Volvo and Land Rover, to evaluate related content about these activities. We found limited disclosure and discussion of those acquisitions. Although, fuller explanations were found in the annual reports at the end of the year, such disclosures are not considered to be as timely given the pace of markets today. The regulatory scheme of a one-size-fits-all reporting procedure applicable across all industries and all firms renders the information content of such disclosures short of market expectations. Hence, we see expanded disclosures on general issues, but less careful elaboration on issues that affect a certain industry (in this case the automotive industry) or company-specific occurrences such as M&A activity. This deficiency in corporate disclosures is a surprise since Ford, relative to other companies, is considered to provide a quality report, complementing its image as a consumer advocate. This reputation is a result of various recognitions the company has received for its quality of disclosures. An example is Ford Motor Company's first place award in Addsion Design's yearly "annual report" ranking, which rank annual reports based on many criteria (including financial and non-financial disclosures).

In this study, we have attempted to look at Ford's disclosures across time, while it is difficult to draw unambiguous conclusions and implicative inferences, the findings may not be generalizable to other firms and industries. For a better prognosis, an analysis of forward and future looking information is desired, and information about intangibles should be carefully analyzed. We assert that a company's value drivers that affect performance and competitive outlook have to be explained and consistently disclosed. As more company disclosures are studied across different industries and economic sectors, the benefits of "value driver" reporting tailored to firm and industry specific attributes will be comprehended. The interest of financial executives, regulators and standard setters to provide investors with 'key performance indicators' may be served by articulating "value drivers" as a step in the process toward such indicators. Value drivers as an observational device assist in identifying patterns of information useful in improving specifications about non-financial as well as financial performance measures.

NOTES

1. These are 1998 figures, before the acquisitions of Volvo and Land Rover, and the controlling stake in Mazda.

2. For a complete listing of the value drivers recommended by the FASB task force, please see Appendix B.

3. For a complete listing of issues evaluated by sell-side analysts in evaluating equity securities, please see Appendix A.

4. Please see Appendix C for items discussed in analyst reports.

5. Please see Appendix C for this list of automotive global value drivers considered relevant to users/investors.

REFERENCES

Anderson, S. P., & de Palma, A. (2000). From Local to Global Competition. *European Economic Review, 44*, 423–424.

American Institute of Certified Public Accountants (AICPA) (1993). *The Information needs of Investors and Creditors*. Special Committee on Financial Reporting.

Barney, J, (1991). Firm Resources and Sustained Competitive Advantage. *Journal of Management, 17*(2), 99–120.

Bartlett, C. A., & Ghoshal, S. (1989). *Managing Across Borders: The transnational Solutions*. Cambridge: Harvard Business School Press.

Belcher, T., & Nail, L. (2000). Integration Problems and Turnaround Strategies in a Cross-Border Merger: A Clinical Examination of the Pharmacia-Upjohn Merger. *International Review of Financial Analysis, 9*(2), 219.

Braid, R. M. (1999). The Price and Profit Effects of Horizontal Mergers in Two-Dimensional Spatial Competition. *Economic Letters, 62*, 117–118.

Bricker, R., Grant, J., Fogarty, T., & Previts, G. (1999). Determinants of Analyst Following. *Journal of Corporate Communications*.

Botosan, C. (1997). Disclosure Level and the Cost of Equity Capital. *The Accounting Review, 72*(3), 323–349.

Buxey, G. (2000). Strategies in an era of Global Competition. *International Journal of Operations & Production Management, 20*(9), 997.

Campbell, A., & Alexander, M. (1997). What's Wrong with Strategy? *Harvard Business Review, 75*(6), 46–51.

CCH (2001). SEC Chief Accountant Discusses Financial Reporting, SEC Accounting Rules, No. 378, (February 13), p. 2.

Celik, O. (1999). *Sirket Birlesmeleri ve Birlesmelerde Sirket Degerlemesi*. Ankara: Turhan Kitabevi.

Chang, L. S., & Most, K. S. *The Perceived Usefulness of Financial Statements for Investors' Decisions*. Miami: University Presses of Florida.

Chugh, L. C., & Meador, J. W. (1984). The Stock Valuation Process: The Analysts' View. *Financial Analysts' Journal, 40*, 41–48.

Dent, D. F. (1996). Global Competition: Challenges for Management Accounting and Control. *Management Accounting Research, 7*(1).

Dunning, J. H. (1993). *Multinational Enterprises and the Global Economy*. Wokingham: Addison Wesley.

Financial Accounting Standards Board (2001). Improving Business Reporting: Insights into Enhancing Voluntary Disclosures. Connecticut: FASB, Steering Committee Report, Business Reporting Project.

Fawcett, E. F., Calantone, R. J., & Roath, A. (2000). Meeting quality and cost imperatives in a global market. *International Journal of Physical Distribution & Logistics Management*, *30*(6), 473–480.

Haas, E. A. (1987). Breakthrough Manufacturing. *Harvard Business Review*, *65*(2), 75–81.

Healy, P., Hutton, A., & Palepu, K. (1999). Stock Price and Intermediation Changes Surrounding Sustained Increases in Disclosure. *Contemporary Accounting Research*, *16*(3), 485–520.

Juran, J. M., & Gryna, F. M. (1980). *Quality Planning and Analysis*. New York: McGraw-Hill.

KPMG (2000). *The New Art of the Deal: How Leading Organizations Realize Value from Transactions* (www.kpmg.com).

Lang, M., & Lundholm, R. (1996). Corporate Disclosure Policy and Analyst Behavior. *The Accounting Review*, *71*(4), 467–492.

Lockamy, A., & Cox, J. (1995). An Empirical Study of Division and Plant Performance Measurement Systems in Selected World Class Manufacturing Firms: Linkages for Competitive Advantage. *International Journal of Production Research*, *33*(1), 2133–2135.

Marquardt, M. (1999). *The Global Advantage: How World-Class Organizations Improve Performance Through Globalization*. Houston: Gulf Publishing Company.

Matlay, H., & Fletcher, D. (2000). Globalization and Strategic Change: Some Lessons from the U.K. Small Business Sector. *Strategic Change*, *9*, 437–449.

Morales, R. (1999). *Flexible Production: Restructuring of the International Automotive Industry*. Cambridge: Polity Press.

Morosini, P. (1994). Post-Cross-Border Acquisitions: Implementing 'National Culture-Compatible' Strategies to Improve Performance. *European Management Journal*, *12*(4).

Napier, N., Schweiger, D., & Kosglow, J. (1993). Managing Organizational Diversity: Observations from Cross-Border Acquisitions. *Human Resource Management*, *23*(4), 505–523.

Opdyke, J. D. (July 25, 2000). The Winningest Pros of Them All. *Wall Street Journal*.

Porter, M. (1986). Changing Patterns of International Competition. *California Management Review*, (Winter).

Previts, G., Bricker, R., Robinson, T., & Young, S. A (1993). *Content Analysis of Sell-Side Financial Analyst Company Reports*. Cleveland: Case Western Reserve University.

Scott, M. C. (1998). *Value Drivers*. Chichester: John Wiley & Sons.

SRI International (1987). *Investor Information Needs and the Annual Report*. Morristown: Financial Executives Research Foundation.

UNCTAD (2000). *World Investment Report 2000: Cross-Border Mergers and Acquisitions and Development*. New York: United Nations.

Tan, K. C., Kannan, V. R., Handfield, R. B., & Ghosh, S. (2000). Quality, Manufacturing Strategy, and Global Competition: An Empirical Analysis. *Benchmarking: An International Journal*, *7*(3), 174–180.

Vastag, G., Kasarda, J., & Boone, T. (1994). Logistical Support for Manufacturing Agility in Global Markets. *International Journal of Operations & Production Management*, *14*(11), 73–85.

Wiegold, C. et al. (2000). Industry by Industry: A Talk with Stock Pickers. *Wall Street Journal*, July 25.

Yang, X. (1995). *Globalization of the Automobile Industry*. Westport: Proeger, 1995.

APPENDIX A

Principal Findings Related to Sell-Side Financial Analysts' Evaluation of Company Equity Securities from Financial and Other Information

1. Analysts frequently adjust reported earnings to determine company core earnings. Analysts are stricter than GAAP in distinguishing between recurring and non-recurring income items. This is also reflected in per share calculations made by analysts, which are often adjusted for non-earnings items. "Adjusted" or "Operating" EPS are often computed.
2. Analysts identify company risks and concerns, which are broader and less quantifiable potential sources of charges against stockholders' equity than are liabilities, obligations, or contingencies.
3. Analysts consider the effect of a company's anticipated eggs on future earnings, including those related to products, projects, restructurings, etc.
4. A large amount of nonfinancial information is assessed, including market share, competitive position, industry and economic conditions, competitors' capabilities and products, and the strategies and quality of company management (particularly changes in management and corporate strategies).
5. Income statement and performance analysis continue to dominate analyst evaluation of companies.
6. Analysts do not define accounting earnings quality terms of representationally faithful financial reports, a correspondence between net income and cash flow, or conservative accounting methods, per se. Instead analysts most frequently refer to accounting earnings quality in terms of a company's ability to manage earnings through the establishment and adjustment of conservative, discretionary reserves, allowances, and OBSAs which provides analysts a low-risk earnings platform for making stock price forecasts and buy/sell/hold recommendations.
7. Many analysts make Non-GAAP cash flow analyses, including discretionary and free cash flow. Per share calculations are common, including operating cash flow per share and free cash flow per share. Price to cash flow, or price to operating-cash-flow calculations are common.
8. Company balance sheets are usually evaluated on a cost basis. Exceptions are: (1) companies with significant off-balance-sheet assets, (2) thinly traded companies, (3) "poorly understood" companies, (4) industries with asset quality problems, for example banking, and (5) takeover targets.
9. Analysts disaggregate company performance into a finer set of operating units than specified by GAAP. For instance, mining companies are typically disaggregated on the basis of individual mines, manufacturing companies on the basis of major products, etc.

10. Most income statements are converted to common size reports.
11. Analysts exhibit interest in earnings Momentum, generally defined in terms of earnings growth trends. Potential earnings surprises are noted.
12. Analysts are sensitive to earnings variability. They discuss stock price variability far less frequently, and virtually never discuss Beta.
13. Analysts see obvious management of earnings through accounting methods applications
14. Some analysts question the economic rationality (in a classic sense) of investors. For example, some analysts believe that the investment horizon of investors is not more than two years.
15. Analyst coverage of large and small companies differs markedly. Some small companies are not covered at all. Therefore, in the small-cap market, sell-side analysis of company information cannot be relied upon as a source of price protection for unsophisticated equity investors.

Source: Previts, G., Bricker, R., Robinson, T., and Young, S. (1993). *Content Analysis of Sell-Side Financial Analyst Company Reports*, Case Western Reserve University, sponsored by the AICPA Special Committee on Financial Reporting (Jenkins' Committee).

APPENDIX B

FASB Business Reporting Research Project Report: January 2001

Value Drivers – Automobile OEM (Original Equipment Manufacturers)
- Industry Economic Outlook
- Consistent Historical Comparisons
- Product and Market Share
- New Products
- Capacity Plans
- Regional Profitability and Unit Volumes
- Cash and Capital Plans
- Work Force Relationships
- Management and Shareholders
- Environmental Concerns

Universal Value Drivers
- Strategy Execution
- Management Credibility
- Quality of Strategy
- Innovativeness

- Ability to attract quality people
- Market Share
- Management Experience
- Quality of Executive Compensation
- Quality of Processes
- Research Leadership

APPENDIX C

Global Value Drivers

Universal Value Drivers:

Cost of Labor: Discussed in the financial/automotive press

Labor Skills: Discussed in the financial/automotive press

Innovation (New Product) Activities: Discussed in analysts' reports, financial/automotive press

Quality Issues/Policy: Discussed in analysts' reports and in automotive/financial press

Consumer Satisfaction: Discussed in analysts' reports and in automotive/financial press

Managerial experience and expertise: Discussed in analysts' reports and in automotive/financial press

Compensation and other Incentives: Discussed in analysts' reports

Hedging Activities: Discussed in analysts' reports and in automotive/financial press

Global Tax Rates: Discussed in analysts' reports and in automotive/financial press

e-Business Activities: Discussed in analysts' reports and in automotive/financial press

Tariffs and Non-Tariffs Barriers:

Automotive Value Drivers:

Capacity Utilization: Discussed in analysts' reports and in automotive/financial press

Relations with Labor Unions: Discussed in analysts' reports and financial/automotive press

Product/Process Flexibility: Discussed in analysts' reports and in automotive/financial press

Relations with Suppliers: Discussed in analysts' reports and in automotive/financial press

Product Life Cycle Time: Discussed in analysts' reports and in automotive/financial press

Global Distribution Channels: Discussed in analysts' reports and in automotive/financial press

Organizational Heritage: Discussed in automotive/financial press

Environmental Issues: Discussed in analysts' reports and in automotive/financial press

Sales Growth Per Region/Product: Discussed in analysts' reports and in automotive/financial press

Average Product Age: Discussed in analysts' reports and in automotive/financial press

Product Line-Up Management Plan: Discussed in analysts' reports and in automotive/financial press

M&A Value Drivers:

Added Growth Prospects: Discussed in analysts' reports and in automotive/financial press, KPMG "The new art of the deal"

Acquisition of Strategic R&D: Discussed in analysts' reports and in automotive/financial press, KPMG "The new art of the deal"

Reduced SG&A Costs: Discussed in analysts' reports and in automotive/financial press, KPMG "The new art of the deal"

Reduced Capital Expenditures: Discussed in analysts' reports and in automotive/financial press, KPMG "The new art of the deal"

Enhanced Gross Margins: Discussed in KPMG's "The new art of the deal".

APPENDIX D

EXHIBIT A: Disclosure of Global Value Drivers
(10-Ks)

	1995 Page(s)		1996 Page(s)		1997 Page(s)		1998 Page(s)		1999 Page(s)		2000 Page(s)
Universal Value Drivers												
Cost of Labor	√√√	39	√√√	28	√√√	31	√√√	39	√√√	38	√√√	35
Skills of Labor	Ø		Ø		Ø		Ø		Ø		Ø	
Innovation (New Product) Activities	√√	22, 30, 42	√√	20, 29	√√	8, 38	√√	21	√√	16	√	8
Quality Policy	Ø		Ø		Ø		Ø		Ø		Ø	
Customer Satisfaction	√	4, 11	√	4, 12	√	4, 11	√	4, 11	√	11	√√	8
Managerial Experience and Expertise	√√√	37	√√√	26	√√√	29	√√√	31	√√√	35,36	√√√	32
Non-Financial Incentives and Compensation	√√√	48, 120-132	√√√	37, 103-112	√√√	42, 114-139	√√√	50, 112, 124, 125	√√√	51, 104, 105, 106,107	√√√	96, 97, 98, 99
Hedging Activities	√√√	66, 67	√√√	36, 54, 55	√√√	40, 41, 61, 62	√√√	48, 49, 69, 70	√√√	48,50, 51, 71, 72	√√√	47, 48, 49, 50, 51, 79
Global Tax Rates	√√√	76, 77	√√√	62, 63, 64	√√√	69, 70	√√√	78, 79	√√√	79,80	√√√	115, 116
e-Business Activities	Ø		Ø		Ø		Ø		√√√	12	√	8
Tariff and Non-Tariff Barriers	√	4	√	4	√	4	√	4	√	4	√	4
Automotive Value Drivers												
Capacity Utilization	Ø		Ø		Ø		Ø		√	10	Ø	
Relations with Labor Unions	√√√	29, 30	√√√	19	√√√	18	√√√	21	√√√	22,41	√√√	18
Product\Process Flexibility	Ø		Ø		Ø		Ø		Ø		Ø	
Relations with Suppliers	Ø		Ø		Ø		Ø		Ø		Ø	
Product Life Cycle Time	Ø		Ø		Ø		Ø		Ø		Ø	

Exhibit A: Continued.

	1995 Page(s)	1996 Page(s)	1997 Page(s)	1998 Page(s)	1999 Page(s)	2000 Page(s)
Global Distribution Channels	Ø	Ø	Ø	Ø	Ø	Ø
Organizational Heritage	√ 3	√ 3	√ 3	√ 3	√ 3	√ 3
Environmental Issues	√√√ 21, 22, 23, 24, 25, 26, 27, 28	√√√ 15, 16, 17, 18	√√√ 13, 14, 15, 16	√√√ 14, 15, 16, 17, 18, 19, 20, 23	√√√ 8, 10, 15, 16, 17,18	√√√ 13, 14, 15, 16
Sales Growth Per Region\Product	√√√ 5, 6, 7, 8, 9, 10, 39, 59	√√√ 5, 6, 7, 8, 9, 29, 32, 33, 34	√√√ 4, 5, 7, 8, 31, 34, 35, 36, 39, 54	√√√6, 7, 8, 9, 34, 38, 39, 62, 63	√√√ 5, 9, 10, 39, 44, 45, 46	√√√ 7, 8, 36, 37, 38, 61
Average Product Age	Ø	Ø	Ø	Ø	Ø	Ø
Product Line-Up Management Plan	Ø	Ø	Ø	Ø	Ø	Ø
M&A Value Drivers						
Added Growth Prospects	Ø	Ø	Ø	Ø	√√ 7,75,46	Ø
Acquisition of Strategic R&D	Ø	Ø	Ø	Ø	Ø	Ø
Reduced SG&A Costs	Ø	Ø	Ø	Ø	Ø	
Reduced Capital Expenditures	Ø	Ø	Ø	Ø	Ø	
Enhanced Gross Margins	Ø	Ø	Ø	Ø	Ø	

Ø: No disclosure
√: Partial disclosure less than 50%.
√√: Partial disclosure more than 50%
√√√: Full disclosure.

EXHIBIT B: Disclosure of Global Value drivers
(Annual Reports)

	1995	Page(s)	1996	Page(s)	1997	Page(s)	1998	Page(s)	1999	Page(s)	2000	Page(s)
Universal Value Drivers												
Cost of Labor	√√√	59	√√√	65	√√√	67	√√√	71	√√√	75	√√√	83
Labor Skills	Ø		Ø		Ø		Ø		Ø		Ø	
Innovation (New Product) Activities	√	5	√√√	4, 7, 10, 11	√√√	3	√√√	5, 14, 30	√√√	5, 14, 17	√√	3,4
Quality Policy	√	5	√√√	2, 3, 6, 8, 9	√√√	3, 13, 14	√	3	√	4	√	5
Consumer Satisfaction	√√√	4, 13, 23, 24, 25, 26, 27	√√√	2, 12, 13	√√√	9, 10	√√√	2, 4, 7, 8, 10, 11, 29	√√√	3, 4, 5, 6, 7, 8, 10, 20, 78	√√√	4, 5, 6, 9, 11, 13
Managerial Experience and Expertise	√√	21	√√√	22, 23	√√√	25, 26	√√√	16, 17, 24, 25, 26	√√√	28, 29, 30, 31	√√√	30, 31, 32, 33
Non-Financial Incentives and Compensation	Ø		Ø		Ø		Ø		Ø		Ø	
Hedging Activities	√√√	36, 37, 53	√√√	32, 39, 40	√√√	37, 44, 45	√√√	41, 42, 49, 50	√√√	44, 45, 51, 52	√√√	46, 47, 48, 57
Global Tax Rates	√√√	43, 44	√√√	46, 47	√√√	50, 51	√√√	55, 56	√√√	58	√√√	64, 65
e-Business Activities	Ø		Ø		√	9	√√√	4, 12	√√√	3, 4, 6, 18, 22, 24	√√√	5, 6, 9, 21
Tariff and Non-Tariff Barriers	Ø		Ø		Ø		Ø		Ø		Ø	
Automotive Value Drivers												
Capacity Utilization	Ø		Ø		Ø		Ø		Ø		Ø	
Relations with Labor Unions	Ø		Ø		Ø		Ø		Ø		√√√	3, 23
Product\Process Flexibility	Ø		Ø		Ø		Ø		Ø		Ø	
Relations with Suppliers	Ø		Ø		Ø		Ø		Ø		√√√	5, 14, 15

Exhibit B: Continued.

	1995	Page(s)	1996	Page(s)	1997	Page(s)	1998	Page(s)	1999	Page(s)	2000	Page(s)
Time of Product Life Cycle	Ø		√	10	Ø		Ø		√	9	Ø	
Global Distribution Channels	Ø		Ø		Ø		√	19	√	9	Ø	
Organizational Heritage	√√√	7, 19	√√√	6, 15	√√√	7, 14	√√√	2, 3, 5, 12, 13, 14	√√√	3, 8, 10, 33	√√√	2, 3, 36
Environmental Issues	√√	17	√√√	14, 15	√√√	3, 13	√√√	2, 4, 15	√√√	6, 13, 14	√√√	3, 4
Sales Growth Per Region\Product	√√√	2, 3, 9	√√√	1, 27, 28, 29, 30, 31, 63	√√√	1, 2, 7, 30, 31, 32, 33, 34, 68	√√√	1, 20, 32, 33	√√√	1, 13, 26, 35, 38, 39, 40, 73	√√√	1, 37, 38, 40, 41, 42, 82
Average Product Age	Ø		Ø		Ø		Ø		Ø		Ø	
Product Line-Up Management Plan	Ø		Ø		Ø		Ø		Ø		Ø	
M&A Value Drivers												
Added Growth Prospects	Ø		Ø		Ø		Ø		Ø		Ø	
Acquisition of Strategic R&D	Ø		Ø		Ø		Ø		Ø		Ø	
Reduced SG&A Costs	√√	1, 4, 5, 11	√√	4, 6, 11, 29	√√	2	√	33	√	38	Ø	
Reduced Capital Expenditures	Ø		Ø		Ø		√	36	√	43	√	44
Enhanced Gross Margins	Ø		Ø		Ø		Ø		Ø		Ø	

Ø: No disclosure
√: Partial disclosure less than 50%
√√: Partial disclosure more than 50%
√√√: Full disclosure.

Exhibit C: Disclosure of Global Value Drivers
(Combined)

	1995 Source		1996 Source		1997 Source		1998 Source		1999 Source		2000 Source
Universal Value Drivers											
Cost of Labor	√	10-K, AR	√	10-K, AR	√	10-K, AR	√	10-K, AR	√	10-K, AR	√	10-K, AR
Labor Skills	Ø		Ø		Ø		Ø		Ø		Ø	
Innovation (New Product) Activities	√	10-K, AR	√	10-K, AR	√	10-K, AR	√	10-K, AR	√	10-K, AR	√	10-K, AR
Quality Policy	√	AR	√	AR	√	AR	√	AR	√	AR	√	AR
Consumer Satisfaction	√	10-K, AR	√	10-K, AR	√	10-K, AR	√	10-K, AR	√	10-K, AR	√	10-K, AR
Managerial Experience and Expertise	√	10-K, AR	√	10-K, AR	√	10-K, AR	√	10-K, AR	√	10-K, AR	√	10-K, AR
Non-Financial Incentives and Compensation	√	10-K	√	10-K	√	10-K	√	10-K	√	10-K	√	10-K
Hedging Activities	√	10-K, AR	√	10-K, AR	√	10-K, AR	√	10-K, AR	√	10-K, AR	√	10-K, AR
Global Tax Rates	√	10-K, AR	√	10-K, AR	√	10-K, AR	√	10-K, AR	√	10-K, AR	√	10-K, AR
e-Business Activities	Ø		Ø		√	AR	√	AR	√	10-K, AR	√	10-K, AR
Tariff and Non-Tariff Barriers	√	10-K	√	10-K	√	10-K	√	10-K	√	10-K	√	10-K
Automotive Value Drivers											
Capacity Utilization	Ø		Ø		Ø		Ø		√	10-K	Ø	
Relations with Labor Unions	√	10-K	√	10-K	√	10-K	√	10-K	√	10-K	√	10-K, AR
Product\Process Flexibility	Ø		Ø		Ø		Ø		Ø		Ø	
Relations with Supplier	Ø		Ø		Ø		Ø		Ø		√	AR
Product Life Cycle Time	Ø		√	AR	Ø		Ø		√	AR	Ø	

Exhibit C: Continued.

	1995	Source	1996	Source	1997	Source	1998	Source	1999	Source	2000	Source
Global Distribution Channels	Ø		Ø		Ø		√	AR	√	AR	Ø	
Organizational Heritage	√	10-K, AR	√	10-K, AR	√	10-K, AR	√	10-K, AR	√	10-K, AR	√	10-K, AR
Environmental Issues	√	10-K, AR	√	10-K, AR	√	10-K, AR	√	10-K, AR	√	10-K	√	10-K AR
Sales Growth Per Region\Product	√	10-K, AR	√	10-K, AR	√	10-K, AR	√	10-K, AR	√	10-K, AR	√	10-K, AR
Average Product Age	Ø		Ø		Ø		Ø		Ø		Ø	
Product Line-Up Management Plan	Ø		Ø		Ø		Ø		Ø		Ø	
M&A Value Drivers												
Added Growth Prospects	Ø		Ø		Ø		Ø		√	10-K	Ø	
Acquisition of Strategic R&D	Ø		Ø		Ø		Ø		Ø		Ø	
Reduced SG&A Costs	√	AR	√	AR	√	AR	√	AR	√	AR	√	AR
Reduced Capital Expenditures	Ø		Ø		Ø		Ø		√	AR	Ø	
Enhanced Gross Margins	Ø		Ø		Ø		Ø		Ø		Ø	

Ø: No disclosure
√: Disclosure.

FINANCIAL STATEMENT FRAUD: CAPITAL MARKET EFFECTS AND MANAGEMENT ACTIONS*

Albert L. Nagy

ABSTRACT

The purpose of this research is to examine the effects that financial statement fraud announcements and certain strategic actions have on the perceived validity of financial disclosures. This study posits that: (1) Financial statement fraud announcements damage the perceived validity of financial disclosures, and (2) certain strategic actions performed subsequent to a fraud announcement improve the perceived validity of financial disclosures. The hypotheses are based upon prior literature that uses the earnings response coefficient (ERC) to measure earnings quality. The OLS regression results provide evidence that a financial statement fraud announcement is associated with a decrease in the ERC, and that the strategic actions of changing external auditor and increasing the percentage of outsiders comprising the board of directors following a fraud announcement improve the ERC. These results suggest that financial statement frauds reduce the perceived validity of financial disclosures, and that the strategic actions of changing external auditor and increasing the percentage of outside directors help mitigate this reduction.

* All data are available from public sources.

Research in Accounting Regulation, Volume 15, pages 95–117.
ISBN: 0-7623-0841-9

I. INTRODUCTION

During his testimony concerning H.R. 574, *The Financial Fraud Detection and Disclosure Act*, the then Chairman of the United States Securities and Exchange Commission (SEC) Richard C. Breeden stated that "financial statements provide the basis for the working of our entire market, as they form the basis for the calculation of risk that is fundamental to every extension of credit and every investment." The heavy reliance placed on financial statement information by market participants is well documented in the financial literature, and generally supports Mr. Breeden's statement. A critical component underlying the amount of reliance placed on financial statement data relates to their representational faithfulness or perceived validity (FASB, 1980). Thus, a decline in the perceived validity of financial statement disclosures jeopardizes their reliability, and in turn impairs the efficiency of the market system.

In order to ensure the quality of firm disclosures, managers often adopt different governance mechanisms. For example, mandatory external audits, an active board of directors and audit committees have all been set up to enhance, in part, the validity of company disclosures. The significant costs associated with implementing and maintaining these mechanisms indicate the importance management and shareholders place on preserving financial disclosure validity. Although firms incur significant costs to maintain disclosure validity, there are events that damage this important financial statement characteristic.

One such event, financial statement fraud, is particularly important because it involves management intentionally deceiving financial statement users, and thus directly influences (or diminishes) investors' trust in management's representations.[1] The announcement of financial statement fraud often triggers certain management actions purported to improve the quality or validity of future financial disclosures and/or decrease the likelihood of financial statement fraud from reoccurring.[2] Despite the large volume of anecdotal evidence that suggests financial statement fraud announcements both damage the perceived validity of financial disclosures and trigger ameliorating company actions, there is a limited amount of empirical research examining these effects. This study adds to the empirical fraud research by examining the following two main questions: (1) Do financial statement fraud announcements reduce the perceived validity of financial disclosures, and (2) do certain strategic actions performed by companies subsequent to the fraud announcement improve the perceived validity of financial disclosures?

Over the past several years, the SEC has placed a high priority on detecting and deterring fraudulent financial reporting. During his now infamous "Numbers Game" speech, former SEC Commissioner Arthur Levitt suggests that "too many corporate managers, auditors, and analysts are participants in a game of nods and winks. In the zeal to satisfy consensus earnings estimates and project a smooth earnings path, wishful thinking may be winning the day over faithful representation. As a result, I fear that we are witnessing an erosion in the quality of earnings, and therefore, the quality of financial reporting" (Levitt, 1998). Recognizing the importance of quality reporting, Chairman Levitt concludes this speech by detailing a plan on how the financial community can restore the quality of financial disclosures. This plan calls for an improvement in the accounting framework, an improvement in the outside auditing and financial reporting processes, and a need for a cultural change.

Triggered from this speech, the SEC has increased regulation over several key corporate governance functions that promote quality financial reporting. The SEC recently revised the rules on auditor independence, limiting certain services of the external auditor and calling for greater disclosure on any non-audit services provided. In an effort to improve the strength and independence of audit committees, the SEC recently finalized new rules concerning audit committees' compositions, activities, and reporting requirements. The SEC has also stepped up their enforcement over fraudulent reporting, making financial fraud and reporting cases the Division of Enforcement's number one focus (Hunt, 2000). By increasing regulation over the external audit and audit committee functions, as well as increasing the enforcement over the financial reporting process, the SEC hopes to improve the quality of financial disclosures and deter fraudulent reporting. Hopefully, the insights provided by this study regarding the association among fraudulent reporting, disclosure quality, and certain corporate governance functions will assist regulators in their quest to improve the financial reporting process.

The next section of this paper describes and lists the study's hypotheses. Section III discusses the related event date and window, and Section IV describes the empirical model. The sample and some descriptive statistics are discussed in Sections V and VI, respectively. Section VII presents the empirical results, and the final section provides a summary of the findings and conclusions.

II. HYPOTHESES

The American Institute of Certified Public Accountants (AICPA) defines financial statement fraud as intentionally misstating or omitting amounts or disclosures in financial statements to deceive financial statement users (AICPA, 1997). Based on this definition, financial statement fraud is a direct violation of investors' trust in the validity of financial disclosures. This study empirically examines the effects that financial statement fraud, along with certain strategic actions, has on the perceived validity of financial disclosures by comparing pre- and post-fraud announcement earnings response coefficients (ERCs).

The ERC measures the correlation between unexpected earnings and abnormal changes in stock prices in response and is a common measure of earnings quality used in prior studies. Prior research documents an inverse relation between the ERC and level of noise in the firm's present and future earnings numbers (Holthausen & Verrecchia, 1988) and a positive relation to earnings persistence (Kormendi & Lipe, 1987; Lipe, 1990). Consistent with Choi and Jeter (1992), this study does not attempt to distinguish between these two explanations for a decline in ERC. However, the level of perceived validity or representational faithfulness of earnings disclosures is expected to be inversely related to the amount of noise in the earnings disclosure and positively related to the level of earnings persistence. Thus, a decline in the ERC following a fraud announcement would be consistent with a decline in the perceived validity of earnings disclosure and leads to the following hypothesis:

H1: The announcement of financial statement fraud is associated with a decrease in the company's ERC.

Prior research provides evidence that certain types of actions effectively improve earnings quality and/or deter future frauds from occurring. Specifically, prior literature suggests that the quality level of the external auditor (Ettredge et al., 1988; Teoh & Wong, 1993; Moreland, 1995), the formation of an audit committee (Wild, 1996; Dechow et al., 1996), and the percentage of outsiders on the board of directors (Dechow et al., 1996) are positively related to the informativeness of the financial disclosures. Furthermore, Klein (2000a, b) provides evidence that audit committee independence is positively related to the informativeness of financial disclosures, and Beasley (1996) provides evidence that the percentage of outsiders on the board of directors is negatively related with the occurrence of financial statement fraud. Based upon this research, certain strategic actions performed by companies recently subjected to a financial statement fraud are expected to improve the informativeness of financial disclosures and/or deter future frauds from occurring. In either event, these actions are expected to improve the perceived validity of financial disclosures and leads to the following three hypotheses:[3]

H2: The act of changing external auditor following the announcement of financial statement fraud is positively related to ERCs.

H3: The act of increasing the percentage of outsiders[4] on the board of directors following the announcement of financial statement fraud is positively related to ERCs.

H4: The act of forming an audit committee following the announcement of financial statement fraud is positively related to ERCs.

Intuitively, the group most responsible for the occurrence of financial statement fraud is upper management. Whether due to direct involvement in the fraud or negligence in their monitoring duties, upper management must assume some or all of the responsibility for the occurrence of financial statement fraud. Thus, changing upper management is expected to improve the perceived validity of financial disclosures following a financial statement fraud announcement. This discussion leads to the following hypothesis:

H5: The act of changing upper management following the announcement of financial statement fraud is positively related to ERCs.

To test the five stated hypotheses, this study examines ERCs surrounding the date in which news of the financial statement fraud became publicly available. The details regarding the selection and identification of this event date (financial statement fraud announcement) are discussed next.

III. THE EVENT DATE AND WINDOW

The SEC's Division of Enforcement is constantly investigating suspicious market actions that may be in violation of the federal securities laws. These investigations are commonly triggered by enforcement leads often provided from the following sources: (1) market surveillance programs, (2) public complaints, tips, referrals from other law enforcement agencies, and financial press information; and (3) reviews of 1933 and 1934 Securities Acts filings (Pincus et al., 1988). Upon receipt of an enforcement lead, an SEC analyst scrutinizes reports for violations of routine screening criteria and for suspicious subjective factors, and then decides if an informal investigation is necessary (Feroz et al., 1991). Informal investigations by the SEC involve persons with relevant information voluntarily providing documentation and testimony. As a matter of policy to protect firms cleared by the inquiry, the SEC does not make informal investigations publicly known (Feroz et al., 1991).

The results from the informal investigation determine whether the SEC begins a formal investigation. The federal securities laws empower the SEC to perform formal investigations, providing subpoena power to compel testimony and the production of documents (SEC, 1996). Target firms are formally notified of the formal investigation, and the public announcement of the investigation is made soon after this notification.[5] A summary of the enforcement actions and other conclusions from the formal investigations are

stated in the Accounting and Auditing Enforcement Releases (AAERs), which
are issued by the SEC.

The SEC is believed to have more targets for formal investigations than it
can practically pursue, and thus it investigates only material cases that have a
high probability of success (i.e. ending with a sanction) (Feroz et al., 1991).[6]
Therefore, the announcement of an SEC formal investigation signals to the
public that the target company has been accused of a material reporting
violation and that a future SEC sanction is likely. News of the SEC formal
investigation may be the first time allegations of fraudulent reporting activity
by the target firm is publicly disseminated, or it may merely confirm market
participants' suspicions of fraudulent reporting by the target firm. In either event,
the beginning of a formal SEC investigation announces to the public that a
credible agency has accused the target company of a material reporting
violation, and thus it is the event date used for this study. The ERCs are
measured over four pre-fraud and four post-fraud quarterly earnings announcements surrounding this event date.[7] Figure 1 presents a timeline showing the
event window.

IV. MODEL DEVELOPMENT

Consistent with Choi and Jeter (1992) who study the effects of qualified audit
opinions on ERCs, this study uses a pooled cross-sectional time-series regression that is estimated using the OLS method. The dependent variable of the
regression model is abnormal stock returns (UR) and the independent variable
is unexpected earnings (UE). Five test variables are included to capture the
effects that the fraud announcement and the strategic actions have on the ERC.
The test variables are FRD, AUD, OUT, AC, and MGMT and are defined in
the Appendix. The effects that financial statement fraud announcements and the
strategic actions have on ERCs are examined by including interaction terms
(the test variable * unexpected earnings) in the regression model.

The data are pooled across firms so factors identified by prior literature as
affecting ERCs should be controlled for in the regression. Prior literature
provides evidence that ERCs are positively related to growth prospects (Collins
& Kothari, 1989) and the persistence of earnings (Kormendi & Lipe, 1987;
Lipe, 1990), and negatively associated with systematic risk (Collins & Kothari,
1989; Easton & Zmijewski, 1989), and the amount of predisclosure firm
information (Atiase, 1985). Additionally, Salamon and Stober (1994) provide
evidence that fourth-quarter earnings announcements have smaller ERCs than
the other three interim quarters. Control variables are included in the regression to control for these effects. A further explanation of these variables, along

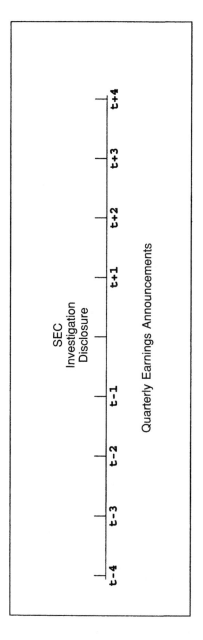

Fig. 1. Event Timeline.

Table 1.   Variable Definitions.

Variable	Variable Type	Description
UR	Dependent	The two-day cumulative unexpected return.
FRD	Independent	A dummy variable equaling 1 if the quarterly earnings announcement is subsequent to the fraud announcement date, and 0 otherwise.
UE	Independent	The unexpected quarterly earnings computed from a seasonal random walk model of earnings scaled by price.
AUD	Independent	For post-event periods, this variable equals 1 if the company changed its external auditor, and 0 otherwise. For pre-event periods this variable equals 0.
OUT	Independent	For post-event periods, this variable equals the increase in the percentage of outside directors serving as board members from the beginning of the event window. For pre-event periods this variable equals 0.
MGMT	Independent	For post-event periods, this variable equals 1 if the company changed an upper management position (CEO, COO, CFO, or CAO), and 0 otherwise. For pre-event periods this variable equals 0.
AC	Independent	For post-event periods, this variable equals 1 if an audit committee was formed, and 0 otherwise. For pre-event periods this variable equals 0.
MBRAT	Independent	Market-to-book value of equity. This variable proxies for both growth and earnings persistence.
RISK	Independent	Systematic risk of the firm is measured per the market model beta.
SIZE	Independent	Size is the natural log of the market value of equity at the beginning of the quarter and proxies for the noise in the predisclosure environment
QTR	Independent	A dummy variable equaling 1 if the quarterly announcement is a fourth period announcement (fiscal year-end), and 0 otherwise.

with the multiple regression model, may be found in the Appendix. A summary of all of the variable definitions is presented in Table 1.

V. SAMPLE AND DATA COLLECTION

Fraud firms were identified by examining AAERs issued between 1/1/90 and 1/31/98 for firms sanctioned by the SEC for violating either Section 13(a) or Rule 10(b)-5 of the Securities Act of 1934.[8] Section 13(a) requires issuers, whose securities are registered with the SEC, to file reports as required by the SEC rules and regulations. The financial statements contained in these filings are required to conform with GAAP.[9] Violation of Rule 10(b)-5 of the 1934 Securities Act requires the intent to deceive, manipulate, or defraud.

In addition to the AAER examination, a full-text Wall Street Journal search was performed for 1995 and 1996 to identify companies currently under investigation by the SEC, but not yet sanctioned.[10] The SEC is believed to pursue cases where their probability of success is high and where the allegations involve material violations (Feroz et al., 1991). Therefore, it is reasonable to assume that the sample obtained for this study consists of publicly-traded firms accused of material reporting violations by the SEC.

Panel A of Table 2 summarizes the sample selection procedure used to obtain firms for empirical analyses. The AAER examination produced a total of 284 companies that were sanctioned by the SEC for violating Section 13(a) and/or Rule 10(b)-5. After considering the availability of Compustat and CRSP data, 58 firms remained.[11] An additional 11 firms were identified per the *WSJ* search and met the data requirements. The final sample consists of 69 companies, of which 17 were sanctioned by the SEC for violating Section 13(a) only.

The following procedures were performed for each of the sampled companies to determine this study's event date (i.e. the announcement of an SEC formal investigation for reporting violations): (1) a full text search was performed via Dow Jones *News/Retrieval* of the *Wall Street Journal* and

Table 2. Sample Information.

Panel A: Sample Selection Summary		
Firms selected from AAERs (No. 251–No. 1011)		
issued between 1/1/90 and 1/31/98		284
less firms with incomplete CRSP data	217	
less firms not listed on COMPUSTAT	9	
plus firms selected from the WSJ search		11
Final Sample		69
Panel B: Summary of Final Data Set		
Potential Observation Points (69 firms * 8 quarters)		552
less missing data items	10	
less extreme UE values		
(greater than 1 or less than –1)	8	
less extreme RISK values		
(greater than 3.5 or less than –0.1)	14	
less extreme MBRAT values (greater than 100)	3	
less influential outliers	15	
Final Sample of Observations		502

numerous industry trade journals beginning with the reporting violation date and ending with the AAER issuance date for each of the sampled companies,[12] (2) forms 10-Ks, 10-Qs and 8-Ks were searched using Lexis-Nexis for an SEC investigation disclosure over the same period.[13]

Panel B of Table 2 summarizes the final set of observations used to perform the empirical analyses. This study attempts to examine eight data points (four quarters before and four quarters after the event date) for each of the sampled companies. With 69 firms in the sample, the possibility of 552 observations exist (8 data points * 69 firms). A total of 50 observations were excluded from analyses for the following reasons: missing data item (10), extreme unexpected earnings amount (8), extreme RISK (market model Beta) variable amount (14), extreme market-to-book ratio (3), influential outlier (15).[14] After these considerations, a total of 502 observations remained for analyses.

The following procedures were performed to capture the date at which information regarding the strategic actions was disseminated to the public. First, auditor and upper management data were obtained from Form 10-Ks issued immediately before the beginning of the event window, and audit committee and board of director data were obtained from proxy statements issued immediately before the event window. Then, the same information was obtained from Form 10-Ks, 8-Ks and proxy statements issued during and immediately after the event window to determine the status of the strategic action variables throughout the event window. Next, in order to identify the first disclosure date concerning these actions, the Dow Jones *News/Retrieval* search engine was used to perform a full text search of the Wall Street Journal, news wire, and industry trade journals for each of the sampled companies to identify disclosures concerning the strategic actions during the event window. The strategic action variables were calculated based upon when the information became publicly known. Descriptive statistics about these variables are discussed next.

VI. DESCRIPTIVE STATISTICS

Table 3 presents the overall mean and median amounts, along with pre-event and post-event mean amounts for unexpected returns (*UR*), unexpected earnings (*UE*), the control variables *RISK* and *MBRAT*, and the market value of equity *MVEQU*. All three of the presented mean amounts (overall, pre-event, and post-event) for both unexpected returns (*UR*) and unexpected earnings (*UE*) are not significantly different from zero at any conventional level.[15] Additionally, the pre-event mean amount is not significantly different from the post-event mean amount at any conventional level for any of the presented variables.

Table 3. Descriptive Statistics.

Variable	Overall Mean	Overall Median	Pre-Event Mean	Post-Event Mean
UR	0.0008	0.0015	−0.0049	0.0068
UE	−0.0068	−0.0028	−0.0058	−0.0079
MBRAT	3.599	2.049	3.357	3.849
RISK	1.095	1.009	1.112	1.077
MVEQU	553.325	173.3	560.751	545.655

UR	= Cumulative unexpected return surrounding quarterly earnings announcement computed via the market model.
UE	= Unexpected quarterly earnings computed from a seasonal random walk model $((EPS_t - EPS_{t-4})/P_t)$.
MBRAT	= Market-to-book value of equity ratio.
RISK	= Systematic risk measured per the market model beta.
MVEQU	= The market value of equity (in millions of dollars) at the beginning of the quarter.

Table 4 presents some descriptive statistics on the four ameliorating action variables examined in this study. Panel A indicates that 23 of the sampled companies (33%) changed their external auditor sometime during the measurement period. Of the 23 companies changing auditors, 16 companies (69%) changed to an auditor of the same quality,[16] five companies (22%) changed to an auditor of higher quality, and two companies (9%) changed to an auditor of lower quality. Of the 69 sampled companies, 58 companies (84%) began the event period with a Big 6 auditor and 11 companies (16%) began the period with a non-Big 6 auditor.

Panel B of Table 4 presents some descriptive statistics on the board of directors and audit committees for the sampled companies. The first column shows that at the beginning of the measurement period $(t - 4)$ the sampled companies' board of directors, on average, consisted of 45% outside directors.[17] By the end of the measurement period $(t + 4)$ this average increased to 52%. Overall, the sampled companies increased the percentage of outsiders comprising their board of directors by an average of 7.7%.

The second column of Panel B presents information about audit committees for the sampled companies. A total of nine companies began the event period without an audit committee. Of these nine companies, six (67%) formed an audit committee soon after the financial statement fraud announcement.

The number of executive officers disclosed in the annual Form 10-Ks varied among the sampled companies. Of the sampled companies, I was able to track all four positions (CEO, CFO, COO, CAO) for 22 companies, three positions for 30 companies, two positions for 15 companies, and only the Chief Executive

Table 4. Descriptive Statistics of Ameliorating Action Variables.

Panel A: Auditor Changes

Period	Higher Quality Change	Same Quality Change	Lower Quality Change	Total
Pre-Event	0	3	0	3
t + 1	1	6	0	7
t + 2	4	4	0	8
t + 3	0	0	0	0
t + 4	0	3	2	5
Total	5	16	2	23

Period t + n represents the n quarter following event date t (SEC investigation announcement).
Higher quality change reflects changing from a non-Big 6 audit firm to a Big 6 audit firm, same
quality change reflects changing within these groups, and lower quality change reflects changing
from a Big 6 auditor to a non-Big 6 auditor.

Panel B: BOD Compositions and Audit Committees

Period	% of Outsiders on BOD	Companies without an Audit Committee
t − 4	45	9
t + 4	52	3

Period t + n represents the n quarter following event date t (SEC investigation announcement).

Panel C: Upper Management Changes

Period	Replaced CEO	Replaced CFO	Replaced COO	Replaced CAO	At least one position replaced
t + 1	26%	45%	26%	36%	49%
t + 2	29%	50%	38%	40%	58%
t + 3	32%	58%	46%	50%	65%
t + 4	40%	63%	62%	50%	72%

Period t + n represents the n quarter following event date t (SEC investigation announcement).

Officer (CEO) position for two of the companies. Arguably, if the position is
not listed in the Form 10-K, either the position does not exist for that particular company or it is not considered to be an upper level managerial position.
This study is concerned with the ameliorating effects of upper management
changes, and thus it appears reasonable to track only the executive positions
disclosed in the company's Form 10-K.

Panel C of Table 4 presents descriptive statistics regarding managerial changes made by the sampled companies. The rows represent the periods subsequent to the event date and the columns represent the management positions tracked for this study. The percentage amounts reflect the percentage of sampled companies that had changed the applicable column's managerial position as of the stated period. For example, the percentage amount found under the column Replaced CFO and at row t + 3 reflects that 58% of the sampled companies had changed their CFO as of the third quarter following the event date. By the end of the measurement period (t + 4), 40% of the companies had replaced their CEO, 63% had replaced their CFO, 62% had replaced their COO, and 50% had replaced their CAO sometime during the measurement period. Overall, approximately 72% of the sampled companies had replaced at least one of the four positions during the measurement period. In summary, the descriptive statistics presented in Table 4 provide evidence that a reasonable number of sampled companies performed the ameliorating actions examined in this study.[18] The empirical analyses attempt to determine whether these actions were effective in improving the perceived disclosure validity subsequent to a financial statement fraud announcement. The results from these analyses are discussed next.

VII. EMPIRICAL RESULTS

Table 5 presents the results of the OLS regression analyses. Column (a) of Table 5 shows the results from the full regression model presented in the Appendix. Two of the strategic actions, changing external auditor and increasing the percentage of outsiders on the board, have significant interaction terms in the predicted direction. Specifically, the significant and positive coefficient on the interaction term $UE*AUD$ (p-value = 0.002) suggests that the act of changing external auditor following the fraud announcement improves the *UR-UE* relation, and supports H2. The significant and positive coefficient on the interaction term $UE*OUT$ (p-value = 0.028) suggests that the act of increasing the percentage of outsiders comprising the board of directors following the fraud announcement improves the *UR-UE* relation, and supports H3.

The audit committee interaction term (UE*AC) coefficient is not significant at any conventional level (p-value = 0.33), and thus H4 is not supported. This lack of significance may be due to a lack of variation of the *AC* variable (i.e. only six of the sampled companies formed an audit committee during the measurement period). The coefficient of the management change interaction variable ($UE*MGMT$) is significant and negative, which is opposite the direction predicted in H5. Additionally, the $UE*FRD$ variable is not significant

Table 5. OLS Regression Results.

(dependent variable = UR)

Variable	Predicted Direction	Column (a) Coefficient (Std Error)	Column (b) Coefficient (Std Error)
Intercept	none	0.012753 (.0147)	0.012269 (0.0147)
FRD	none	0.013302 (0.0110)	0.015447* (0.0093)
UE	positive	0.129681*** (0.0563)	0.130312*** (0.0564)
UE*FRD	negative	0.004132 (0.1257)	–0.153588** (0.0892)
AUD	none	–0.018735 (0.0140)	–0.015915 (0.0136)
UE*AUD	positive	0.556735*** (0.1915)	0.526046*** (0.1909)
OUT	none	0.036639 (0.0669)	0.040445 (0.0664)
UE*OUT	positive	2.58235** (1.3429)	1.825633* (1.2865)
AC	none	–0.019130 (0.0204)	–0.017884 (0.0204)
UE*AC	positive	0.277407 (0.6498)	0.241677 (0.6507)
MGMT	none	0.006685 (0.0121)	
UE*MGMT	positive	–0.253853 (0.1398)	
MBRAT	positive	0.000498 (0.0007)	0.000489 (0.0007)
RISK	negative	–0.012263** (0.0065)	–0.013484*** (0.0065)
SIZE	negative	–0.001318 (0.0023)	–0.001013 (0.0023)
QTR	negative	0.007575 (0.0092)	0.008628 (0.0092)
Sample Size		502	502
R-Square		0.07	0.06
F-Ratio		2.43	2.51

***, **, * Statistically significant at less than the 0.02, 0.05, and 0.10 levels, respectively. Based on one-tailed (two-tailed) tests for variables whose relation to the dependent variable is (is not) predicted.

at any conventional level, and thus H1 is not supported. However, further analysis reveals that the management change variable (*MGMT*) appears to be capturing similar effects as the *FRD* variable. The correlation amounts between *MGMT* and *FRD* (0.66) and between *UE*MGMT* and *UE*FRD* (0.85) are both highly significant. Additionally, the variance inflation factors (VIFs) of the terms *UE*FRD* and *UE*MGMT* are 4.65 and 4.14, respectively.[19] The VIFs of these two terms are twice as large as the next highest VIF (1.97) associated with the remaining variables, which suggests that the variables measuring fraud effects and management change effects are highly collinear.

Perhaps the act of changing upper management subsequent to the fraud announcement is an action that market participants expect companies accused by the SEC of a material reporting violation to perform. That is, if the market perceives the changing of upper management as an expected and necessary action following the announcement of financial statement fraud, the market effects of the fraud announcement and the changing of upper management would be similar. The high percentage of sampled companies that changed upper management (72%) supports this notion. To address this issue, the model was employed excluding the managerial change variables.

Column (b) of Table 5 presents the results of the regression model excluding the managerial change variables (*MGMT* and *UE*MGMT*). The coefficient of the interaction term *UE*FRD* is now significant (*p*-value = 0.04) in the predicted direction, thus supporting H1. The coefficient of the interaction term *UE*OUT* reduces slightly in significance (*p*-value = 0.08), and the coefficient of the *RISK* variable improves slightly in significance (*p*-value = 0.02). The coefficient of the *FRD* variable becomes marginally significant (*p*-value = 0.10) in this model. The direction and significance of the coefficients for the remaining variables are consistent with model (a).

In summary, after excluding the management change variables, the results suggest that the announcement of financial statement fraud is associated with a decrease in the earnings response coefficient. Furthermore, the strategic actions of changing external auditor and increasing the percentage of outsiders comprising the board of directors following the announcement of financial statement fraud improves the earnings response coefficient. These results support H1, H2 and H3, but do not support H4 and H5.[20]

VIII. SUMMARY AND CONCLUSIONS

This study examines the effects that financial statement fraud announcements and certain strategic actions have on the perceived validity of financial disclosures. The hypotheses are based upon the prior literature that uses the earnings response coefficient to measure earnings quality. In a similar light, this study uses the ERC to measure the perceived validity of financial disclosures. The first hypothesis proposes that the announcement of a financial statement fraud is associated with a decrease in the company's ERC. The remaining hypotheses propose that certain strategic actions performed by companies following a fraud announcement improve the ERC. The hypotheses were tested by examining the ERCs associated with the quarterly earnings announcements surrounding a financial statement fraud announcement.

The results suggest that a financial statement fraud announcement is associated with a decrease in the ERC, and support H1. Additionally, the results suggest that the strategic actions of changing external auditor and increasing the percentage of outsiders comprising the board of directors following a fraud announcement improve the ERC, and support H2 and H3. The hypotheses regarding the two strategic actions of forming an audit committee (H4) and changing upper management (H5) were not supported by the results. Based on this evidence, financial statement frauds appear to damage the perceived validity of financial disclosures, and the strategic actions of changing external auditor and increasing the percentage of outsiders on the board of directors appear to ameliorate this damaged validity. The robustness of these results was tested by performing several sensitivity analyses.

This study is subject to several limitations. First, only 69 companies were available for analyses, and thus the power of the statistics and the ability to generalize the results may be questioned.[21] Second, a pooled cross-sectional regression is used to analyze the earnings response coefficients of the selected companies. Although control variables are included to attempt to control for any firm-specific effects, omitted correlated variables may exist which would lead to incorrect conclusions. Third, only four strategic actions are considered for examination. Arguably, companies accused of a material reporting violation perform other ameliorating actions than those examined. If another type of strategic action is correlated with one of the actions examined, the presented results may lead to erroneous conclusions. Fourth, although careful attention was given toward the identification of the event date (SEC investigation announcement), leakage of information may have occurred prior to the date identified. This would add noise to the data and the regression estimates. Fifth, this study examines strategic actions performed over four quarters subsequent to the announcement of financial statement fraud, and thus a survivorship bias exists.

Overall, this study is one of the first attempts to empirically examine financial statement fraud effects on the validity of earnings disclosures. The results suggest that fraud announcements damage the perceived validity of financial disclosures, and that certain strategic actions effectively ameliorate this negative effect. I hope these results will encourage further research in this area

NOTES

1. For example, news of an SEC investigation for reporting violations prompted PaineWeber analyst Steve Fortuna to question the credibility of Sensormatic management (*Sensor Business News*, 1995). After news of a financial statement fraud, Price Waterhouse told PerSeptive Biosystems that it could no longer rely on certain management representations (*Wall Street Journal*, 1995). Additionally, an independent analyst said that the change in management following fraud allegations would help Bolar Pharmaceutical Co. restore its credibility with investors (*Wall Street Journal*, 1990).

2. For example, Cal Micro changed its senior management and fired several board members soon after disclosure of their alleged fraud (Richards, 1996). Sunrise Medical Inc. reported that they fired the vice president of finance, changed its management bonus schemes and planned to strengthen the company's financial controls shortly after being accused of fraudulent reporting (Rundle, 1996). Additionally, Comptronix Corp. fired members of its top management along with their independent auditor after a disclosure described their involvement in financial statement fraud (*Wall Street Journal*, 1993).

3. The proposed hypotheses do not consider auditor quality or audit committee composition effects. It is assumed that the perceived quality of the incumbent auditor is severely damaged from the fraud occurrence and that any change of auditor is perceived as an improvement in quality. Audit committee composition effects and auditor quality effects are considered in sensitivity analyses that are discussed later in the paper.

4. Outside directors are those directors who have no other affiliation with the firm other than the affiliation from being on the board of directors. Thus, those directors who have some non-board affiliation with the firm (i.e. 'grey' directors) are not considered as outside directors for this study.

5. According to Feroz et al. (1991), the SEC makes its enforcement activities public only when it files a formal complaint alleging securities law violations and seeks settlement with the enforcement target. However, the *1934 Act Release No. 5092* requires the public disclosure by companies of material information, which would include formal investigations by the enforcement division.

6. Feroz et al. (1991) point out that of 43 accounting-based formal investigations completed in 1989, only two did not result in an SEC 'win'.

7. The reasoning that four subsequent periods are examined is twofold. First, the quarterly financial statement data disclosed immediately after the fraud announcement may include significant accounting adjustments due to the fraud, which may reduce its informativeness to investors. Second, the examination of four post-fraud quarters may lend insights about the persistence of the perceived validity damage caused by fraud announcements. Additionally, an adequate time frame is necessary to allow ample time for the strategic actions to be performed and for the market to react to these actions. Four pre-fraud periods are examined in order to balance the model and to have an adequate number of observations to provide reasonable earnings response metrics prior to the fraud announcement.

8. This period is chosen for examination in order to ensure that the data obtained are current and that the sample is large enough for meaningful analysis.

9. Section 13(a) violations are arguably not as severe as Rule 10(b)-5 violations. However, Dechow et al. (1996) state that the SEC only pursues Section 13(a) cases where it can demonstrate that management knew or should have known through better internal controls about the reporting violation. The authors conclude that it is reasonable to assume that firms facing enforcement actions by the SEC knowingly and intentionally engaged in earnings manipulation. Additionally, the SEC investigation disclosure (the event date for this study) only mentions that some type of reporting violation has occurred, and does not identify the type of violation the target allegedly violated. The inclusion of Section 13(a) violation firms is necessary in order to obtain a large enough sample for meaningful analyses. A sensitivity test is performed to examine for possible differences between Section 13(a) violators (17 sampled companies) and Rule 10(b)-5 violators (52 sampled companies).

10. Dow Jones *News/Retrieval* was used for the full-text search. The search involved examining articles in which the words investigation, inquiry, or probe were within 25 words of the words Exchange Commission or SEC. This period (1995–1996) was searched in order to ensure that a long enough period exists after the fraud announcement to examine the effects of the subsequent strategic actions.

11. This amount is somewhat consistent with Dechow et al. (1996) whose final sample consisted of 92 firms generated from AAERs issued between 1982 and 1992. Their average number of firms per AAER year examined is slightly higher than this study's (8.36 vs. 7.25). This difference is probably due to Dechow et al. (1996) having a shorter market data window (i.e. one day) and thus a less demanding data requirement.

12. For companies identified via the *WSJ* search, the Dow Jones *News/Retrieval* search period extended back a period of two years using the company name as a keyword.

13. For companies not included in the Lexis-Nexis database, form 10-Ks were examined via Q-Data SEC files.

14. Extreme amounts were determined as follows: UE amounts greater than 1 or less than −1; *RISK* amounts greater than 3.5 or less than −0.10; and *MBRAT* amounts greater than 100. Influential outliers were determined by examining the studentized residuals and the Cook's D Influence variables for the sampled observations.

15. *T*-statistics were calculated (although not reported) to test the significance of the difference between the mean levels of the variables.

16. Consistent with DeAngelo's (1981) argument that auditor size is a reasonable proxy for quality, this study considers Big 6 audit firms to be of higher quality than non-Big 6 audit firms.

17. This amount is consistent with Dechow et al. (1996), whose sample had an average of 53% insiders on the board of directors.

18. Prior research provides some evidence that the frequency of the ameliorating actions for the sampled companies is greater than that of the general population. For example, prior research suggests that around 6% of companies change auditors in a given year (Krishnan, 1994) (versus 33% of the sampled companies who changed their auditor), and that around 6%–12% of companies change their CEO in a given year (Denis et al., 1997; *WSJ*, 1996) (versus 40% of the sampled companies who changed their CEO). Information regarding population percentages for audit committee formation and board of director compostion changes was not readily available.

19. VIFs represent the inflation that each regression coefficient experiences above ideal. Large VIFs suggest that collinearity may be problematic.

20. The following sensitivity tests were performed to test for the robustness of these results: (1) the immediate quarters surrounding the event date (t − 1 and t + 1) were excluded from the sample; (2) two alternative measurements of the *MGMT* variable were considered; (3) auditor quality effects (i.e. the effectiveness of auditor change depends on the type of change) were examined; (4) and differences between Section 13(a) and Rule 10(b)-5 violations were examined. The results from these sensitivity analyses are similar to those presented. Additionally, the variables controlling for auditor quality and Section 13(a) violations were insignificant. Another sensitivity test involved measuring the effects of changes in audit committee composition (i.e. the change in the percentage of outsiders on the audit committee). The results from this test were similar to those presented except that the interaction variable UE*OUT loses significance. This is apparently due to the introduction of multicollinearity into the model resulting from the significant correlation between the audit committee composition and board of director composition variables (0.36). Additionally, the audit committee composition variable was insignificant. Based on these sensitivity analyses, the presented results appear to be robust.

21. As a sensitivity test, the regression was estimated after eliminating sampled firms that had at least one influential outlier observation. This left a sample size of 58 firms and a total of 431 observations. The results from this regression support H2 (the external auditor effect), but no longer support H1and H3. Thus, the reduction in sample size by 11 firms (16%) weakens the results and conclusions presented.

22. For quarterly earnings announcements prior to the fraud announcement, the 200 day estimation period ended the day before the quarterly announcement. For quarterly earnings announcements after the fraud announcement, however, the 200 day estimation period had to cover a period surrounding the earnings announcement due to the event date (i.e. fraud announcement) being within 200 days of the subsequent quarterly announcement. In order to exclude the effects of the fraud announcement, a 10 day period surrounding the fraud announcement was excluded from the market model estimation period.

23. A separate persistence of earnings measure is not included due to the sampled firms lacking an earnings history that is necessary to calculate a persistence variable. Kormendi and Lipe (1987) used 35 consecutive earnings observations per firm, and Easton and Zmijewski (1989) used 20 earnings observations per firm to measure persistence. This study would require a similar number of earnings from each period (pre-announcement and post-announcement) to measure a persistence variable, and such an amount is not available for many of the sampled companies. Therefore, the market-to-book value of equity ratio is used to proxy for both growth potential and earnings persistence. Collins and Kothari (1989) suggest that this ratio is likely to be affected by earnings persistence, and prior empirical studies have used the market-to-book ratio to proxy for both growth and earnings persistence (Teoh & Wong, 1993; Wild, 1996).

ACKNOWLEDGMENTS

This paper is based on my dissertation at the University of Tennessee. I would like to thank the members of my dissertation committee: Joseph Carcello (Chairman), Susan Ayers, Bruce Behn, Ron Shrieves, and Jan Williams. I would also like to thank Kevin James, LeAnn Luna, Terry Neal, Dick Riley, and two anonymous referees for their helpful comments.

REFERENCES

American Institute of Certified Public Accountants (AICPA) (1997). *Consideration of Fraud in a Financial Statement Audit*. Statement on Auditing Standards No.82. New York, NY: AICPA.

Atiase, R. (1985). Pre-disclosure information, firm capitalization, and security price behavior around earnings announcements. *Journal of Accounting Research*, (Spring), 21–36.

Beasley, M. (1996). An empirical analysis of the relation between the board of director composition and financial statement fraud. *The Accounting Review*, (October), 443–465.

Choi, S., & Jeter, D. (1992). The effects of qualified audit opinions on earnings response coefficients. *Journal of Accounting and Economics*, *15*, 229–247.

Collins, D., & Kothari, S. P. (1989). An analysis of intertemporal and cross-sectional determinants of earnings response coefficients. *Journal of Accounting and Economics*, *11*, 143–181.

DeAngelo, L. (1981). Auditor size and audit quality. *Journal of Accounting & Economics*, *3*(December), 183–199.

Dechow, P., Sloan, R., & Sweeney, A. (1996). Causes and consequences of earnings manipulation: An analysis of firms subject to enforcement actions by the SEC. *Contemporary Accounting Research*, (Spring), 1–36.

Denis, D., Denis, D., & Sarin, A. (1997). Ownership structure and top executive turnover. *Journal of Financial Economics*, *45*, 193–221.

Easton, P., & Zmijewski, M. (1989). Cross-sectional variation in the stock market response to accounting earnings announcements. *Journal of Accounting and Economics*, *11*, 117–141.

Ettredge, M., Shane, P., & Smith, D. (1988). Audit firm size and the association between reported earnings and security returns. *Auditing: A Journal of Practice & Theory*, (Spring), 29–42.

Feroz, E. H., Park, K., & Pastena, V. S. (1991). The financial and market effects of the SEC's accounting and auditing enforcement releases. *Journal of Accounting Research*, *29*(Suppl.), 107–142.

Financial Accounting Standards Board (1980). *Statement of Financial Accounting Concepts No. 2: Qualitative Characteristics of Accounting Information*. Stamford, Conn.: FASB.

Holthausen, R., & Verrecchia, R. (1988). The effect of sequential information releases on the variance of price changes in an intertemporal multi-asset market. *Journal of Accounting Research*, *26*(Spring), 82–106.

Hunt, I. (2000). Remarks delivered at "SEC Speaks in 2000". March 3. Washington, D.C.: SEC.

Klein, A. (2000a). Causes and consequences of variations in audit committee composition. Working Paper. New York University.

Klein, A. (2000b). Audit committee, board of director characteristics, and earnings management. Working Paper. New York University.

Kormendi, R., & Lipe, R. (1987). Earnings innovations, earnings persistence, and stock returns. *Journal of Business*, (July), 323–345.

Krishnan, J. (1994). Auditor switching and conservatism. *The Accounting Review*, (January), 200–215.

Lipe, R. (1990). The relation between stock returns and accounting earnings given alternative information. *The Accounting Review*, (January), 49–71.

Levitt, A. (1998). The numbers game. Remarks delivered at the NYU Center for Law and Business, New York, NY, September 28. Washington, D.C.: SEC.

Moreland, K. (1995). Criticisms of auditors and the association between earnings and returns of client firms. *Auditing: A Journal of Practice & Theory*, (Spring), 94–104.

Pincus, K., Holder, W. H., & Mock, T. J. (1988). *Reducing the incidence of fraudulent financial reporting: The role of the Securities and Exchange Commission*. Los Angeles: SEC and Financial Reporting Institute of the University of Southern California.

Richards, B. (1996). Former officials at California Micro face SEC charges. *Wall Street Journal*, (September 27), B7.

Rundle, R. (1996). Sunrise, restating sharply downward two years of profit, alleges faked data. *Wall Street Journal*, (January 5), A2.

Salamon, G., & Stober, T. (1994). Cross-quarter differences in stock price responses to earnings announcements: Fourth-quarter and seasonality influences. *Contemporary Accounting Research*, (Fall), 297–330.

Securities and Exchange Commission (1996). *Annual report of the SEC*. Washington, D.C.: Government Printing Office.

Sensor Business News (1995). Sensormatic Corp. sees earnings drop, faces SEC probe of financial practices. (November 8).

Teoh, S., & Wong, T. (1993). Perceived auditor quality and the earnings response coefficient. *The Accounting Review*, 68(April), 346–366.

Wall Street Journal (1990). Bolar's Shulman resigns as president, sources say, as Mylan seeks to buy drug. (February 13), A2.

Wall Street Journal (1993). Comptronix settles shareholder claims, reaches restructuring pact with banks. (March 9), B4.

Wall Street Journal (1995). SEC is seeking information from Massachusetts firm. Wall Street Journal (January 11).

Wall Street Journal (1996). Executive Pay Survey Results. (April 11), R16–R17.

Wild, J. (1996). The audit committee and earnings quality. *Journal of Accounting, Auditing & Finance*, (Spring), 247–276.

APPENDIX: MODEL AND VARIABLES

Overview of the estimated multiple regression model

$$UR_{ia} = \beta_0 + \beta_1 FRD_{ia} + \beta_2 UE_{ia} + \beta_3 (UE_{ia} * FRD_{ia}) + \beta_4 AUD_{ia} + \beta_5 (UE_{ia} * AUD_{ia})$$
$$+ \beta_6 OUT_{ia} + \beta_7 (UE_{ia} * OUT_{ia}) + \beta_8 MGMT_{ia} + \beta_9 (UE_{ia} * MGMT_{ia}) + \beta_{10} AC_{ia}$$
$$+ \beta_{11} (UE_{ia} * AC_{ia}) + \beta_{12} MBRAT_{ia} + \beta_{13} RISK_{ia} + \beta_{14} SIZE_{ia} + \beta_{15} QTR_{ia} + \varepsilon_{ia}.$$

Dependent variable

UR_{ia}. The cumulative unexpected return for firm i surrounding quarterly earnings announcement a. Unexpected returns are estimated through the following market model:

$$UR_{ja} = \sum_{t=-1}^{0} (R_{jt} - \hat{\gamma}_{j0} - \hat{\gamma}_{j1} R_{Mt}),$$

where $t = 0$ is the day of the firm's quarterly earnings announcement, j denotes firm and a denotes quarter. R_{jt} is the rate of return of firm j at day t, R_{Mt} is the Center for Research in Security Prices (CRSP) value-weighted index, and γ_{j0} and γ_{j1} are parameter estimates from a firm specific market return model. These parameters are estimated over a 200 trading day period.[22] These variables were obtained from the daily CRSP tapes.

Test variables

UE_{ia}. The unexpected quarterly earnings for firm i at announcement a. Unexpected earnings are computed from a seasonal random walk model of earnings, scaled by price:

$$UR_{ia} = (EPS_{ia} - EPS_{ia-4})/P_{ia},$$

where EPS_{ia} is the earnings per share for firm i for quarter a, and EPS_{ia-4} is prior period's earnings per share (i.e. prior year's EPS for the same quarter). P_{ia} is the price per share of firm i's stock at the beginning of the quarter. These variables were obtained from the Compustat quarterly tapes.

FRD_{ia}. A dummy variable equaling 1 if the quarterly earnings announcement is subsequent to the fraud announcement, and 0 otherwise. A negative coefficient on this variable's interaction term ($UE*FRD$) would support H1.

AUD_{ia}. For subsequent fraud announcement periods, this variable equals 1 if company i changed its external auditor, and 0 otherwise. For prior fraud announcement periods, this variable equals zero. A positive coefficient on this variable's interaction term ($UE*AUD$) would support H2.

OUT_{ia}. For subsequent fraud announcement periods, this variable equals the increase in the percentage of outside directors serving as board members from the beginning of the measurement period. For prior fraud announcement periods, this variable equals zero. A significant and positive coefficient on this variable's interaction term ($UE*OUT$) would support H3.

AC_{ia}. For subsequent fraud announcement periods, this variable equals 1 if an audit committee was formed, and 0 otherwise. For prior fraud announcement periods, this variable equals zero. A positive coefficient on this variable's interaction term ($UE*AC$) would support H4.

$MGMT_{ia}$. For subsequent fraud announcement periods, this variable equals 1 if the company changed an upper management position (CEO, COO, CFO, CAO) subsequent to the fraud announcement, and 0 otherwise. For prior fraud announcement periods, this variable equals zero. A positive coefficient on this variable's interaction term ($UE*MGMT$) would support H5.

Control Variables

$MBRAT_{ia}$. The market-to-book value of equity ratio for firm i at quarter a. This variable proxies for both growth and earnings persistence and is expected to have a positive coefficient.[23]

$RISK_{ia}$. The systematic risk of firm i measured per the market model beta. The estimated market model is discussed above in the definition of *UR*. The coefficient of this variable is expected to be negative.

$SIZE_{ia}$. The natural log of the market value of equity at the beginning of quarter a. This variable proxies for the noise in the predisclosure environment and is expected to have a negative coefficient.

QTR_{ia}. A dummy variable equaling one if the quarterly announcement is a fourth period (i.e. fiscal year-end) announcement and 0 otherwise. The coefficient of this variable is expected to be negative.

ε. The disturbance term.

EVIDENCE OF EARNINGS MANAGEMENT WITH THE SELECTION OF THE DISCOUNT RATE FOR PENSION ACCOUNTING: THE IMPACT OF A SEC LETTER

David R. Vruwink

ABSTRACT

In September 1993, the Securities Exchange Commission (SEC) sent the Financial Accounting Standards Board (FASB) a letter, which made the charge that many companies were not following current accounting standards in the selection of the discount rate for computing pension liabilities and pension expense. This study compares the discount rates, before and after the SEC letter, of firms with rapid earnings growth to those firms that had declining earnings from the previous year for the 1991 to 1995 time period. The results provide some evidence that prior to the SEC letter, firms with positive earnings were influenced by past operating performance in selecting the discount rate. After the SEC letter, no significant difference was found between the discount rates for the two groups of firms. This outcome supports the view that the SEC letter appears to have been successful in influencing more companies to follow current accounting standards in selecting the discount rate.

Research in Accounting Regulation, Volume 15, pages 119–132.

1. INTRODUCTION

In the early 1990s, there were numerous allegations in national news magazines, newspapers and on network TV that many companies were abusing pension accounting standards. The stories usually focused on firms using very high interest rates in their discounting calculations to determine the amount of pension liabilities and pension expense. At the time there were concerns that companies would not be able to provide pension benefits earned by their employees (Blankley & Swanson, 1995).

In support of these allegations, Walter P. Schuetze, the SEC's chief accountant, sent a letter to the Emerging Issues Task Force of the Financial Accounting Standards Board (FASB), on September 20, 1993. The letter charged that many companies and their auditors were not following current accounting standards in determining the proper discount rate for estimating pension liabilities. The SEC staff found that a sizable number of companies were using out-dated and much higher interest rates than dictated by current interest rates. Consequently, the SEC letter recommended that companies follow a more narrow interpretation of SFAS No. 87 by selecting a discount rate that reflected the interest rate of a fixed-income security of at least AA quality (Bergsman, 1994).

A firm's reluctance to reduce its discount rate to reflect the lower interest rates of recent years is understandable when considering that even a small downward adjustment of the discount rate increases significantly the pension liabilities and related pension expense. For example, a general rule-of-thumb is that pension expense is increased by 4 to 7% for each one-quarter point decrease in the interest rate (Winklevoss, 1977; Kwon, 1994). While a 4 to 7% change in pension expense could seem insignificant in comparison to total earnings, it should have a much larger impact on the company's expected growth rate of earnings for the current year.

For example, assume a company has earned $1 per share in the past year and had increased earnings by approximately 12% over the last several years. Management is well aware that shareholders are expecting that rate of earnings growth to continue. If business conditions look bleak at the beginning of the year, management may be tempted to get at least part of that expected earnings growth through manipulating the discount rate by one-quarter of a percent or more.

(i) Goals of the Study

From the many claims of pension abuse and the SEC letter previously mentioned, it appears that the management of a number of companies were "managing" earnings through the selection of the discount rate for pension liabilities. Too much flexibility in selecting a discount rate appears to have been allowed under SFAS No. 87, "Employer's Accounting for Pensions" (1985). In theory, the discount rate should be almost identical for all U.S. companies. Assuming a positive yield curve, the age, mortality, retirement age, etc. of a company's workforce should have only a small impact on the selection of the discount rate. However, in actual practice, the discount rate varies widely.

Therefore, the two main goals of this study are first to determine the extent (if any) that companies used the selection of the discount rate to influence earnings, and second to measure how successful the SEC letter was on encouraging companies to follow GAAP guidelines in selecting the discount rate. If a company had always been using a relatively higher (lower) discount rate than other companies, then it was not following SFAS No. 87 guidelines. That is why the SEC letter is such a great event to measure the change in behavior by the firms. Management knew that the SEC was now watching their selection of the discount rate.[1]

2. REVIEW OF PENSION ACCOUNTING

There are two general types of pension plans in the United States: (1) defined contribution plans, and (2) defined benefit plans. The accounting for a defined contribution plan is quite simple. The pension cost is equal to the company's required contribution. Any shortfall from the required contribution would be recognized as a liability on the balance sheet. The company does not promise any specific level of future benefits to their employees. The employees are responsible for how their contributions are invested.

Defined benefit plans specify the amount of pension benefits to be paid to the retired employee. The company is responsible for making contributions to a fund and assuming the investment risk in earning a return that will provide the specified benefits to their employees at retirement. The company must estimate each year the pension cost and contributions for the year and whether the company has enough funds for pension benefits earned in prior years.

The focus of the SEC letter and this study is on companies with defined benefit plans. This is due to the large amounts of pension assets and liabilities accumulated by these companies and the potential impact on their financial statements. Current accounting standards require companies with defined benefit plans to disclose in the footnotes of their annual reports the following information: (1) the funded status of the pension plans, (2) the components of pension expense, and (3) the actuarial assumptions used to compute the company's pension liabilities and pension expense.

U.S. companies must report three different measures of pension liabilities for their U.S. pension plans in their pension footnote: (1) the vested benefit obligation (VBO) if all the employees would quit, which is the amount of retirement benefits legally owed to employees on that date, (2) the accumulated benefit obligation (ABO), calculated as the vested benefits obligation plus any benefits earned by employees who have not yet vested, and (3) the projected benefit obligation (PBO), which is the present value of all estimated benefits plus expected future salary increases. The projected benefit obligation (PBO) is probably most often used by investors and shareholders as a company's actual pension liabilities since the PBO figures assume the company will continue to exist indefinitely.

There are three major components of pension expense: (1) service cost, the present value of the pension benefits earned by the company's employees during the current year; (2) the interest cost on the projected benefit obligation, calculated by multiplying the beginning balance of the projected benefit obligation by the discount rate, and (3) the reduction of those costs through the expected return on pension plan assets. Lesser components of pension expense consist of amortization of unrecognized gains or losses from pension plan assets, amortization of prior service cost, and amortization of the transition amount, if any.

Three actuarial assumptions are also disclosed in the pension footnotes for U.S. companies: (1) the expected return on plan assets, (2) the average rate of increase in future compensation, and (3) the discount rate. An increase in the expected return on plan assets will decrease pension expense while an increase in the expected rate of compensation will increase pension expense through an increased amount of both service cost and interest cost from a larger PBO. An increase in the discount rate will decrease both pension liabilities and pension expense. Pension liabilities must decrease because of the higher interest rate used to compute the present value of the future pension obligations. Pension expense decreases because of the decrease in the present value of the service cost earned by the employees for the current year.

(i) Official Guidance – Discount Rate

SFAS No. 87, "Employers' Accounting for Pensions" (1985), requires that in selecting appropriate discount rates, employers should refer to current information on rates used in annuity contracts that could be used to settle pension obligations, including the annuity rates published by the Pension Benefit Guaranty Corporation (PBGC), or use rates of return on high-quality fixed-income investments that are expected to be available through the maturity dates of the pension benefits. A survey conducted in 1991 by Blankley and Swanson (1995) found that firms were using several different rates, including PBGC rates, 30-year Treasury bonds, Merrill Lynch index of high-quality bonds and others. The differences in yields among the different benchmarks were substantial, with PBGC rates being the lowest and most conservative. Companies had a wide range of interest rates from which to select a discount rate.

The SEC letter sent to the FASB on September 20, 1993, made it clear that the SEC wanted the provisions of SFAS No. 87 to be more narrowly interpreted by companies in selecting the discount rate for pension liabilities. For example, the letter stated that fixed-income investments that received one of the two highest ratings given by a recognized rating agency should be used to determine the present value of a sponsor's pension obligations. Thus, the interest rate of a fixed-income investment that received a rating of AA or higher from Moody's would be considered an appropriate discount rate. This new interpretation of SFAS No. 87 by the SEC was intended to greatly narrow the range of interest rates that could be used to measure pension costs and liabilities, and as a result, became quite similar to the provisions of SFAS No.106, "Employer's Accounting for Post-retirement Benefits Other Than Pensions" (1990). SFAS No. 106 recommends a discount rate based on a portfolio of high-quality, fixed-income investments, where those rates incorporate the expected reinvestment rates in the future (para. 186).

Two studies indicate that many companies were already using guidelines similar to SFAS No. 106 in selecting the discount rate for pension liabilities. Amir and Gordon (1996) find that the mean discount rates used by early adopters of SFAS No.106 during the 1991, 1992 and 1993 fiscal years for pensions (8.41, 8.22, 7.38%) are very similar to the discount rates for health care costs (8.39,8.27,7.37%). The standard error of the pension discount rates (0.62%, 0.54%, and 0.40% in 1991, 1992, and 1993) however, is slightly larger than the standard error of the health care rates (0.47%, 0.47%, and 0.38%), indicating that some of their sample firms used more extreme assumptions for the pension discount rates.

Blankley and Swanson (1995) find similar discount rates for pensions in a random sample of 305 firms with defined benefit pension plans. The mean discount rates selected for 1991, 1992, and 1993 (8.41, 8.21, and 7.43) are very similar to the pension discount rates reported by Amir and Gordon. The discount rates in both of these two studies suggest that most firms were already following guidelines similar to SFAS No. 106 during this period for both health care and pensions since the "AA" bond yield was 8.51, 8.30, and 7.30, respectively, at the end of 1991, 1992 and 1993.

3. REVIEW OF PRIOR STUDIES

Goldberg, and Duchac (1996) provide an extensive review of pension studies in the last several years. They find that the greater part of the empirical accounting research in this area examines the motivation for making changes to over-funded defined-benefit pension plans through either plan terminations, settlements or changes in actuarial assumptions. Since legal pension obligations are relatively explicit under a defined-benefit plan, the sponsoring firm may recapture the excess assets either quickly through plan terminations and settlements, or slowly through actuarial assumptions.

During the 1980s, interest rates remained fairly high while the stock market rose significantly, leaving many defined pension plans over-funded. Thus, many companies had pension plan settlements or terminations during this period. Early empirical research (Thomas, 1989; Mittelstaedt, 1989; Healy & Palepu, 1990; and Ghicas, 1990) focus on the motivation behind these actions and find cash flow needs or financial weakening to be the primary factors. With the steep decline in interest rates in the 1990s and the related decline in the over-funding of pension plans, firms appear to have reoriented their efforts toward changes in actuarial assumptions, including the discount rate, to slow the amount of funding to their pension plans. The numerous articles in the financial press on actuarial assumptions during this time period, along with the SEC letter, attest to management's change in focus.

Healy and Palepu (1990) find no evidence that dividend constraints in debt contracts influenced changes in actuarial assumptions by companies during the time period of 1981–1985. This time period is chosen because of a sharp increase in the number of companies that faced dividend constraints as a result of the recession in 1981–1982. Kwon (1994) examine the selection of the discount rate with several firm-related variables for 130 companies over a 1984–1988 period. His major finding is that the level of funding of a pension plan does influence the selection of the discount rate. Companies with under-funded pension plans tend to select higher discount rates, which lower the amount of under-funding. Kwon (1994) did not test any earnings-related variables.

Godwin, Goldberg and Duchac (1996) examine the relationship between the discount rate and a firm's cash flows, earnings, financial leverage and changes in tax benefits of plan funding over a three-year period (1981–1983). The empirical results of their research suggest that managers prefer to increase the discount rate when a company has lower earnings, higher financial leverage, tighter dividend restrictions, or a reduction in tax benefits. Similarly, Amir and Gordon (1996) find that firms with extreme earnings-price ratios were more likely to select lower discount rates for their pension plans than other companies during the 1991–1993 period.

4. HYPOTHESIS AND MOTIVATION FOR THE STUDY

There are several incentives that would explain management behavior in selecting a discount rate to manage or smooth earnings. In an effort to maximize their own wealth, managers must consider the effect that discretionary accrual accounting decisions (such as the selection of the discount rate) have: (1) on their reputation/job tenure (DeFond & Park, 1997; Fundenberg & Tirole, 1995); (2) on reaching their earnings-based bonuses (Guidry, Leone & Rock, 1999; Holthausen, Larcker & Sloan, 1995; Healy, 1985); and (3) increasing the value of their own stockholdings and options (Gaver, Gaver & Austin, 1995).

Some incentives for smoothing earnings are much stronger than others. Lewellen, Loderer and Martin (1987) report that the mean value of manager's stock holdings and options is almost thirty times the mean value of salary plus earnings-based bonuses. Also, Gaver, Gaver, and Austin (1995) report that 91.6% of their firm-year observations, a stock option or restricted stock plan was in place in addition to a bonus plan. Consequently, management's income smoothing decisions should be focused primarily on increasing the stock price of their firm.

Several studies (Michaelson, Jordan-Wagner & Wootton, 1995; Trueman & Titman, 1988; Moses, 1987) suggest that income smoothing leads to higher share prices. The underlying hypothesis is that investors and shareholders have more confidence in management and the company when earnings are less volatile or more stable. Thus, investors are willing to pay a higher stock price for smoother earnings.

Under the income smoothing hypothesis, management searches for accounting procedures (such as the selection of the discount rate in this study) that will help them smooth earnings. It is expected that management of companies with declining earnings from operations would have a strong motivation to select a higher discount rate than desired under SFAS No. 87 in order to reduce pension liabilities and improve reported net income through a lower pension expense. Companies with high growth rates of earnings from operations have an incentive to select a lower discount rate, since it allows them to lower reported net income so that a smoother increase in reported income will occur.[2]

Thus, the proposed hypothesis:

H1: Companies with positive earnings from operations that are declining, will choose a higher discount rate than companies with rapidly growing positive earnings from operations.

If the SEC letter had its desired effect on a company selection of the discount rate, then no significant difference should be found between companies with rapid growing earnings and those firms having declining earnings. This result would indicate that the SEC letter was justified and had the desired effect of pressuring companies to select the proper discount rate for computing pension liabilities and pension expense.

5. SAMPLE FORMATION AND VARIABLE MEASUREMENT

All companies on the Compustat Annual Industrial tapes that reported operating earnings (Compustat data item 13), pension expense (Compustat data item 43), and had a December 31 fiscal year-end were included in a group for each year between 1991 and 1995. A December 31 fiscal year-end was necessary to ensure that the management of all companies in the sample selected a discount rate during the same time period. The study covers the period between 1991 and 1995, two years before and three years after the SEC letter, because there is a lack of pension data for many companies before 1991 on the Compustat tapes.

Variable measurement for each fiscal year included:

• operating earnings + pension expense = adjusted operating earnings (AOE); (1)
• (current year AOE – prior year AOE) / prior year AOE = %
  change in AOE.   (2)

Sample formation for each fiscal year included:

* Companies ranked by percent change in AOE;
* Companies ranked in top quintile were grouped as high growth companies;
* Companies ranked in bottom quintile were grouped as low growth companies.

The pension expense was added to the operating earnings to remove the variable that is hypothesized to be used for earnings management and determine the amount of adjusted operating earnings (AOE). Any company with a negative prior year operating earnings was removed from the sample because of a lack of a meaningful percentage change in earnings and the likelihood that management was not concerned about smoothing income.

6. RESULTS

(i) Descriptive Statistics

All firms in the study are ranked by the percentage change in AOE for each year and then divided into quintiles as shown in Table 1. The percentage of firms reporting the discount rate, the average discount rate of reporting firms, and their median market value of equity, revenues and assets are also reported for each quintile by year.

Several observations can be made from the data. First, the average discount rates for the low growth companies (quintile 1) were noticeably higher than the other groups before the SEC letter (1991 & 1992), but dropped back with the other groups in 1993, 1994 and 1995. The high growth companies (quintile 5) had much lower discount rates than the low growth companies before the SEC letter but were more similar to the other groups throughout the study period.

Second, there appear to be no major differences between the low and high growth companies (quintiles 1 & 5 respectively) in terms of revenue and total assets. The market value of firms in the bottom quintile was much less than firms in the top quintile because of declining operating earnings. Also, in comparison with the other companies in the sample, the low and high growth companies are much smaller, and thus, more easily show rapid earnings growth in comparison to larger companies but are also more likely to have larger declines in earnings from operations.

Table 1 also shows the percentage change in operating income and the percentage of firms for each group reporting the discount rate each year. Note that the rise in the median AOE for the top quintile rises each year from 1991 through 1995, as the U.S. economy continued to expand. Another trend revealed by Table 1 is the decline in the percentage of firms in the top and bottom quintiles that reported the discount rate after 1993. The number of firms that adopted defined contribution plans is the probable reason for this trend. By adopting defined contribution plans instead of defined benefit plans, companies transfer the risk of owning equity securities (and the potential pension liabilities) to their employees.

The average discount rates for the top and bottom quintiles of companies in this study, the average discount rates of two prior studies and the end-of-year AA bond yield are shown in Table 2. In 1991 and 1992, before the SEC letter, firms with rapidly growing operating earnings used much lower interest rates than companies in the other studies and companies with declining operating earnings. After the SEC letter in 1993, the major impact on the companies in this study was that all companies appear to be following the narrower

Table 1. Summary Data for Firms Ranked by Percent Change in Adjusted Operating Earnings (AOE). (Dollar amounts in millions.)

Year		% Reporting Discount Rate[1]	Average Discount Rate	AOE Change	Market Value	Revenues	Assets
				Medians			
1991	Quintile 1	41.6%	8.383	−47.6%	77.729	174.490	198.30
	Quintile 2	52.3%	8.398	−13.2%	315.828	481.285	478.067
	Quintile 3	65.4%	8.243	3.9%	629.724	637.288	1141.13
	Quintile 4	56.2%	8.329	15.3%	619.697	514.533	914.807
	Quintile 5	39.5%	8.268	50.6%	137.453	147.315	168.131
1992	Quintile 1	41.7%	8.323	−39.8%	65.32	127.663	141.105
	Quintile 2	64.8%	8.130	-3.8%	728.402	876.726	1282.385
	Quintile 3	61.5%	8.138	8.6%	774.89	744.072	1199.56
	Quintile 4	54.2%	8.197	21.6%	375.27	370.935	450.068
	Quintile 5	39.1%	8.170	73.3%	147.798	150.253	154.399
1993	Quintile 1	42.4%	7.389	−35.7%	62.827	100.040	105.052
	Quintile 2	61.1%	7.394	0.1%	666.722	760.500	1068.001
	Quintile 3	66.9%	7.412	11.2%	957.325	719.828	1454.480
	Quintile 4	47.7%	7.440	27.1%	432.794	393.033	445.454
	Quintile 5	31.2%	7.414	87.3%	161.747	123.481	133.523
1994	Quintile 1	35.0%	8.170	−35.6%	81.366	101.637	141.090
	Quintile 2	63.4%	8.207	2.8%	592.433	588.061	1071.595
	Quintile 3	56.0%	8.146	15.3%	666.899	668.279	1015.990
	Quintile 4	45.7%	8.115	32.9%	302.818	331.352	346.288
	Quintile 5	32.3%	8.163	82.6%	159.713	136.695	146.796
1995	Quintile 1	31.7%	7.354	−43.3%	69.412	91.349	572.016
	Quintile 2	58%	7.372	0.1%	483.218	524.909	97.130
	Quintile 3	56.1%	7.401	12.8%	771.266	688.424	991.799
	Quintile 4	42.2%	7.418	30.4%	431.667	416.836	445.591
	Quintile 5	28.3%	7.369	93.5%	222.569	149.218	210.929

[1] The percentage of firms for each quintile that reported the discount rate on COMPUSTAT.

guidelines of SFAS No. 106, as recommended in the SEC letter, because the range of discount rates decreased significantly for all groups.

On December 31, 1991 and December 31, 1992, the slope of the yield curve was fairly steep (more than 1% difference in yield between intermediate and long-term interest rates on U.S. government treasuries). By December 31, 1993, the intermediate and long-term treasuries dropped about 1%, but the slope for

Table 2. A Comparison of Average Discount Rates for the Bottom and Top Quintiles of Ranked Firms by Adjusted Operating Income with other Studies and the AA Bond Yield.

Year	AA[1] Bond Yield	Blankley and Swanson	Amir and Gorden	Bottom Quintile	Top Quintile	No. of firms in each Quintile
1991	8.51%	8.41%	8.41%	8.383%	8.268%	281
1992	8.30%	8.21%	8.22%	8.323%	8.170%	304
1993	7.30%	7.43%	7.38%	7.414%	7.389%	339
1994	8.52%	–	–	8.163%	8.170%	380
1995	6.82%	–	–	7.369%	7.354%	438

[1] The end of year AA bond yield recommended in the accounting standards.
Source: Standard and Poor's Security Price Index Record.

this part of the yield curve stayed about the same. Thus, the fact that the slope of the yield curve did not change between 1992 and 1993, yet the range of discount rates selected by companies greatly narrowed after the SEC letter (1993) provides additional evidence of earnings management before the letter.[3]

A second observation in comparing the average discount rates with the changes in the AA bond yield is the apparent "stickiness" of the average discount rates by firms in all of the studies. While most firms follow the direction of changes in the AA bond yield, the discount rates selected by the companies usually lag behind when large changes in the AA bond yield occurs. It appears that these companies wanted to see if changes in interest rates were more "permanent" before adjusting their own discount rates to fully reflect the changes in the AA bond yield.

(ii) Hypothesis Test

Shown in Table 3 are the average discount rates for the bottom and top quintiles of ranked firms by year. In comparing the average discount rates of the two groups of firms, the top quintile of firms had lower average discount rates until the SEC letter in the fall of 1993. Then, at the end of 1993 and 1994, the difference in the average discount rates between the two groups almost disappears. The statistically significant relationship between a firm's AOE growth and its discount rate for pensions for 1992 provides some evidence that firms took recent operating earnings performance into consideration when selecting the discount rate. The statistical relationship between the growth rate of operating earnings and the discount rate ended after the SEC letter to the FASB.

Table 3.   Differences in Average Discount Rates for Firms Sorted by
Percent Changes in Operating Income.

| Year | Average Discount Rates | | Difference in Average Discount Rates | t-Statistic[1] for Difference |
	Bottom Quintile	Top Quintile		
1991	8.383%	8.268%	0.115%	1.50*
1992	8.323%	8.170%	0.153%	1.99**
1993	7.389%	7.414%	−0.025%	0.34
1994	8.163%	8.170%	−0.007%	0.095
1995	7.369%	7.354%	0.015%	0.20

* Significant at the 10 % level.
** Significant at the 5% level.
[1] The reported t-statistics are for a null hypothesis of no difference in average discount rates, assuming independent, identically distributed (normal) observations across both quintiles.

7. CONCLUSIONS

The most significant finding of this study is that prior to the SEC letter of 1993, some evidence of firms with positive earnings from operations that were either declining or rapidly growing, took recent performance of operating earnings into account in selecting their pension discount rates. While these companies in the bottom (declining earnings) and top (fast growing earnings) quintiles had similar market values of equity, revenues and total assets in comparison with each other, they selected significantly different discount rates. Also, it was observed that firms with increasing negative earnings were likely to select discount rates that were much lower than most firms in the sample and substantially below the discount rates recommend in the accounting standards in 1991 and 1992.

The fact that these differences in the discount rates disappeared after the SEC letter provides further support that a significant number of firms were not following current accounting standards and were motivated by other factors including earnings in selecting discount rates. The SEC letter made it quite clear that companies faced the prospect of restating their earnings (and the wrath of investors and shareholders) if the SEC did not think a company was following SFAS No. 87 guidelines.

Recently the SEC's Chief Accountant, Lynn Turner indicated that given the number of interest rate reductions put in place in 2001, the SEC would again by reviewing this area, albeit from the view of companies applying current rates, thus reducing the opportunity for any form of earnings management option.

NOTES

1. Schipper (1989, p 101) points out that "if a set of regulations leads to a particular form of earnings management, changes in regulations should lead to predictable changes in earnings management behavior."

2. Companies with negative earnings were excluded from the study because it appears that most of these companies with large increases in negative earnings used discount rates that were substantially below all other discount rates in the sample and significantly below those discount rates recommended by FASB. For example, if negative earnings firms are included in the bottom quintile, the 27 negative earnings companies in 1991 has an average discount rate of 8.12 compared to 126 companies with positive earnings that had a discount rate of 8.383. In 1992, 20 negative earnings firms in the bottom quintile have an average discount rate of 7.975 compared to 8.323 for 127 companies with positive earnings. The recommended discount rates in the accounting standards for 1991 and 1992 were 8.51 and 8.3 respectively (see Table 2). After the SEC letter, the discount rates for negative earnings firms were quite similar to the other companies in the sample. Thus, mixing negative earnings companies with companies that have positive earnings but are declining hides the fact that both groups have companies that are not following accounting standards. However, the negative earnings companies are using lower discount rates than most companies while the positive but declining earning companies are using discount rates that are much higher.

3. The yield curve had a sharp upward sloping yield curve at the end of 1991, 1992, and 1993. The yield curve was fairly flat at the end of 1994 and 1995.

ACKNOWLEDGMENT

The author appreciates the financial support received from the College of Business at Kansas State University to complete this project.

REFERENCES

Amir E., & Gordon, E. (1996). Firms' choice of estimation parameters: empirical evidence from SFAS No. 106. *Journal of Accounting, Auditing & Finance, 11*(Summer), 427–448.

Bergsman, S. (1994). FASB's influence on pension plans. *Pension Management*, (November), 20–22.

Blankley, A., & Swanson, E. (1995). A longitudinal study of SFAS 87 pension rate assumptions. *Accounting Horizons, 9*(December), 1–21.

DeFond, M., & Park, C. (1997). Smoothing income in anticipation of future earnings. *Journal of Accounting and Economics, 23*, 115–129.

Feldstein, M., & Morck, R. (1983). Pension funding decisions, interest rate assumptions and share prices. In: *Financial Aspects of the United States Pension System* (pp. 177–207). Chicago: University of Chicago Press.

Financial Accounting Standards Board (FASB) (1985). *Employers' Accounting for Pensions. Statement of Financial Accounting Standards No. 87*. Norwalk, CT: FASB.

Financial Accounting Standards Board (FASB) (1990). *Employers' Accounting for Postretirement Benefits Other than Pensions. Statement of Financial Accounting Standards No. 106.* Norwalk, CT: FASB.

Fudenberg, K., & Tirole, J. (1995). A theory of income and dividend smoothing based on incumbency rents. *Journal of Political Economy, 103,* 75–93.

Gaver, J., Gaver, K., & Austin, J. (1995). Additional evidence on bonus plans and income management. *Journal of Accounting and Economics, 19,* 3–28.

Ghicas, D. (1990). Determinants of actuarial cost methods changes for pension accounting and Funding. *The Accounting Review, 65*(April), 384–405.

Godwin, J., Goldberg, S., & Duchac, J. (1996). An empirical analysis of factors associated with changes in pension-plan interest-rate assumptions. *Journal of Accounting, Auditing & Finance, 11*(Spring), 305–322.

Guidry, F., Leone, A., & Rock, S. (1999). Earnings-based bonus plans and earnings management by business-unit managers. *Journal of Accounting and Economics, 26,* 113–142.

Healy, P. (1985). The effect of bonus schemes on accounting decisions. *Journal of Accounting and Economics, 7,* 85–107.

Healy, P., & Palepu, K. (1990). Effectiveness of accounting-based dividend covenants. *Journal of Accounting and Economics, 12*(January), 97–123.

Holthausen, R., Larker, D., & Sloan, R. (1995). Annual bonus schemes and the manipulation of earnings. *Journal of Accounting and Economics, 19,* 29–74.

Kwon, S. (1994). Economic determinants of the assumed interest rate in pension accounting. *Advances in Accounting, 12,* 67–86.

Lewellen, W., Loderer, C., & Martin, K. (1987). Executive compensation and executive incentive problems: An empirical analysis. *Journal of Accounting and Economics, 9,* 287–310.

Michelson, S., Jordan-Wagner, J., & Wootton, C. (1995). A market based analysis of income smoothing. *Journal of Business Finance and Accounting, 22*(December), 1179–1193.

Mittelstaedt, H. F. (1989). An empirical analysis of the factors underlying the decision to remove excess assets from over-funded pension plans. *Journal of Accounting and Economics 11,* 399–418.

Moses, O. (1987). Income smoothing and incentives: empirical tests using accounting changes. *The Accounting Review, 62*(April), 358–377.

Schipper, K. (1989). Commentary on Earnings Management. *Accounting Horizons,* (December), 91–102.

Thomas, J. (1989). Why do firms terminate their over-funded pension plans?. *Journal of Accounting and Economics, 7,* 117–161.

Trueman, B., & Titman, S. (1988). An explanation for accounting income smoothing. *Journal of Accounting Research, 26*(Suppl.), 127–129.

Winklevoss, H. E. (1973). *Pension Mathematics with Numerical Illustrations* (2nd ed.). Philadelphia, PA: University of Pennsylvania Press.

PART II:
RESEARCH REPORTS

SEC AUDIT REQUIREMENTS AND AUDIT FEES

Charles P. Cullinan

ABSTRACT

The SEC has active regulatory oversight of the accounting and disclosure practices of mutual funds (e.g. SEC, 2001; Brown, 2000). Such oversight requires the SEC to consider the costs and benefits of regulatory requirements. There is limited research, however, on the costs of accounting and disclosure regulations in the mutual fund area. The objective of this study is to examine the effects of two SEC mutual fund audit requirements on audit costs. The two requirements are that auditors of mutual funds audit the the valuation of every security held by a fund, and that the auditor provide an opinion on the fund's internal control system. Results suggest that auditing the valuation of every security held results in a small incremental audit cost, even for funds of similar size. The study also indicates that the internal control requirement may be less costly for funds in large fund families due to potential economies of scale.

INTRODUCTION

The Investment Company Act of 1940 provides for U.S. Securities Exchange Commission (SEC) oversight of many aspects of mutual fund operations. Recently, the SEC has focused attention on the accounting and disclosure practices of mutual funds. For example, The SEC recently enacted a requirement

Research in Accounting Regulation, Volume 15, pages 135–150.
Copyright © 2002 by Elsevier Science Ltd.
All rights of reproduction in any form reserved.
ISBN: 0-7623-0841-9

that mutual funds disclose estimated after-tax returns (SEC, 2000). There is also a proposal that mutual funds disclose to individual shareholders the individual shareholder's costs of holding a mutual fund (Brown, 2000). In its regulatory activities, the SEC must consider the potential costs and benefits of their proposed rules. However, there is little empirical evidence regarding the costs and benefits of SEC regulation of mutual fund accounting.

The objective of this research is to empirically examine the cost associated with two existing SEC accounting requirements for mutual funds. The two regulatory requirements examined in this study are: (1) the requirement that mutual fund auditors audit the valuation of *each* of a mutual fund's security holdings, and (2) the requirement that mutual fund auditors prepare an independent accountant's report on the fund's internal control system. These regulatory requirements may affect the audit fees of mutual funds, thus affecting the cost of regulation in a cost/benefit framework.

The remainder of this paper consists of four sections. The next section reviews the relevant literature and identifies how SEC regulation may affect mutual fund audit fees. Control variables are also specified based on existing audit fee literature. A discussion of the data gathering techniques is then presented, followed by the results of empirical testing of the model. The paper closes with a discussion of the study's limitations and conclusions.

LITERATURE REVIEW/MODEL DEVELOPMENT

There is a fairly rich literature on public company audit fees both in the United States (e.g. Simunic, 1980, Francis & Simon, 1987, Gist, 1992), and in other countries (e.g. Anderson & Zhégal, 1992, Chan et al., 1993). Research has also examined audit fees in non-public company settings, such as municipality audit fees (e.g. Ward et al., 1994), and pension plan audit fees (Cullinan, 1997). Thus, there is a rich audit fee literature which can be used as a basis to develop a mutual fund audit fee model. In contrast, there is little research on accounting and auditing aspects of the mutual fund environment (Previts, 1996). The mutual fund research literature outside of accounting has generally focused on mutual fund performance information, rather than fund fee structures.[1] The studies which have examined mutual fund fees typically examined the entire expense ratio (e.g. Malhotra & McLeod, 1997), rather than individual components of fund expenses such as audit fees.

Research examining the effect of regulatory requirements on audit fees has been quite limited. In the not-for-profit environment, Pearson, et al. (1998) examined the effect of Single Audit Act (SAA) requirements on audit fees. Using a 0,1 variable indicating whether the SAA was applicable, they found that the SSA requirements significantly increased audit fees of not-for-profit organizations.

SEC Imposed Requirements

The SEC has regulatory oversight over mutual funds and has imposed at least two specific audit requirements on mutual fund auditors: the requirement that *all* security valuations be audited, and the requirement that a report on the system of internal control must be prepared. This section reviews these requirements, and indicates how the effect of these regulations on mutual fund audit fees is operationalized.

Security Valuation Auditing

A mutual fund is required to disclose the details of each of its security holdings (e.g. individual stocks and bonds) on its statement of net assets, which is one of the basic financial statements of a mutual fund. A mutual fund's statement of net assets and related balance sheet are used to compute the net asset value per share, which is the price at which the mutual fund shares are bought and sold by investors.[2] As such, the SEC considers the valuation of securities (which make up the vast majority of most funds' assets) to be an especially important part of the audit, as evidenced by the SEC's requirement that the auditor examine *all* of the fund's portfolio valuations (AICPA, 1997, ¶ 2.152).

From an audit cost perspective, the cost of verifying the existence and valuation of individual security holdings is likely to vary with the number of securities held. As such, auditing a fund of a given size which holds a large number of securities is expected to cost more than auditing a similarly sized fund with fewer security holdings. Therefore, the total number of different securities held by the fund is included in the audit fee model to measure the effect of the SEC's requirement to audit all security valuations, and is expected to be positively related to the fund's audit fee.[3]

Internal Control Reporting Requirement

Mutual funds are required to obtain an auditor's report on the fund's internal control structure, and provide a copy of the report to the SEC (AICPA, 1997, ¶ 9.10; SEC, 1997, Instructions p. 14). The "standard" auditor's internal control report in the context specifically addresses itself to regulatory requirements twice. First, the report indicates that one of the main purposes of the report is "to comply with the requirements of form N-SAR . . ."[4] Second, the report mentions the SEC as one of three intended users of the internal control report (the other two intended users are management and the board of directors). Excerpts from an auditor's mutual fund internal control report are shown in Fig. 1.

FUND: American Gas Index Fund

To the Board of Directors of American Gas Index Fund, Inc.:

In planning and performing our audit of the financial statement of American Gas Index Fund, Inc. (the "Fund") for the year ended March 31, 1999 (on which we have issued our report dated April 30, 1999) we considered its internal control, including control activities for safeguarding securities, in order to determine our auditing procedures for the purpose of expressing our opinion on the financial statements and to comply with the requirements of Form N-SAR, and not to provide assurance on the fund's internal control.

.
.
.

This report is intended solely for the information and use of management, the Board of Directors, and the Securities Exchange Commission and is not intended to be and should not be used by anyone other than these specified parties.

Deloitte & Touche LLP
Princeton, New Jersey
April 30, 1999

Fig. 1.   Excerpts from Mutual Fund Internal Control Report.

   Mutual funds are often part of "fund families" which usually have the same investment management firm, shareholder servicing companies, and security custodians. Fund families also typically use the same auditor, or a small group of auditors (Abelson, 1997). Therefore, the auditor's study and evaluation of the control system would not have to be repeated for each individual fund, but could be performed once for the fund family, lowering the auditor's cost per fund. The regulatory requirement of an internal control report is likely to cost less for a fund which a part of a larger fund family, than it would for a stand-alone fund, or a fund in a small fund family. The size of the fund family was measured by counting the total number of funds[5] in the fund family (as defined by Morningstar). The log of fund family size is used, and is expected to be negatively related to audit fees.

Control Variables

Size
Audit fees have been found to be correlated with size in virtually every study of audit fees (see for example, Chan et al., 1993, for a review). Larger size mutual fund clients are expected to require a greater amount of audit work,

increasing the auditor's cost and the audit fee. In accord with most other audit fee studies, the measure of size used in this study is the log of total fund assets.

In addition to the scale of an organization, Pearson and Trompeter (1994, p. 122) suggest that size may be a measure of "the *scope* of [an] organization's activities" (emphasis added). In the mutual fund environment, a more direct measure of the scope of the fund's activities is the number of securities held by the fund.

Activity

In the mutual fund environment, funds of similar size can have very different levels of activity in a given period. For example, a fund with a buy and hold strategy (such as an index fund) would have fewer gains and losses on security transactions than those funds which employ a more active trading style. As more securities are sold during a period, the auditor will spend more time examining these transactions, and their impact on the financial statements. This increased auditor time would increase the cost of providing the audit, raising the audit fee. Trading activity is measured in the current study by portfolio turnover, with higher levels of turnover expected to result in higher fees.

Audit Risk/Complexity

Mutual funds differ in their share structures, the extent to which they hold foreign securities, and their investment risk profile, all of which may affect the audit risk[6] and complexity of a mutual fund audit. Mutual funds with multiple share classes are required to separately disclose information for each share class, such as net asset value per class (AICPA, 1997, ¶ 2.24) and annual return per class, as a result of the share classes' differing fee structures.[7] The share class reporting requirements are part of the financial statements, and are therefore subject to audit. An auditor would need to spend more time examining the share class calculations and disclosures of funds with a large number of share classes, resulting in greater cost to the auditor, and a higher audit fee. Therefore, the number of share classes of the mutual fund is included in the audit fee model, and is expected to be positively related to the fund's audit fee.

An additional aspect of complexity which may impact the cost of performing an audit is the extent of the fund's foreign security holdings. All the security holdings of mutual funds are valued at their market value at the end of the fund's reporting period. To determine the value of domestic securities, the number of shares is multiplied by the current market price per share of the securities. For foreign securities, "the [auditor's] tests of such valuations may require special considerations" (AICPA, 1997, ¶ 2.97) because the incremental step of translating the foreign currency value of the foreign securities to U.S. dollars may be necessary. Auditing the value of foreign securities would thus be expected to require more audit time than domestic securities, increasing the audit cost, and the audit fee. Thus, the greater the percentage of foreign security holdings, the higher the expected audit fee.

The percentage of a mutual fund's assets invested in cash may have a negative relationship with audit fee. The valuation of cash is usually not difficult to audit, because there are usually no conversions necessary into dollar values (unless the cash is foreign currency). As such, audits of mutual funds which have a large proportion of assets in cash will be expected to be less costly to audit.

A mutual fund with greater risk could lead an auditor to perform more audit testing to keep audit risk at an acceptable level, or could result in the auditor charging a risk premium to a riskier fund. Morningstar, a fund information service, has developed a measure of fund risk relative to a variety of benchmarks. The Morningstar risk rating[8] is included in the audit fee model, with an expected positive relationship to fund audit fee.

Audit Market: CPA Firm Characteristics
Two CPA firm characteristics are considered in the present study: Big 6 status, and auditor changes. Research has been fairly consistent in showing that Big 6 CPA firms charge higher audit fees than other CPA firms[9] (e.g. Francis & Simon, 1987; Craswell et al., 1995). As in the public company audit market, Big 6 firms have a large market share of the mutual fund audit market. Therefore, Big 6 status of the mutual fund auditor is included in the audit fee model tested in this study, and is expected to be positively related to the audit fee. Research also suggests that a change in auditor often results in a lower audit fee (e.g. Simon & Francis, 1988). The lower fee is presumed to result from competitive pressure resulting in a lowering of the proposed audit fee in order to obtain the client. Whether the CPA firm is new to the audit engagement is also incorporated into the mutual fund audit fee model, with a negative relationship expected between auditor change and the audit fee.

Audit Market: Mutual Fund Characteristics
Another consideration which could potentially affect mutual fund audit fees is the age of the mutual fund. Malhotra and McLeod (1997) suggest that older funds may have lower operating expenses due to their potentially operating more efficiently, reducing costs. With respect to audit fees, however, one may expect newer funds to have lower audit fees. This results

from the competition to obtain a new mutual fund as an audit client. Consistent with the auditor change literature (e.g. DeAngelo, 1981), auditors may charge lower fees in the early years of a fund's life to obtain the client, and charge fees more reflective of their audit costs later in the life of the fund. Simon and Francis (1988) suggest that the incoming auditor may charge a reduced fee for a number of years after they obtain the engagement. Because newer funds are, by definition, newer clients, the fund's age in included in the audit fee model, with the expectation that newer funds will have lower audit fees.

Mutual funds differ widely in their overall cost structures. Some fund families, such as the Vanguard funds, are known for their low costs. Mulvihill (1996) and Tufano and Sevcik (1997) found that funds which pay high trustee fees also have higher expense ratios, suggesting that some funds may not be very cost conscious. If a fund is not cost conscious in other areas, the fund may not be very aggressive in managing its audit fee. Cost consciousness is measured in the current study based on the expense ratio of the fund (i.e. total expenses divided by total assets). Since the audit fee would affect the expense ratio by its inclusion in total expenses, the expense ratio used in the audit fee model is the expense ratio, less the audit fee, divided by total assets. The expected relationship between this modified expense ratio and the audit fee is positive.

Geographic Factors
The costs of doing business can vary depending on the region of the country within which a firm operates. In the public accounting industry, billing rates may vary depending on the office which is performing the audit work. Simunic and Stein (1987) distinguish the audit price, which is the cost per hour of audit work purchased, from the audit fee, which is the audit price per hour multiplied by the quantity of audit hours provided. In this framework, differences in billing rates among different offices of CPA firms relate to the price per hour, which would affect the audit fee, but would not affect the amount of audit work performed.

To measure the comparative size of audit billing rates, the relative cost of living for the city of the CPA firm's office is used. A city's cost of living is likely to be related to an accounting firm's billing rates because an accounting firm operating in the city will pay market rates for office space, professional staff, etc. The cost of living index computed quarterly by ACCRA measures the relative cost of living in most cities in he U.S. The ACCRA index measures cross-sectional differences in cost of living among cities, where the average cost of living in the U.S. is set to 100. Values above (below) 100 indicate a cost of living in that city above (below) the national average. In the current study, cost of living was measured based on the city in which the audit opinion was signed. A positive relationship is expected between the cost of living and audit fee.

RESEARCH METHODS

The data for this study were drawn from four sources: The Morningstar Principia database, the fund's N-SAR, the fund's annual report, and the ACCRA Cost of Living Index. The four sources used were based on the fund's fiscal year 1997. The Morningstar Principia database was used as the population from which the sample was drawn, and for many of the variables in the study. The SEC form N-SAR was used to gather audit fee information and other data. The N-SAR is filed by all mutual funds (or trusts containing mutual funds) with the SEC, and was accessed via the SEC's EDGAR internet searching program. The mutual fund's annual report was obtained to determine where the audit opinion was signed, and if there were any opinion qualifications.[10] The ACCRA survey was the source for the regional cost of living variable. Table 1 provides a summary of the variables in included in the mutual fund audit fee model, and where they were obtained and/or how they were computed.

The initial step in the sampling design was to limit the sample to those equity funds in the Morningstar database which had filed an N-SAR with the SEC.[11] The sample was restricted to equity funds to ensure some degree of comparability of the funds in the sample. The matching of the Morningstar and N-SAR databases yielded an initial sample of 476 funds. After eliminating funds with missing data,[12] the final sample used in this study consists of 323 mutual funds investing primarily in equity securities.

RESULTS

Descriptive Statistics

Descriptive statistics for the sample of mutual funds are displayed in Table 2. These descriptive statistics indicate that the Big 6 firms have a large market presence in the mutual fund audit market (i.e. an 86.42% market share). The number and percentage of auditor changes is fairly low, suggesting that mutual funds may be more likely to retain auditors than public companies. The average cost of living index is greater than the nationwide average of 100. This finding

Table 1. Definition of Variables and Data Sources.

Variable Name	Definition	Data Source(s)
Log of audit fee	Natural log of audit fee	N-SAR
Number of holdings	Total number of security held by fund	Morningstar Principia
Log of funds in fund family	Natural log of number of funds in fund family.	Count of Morningstar Principia
Log of total assets	Natural log of total assets	Morningstar Principia
Portfolio turnover	Portfolio turnover	Morningstar Principia
Share classes	Number of share classes	Count of Morningstar Principia
Percentage foreign assets	% of foreign assets	Morningstar Principia
Percentage of cash	% of cash	Morningstar Principia
Morningstar risk rating	Morningstar 1 year risk rating	Morningstar Principia
Big 6 firm	1 if auditor is Big 6 firm, 0 otherwise	N-SAR or Annual report
Auditor change	1 if auditor changed from previous year, 0 otherwise	N-SAR or Annual report
Modified expense ratio	Expense ratio − (audit fee/assets)	Morningstar Principia and N-SAR
Fund age	The age, in years of the fund, calculated as: 1997 minus the year of the fund's establishment	Morningstar Principia
Cost of living	Cost of living index in the city where the audit report was signed	City of audit report was obtained from annual report; Cost of living index from ACCRA

is in accord with the geographic concentration of the mutual fund industry in larger urban areas, especially in the Northeast,[13] where the cost of living is relatively high.

Results of Empirically Testing the Audit Fee Model

The results of testing the audit fee model using ordinary least squares regression are presented in Table 3. The model has an F value of 31.906, which is significant at 0.0001. An examination of residuals revealed no heteroschedasticity concerns. The largest variance inflation factors for a variable in the model was 1.92, indicating that multi-collinearity is not a major problem with the regression model. The model's R^2 of 0.5175 is reasonable.

Table 2. Descriptive Statistics.

Continuous Variables:

Variable	Median	Mean	Std Deviation
Audit fee	$30,000	$37,297	$33,106
Number of holdings	86	108	85
Funds in complex	21.00	29.98	28.96
Total assets (000)	$256,000	$1,223,070	$3,387,857
Portfolio turnover	56.00%	83.24%	127.14%
Classes	1	1.92	1.17
Percentage foreign assets	6.70%	24.84%	35.12%
Percentage of cash	4.80%	6.76%	7.41%
Morningstar risk rating	0.83	1.10	0.82
Modified expense ratio	1.15%	1.34%	1.04%
Age	12 years	18 years	16 years
Cost of living index	126.90	149.24	50.08

Ordinal/Nominal variables:

Variable:		Value	Number of funds	
Big 6	Non-Big 6 auditor	0	44	13.6%
	Big 6 auditor	1	279	86.4%
Auditor change	No auditor change	0	315	97.5%
	Auditor change	1	8	2.5%

Regulatory requirement variables

Both of the regulatory variables are significant, and in the expected direction. The result for the number of holdings variable is significantly positive, as expected. This finding indicates that auditing each security holding, as required by the SEC, increases audit fees. For one additional security holding, the incremental effect on the log of audit fee is expected to increase the log of audit fee by 0.0016, which, when taking the anti-log, translates to an effect on the audit fee of approximately $1.00 for each incremental security held. For the average fund in the sample, which consists of 108 securities, this would suggest that the incremental impact of auditing *each* of the security valuations is $108.

Results for the fund family variable is consistent with the idea that the audit fees charged to mutual funds are affected by the economies of scale of assessing and reporting on the control system of a fund family. Specifically, results are consistent with the notion that the SEC mandated internal control reporting requirements costs less for larger fund families that for smaller fund families.

Table 3. OLS Regression Results Dependent Variable: Natural Log of
Audit Fee in Thousands.

Variable	Expected Sign	Parameter estimate	Standardized parameter estimate	T value	One tail Prob > T
Intercept		1.3347	0	8.523	0.0001
SEC audit requirements:					
Number of holdings	+	0.0016	0.1966	4.345	0.0001
Log of funds in fund family	−	−0.0510	−0.1113	−2.012	0.0225
Size/Activity:					
log of Total assets	+	0.1443	0.4339	8.194	0.0001
Portfolio turnover	+	0.0001	0.0267	0.645	0.2597
Audit risk:					
Share classes	+	0.1957	0.3388	7.222	0.0001
Percentage foreign assets	+	0.0043	0.2212	5.000	0.0001
Percentage of cash	−	−0.0082	−0.0903	−2.286	0.0115
Morningstar risk rating	+	−0.0113	−0.0138	−0.337	0.7367
CPA Firm Characteristics:					
Big 6 firm	+	0.2571	0.1307	2.874	0.0022
Auditor change	−	−0.3790	−0.0873	−2.112	0.0178
Mutual Fund Market Characteristics:					
Modified expense ratio	+	0.0556	0.0855	1.835	0.0338
Fund age	+	0.0050	0.1213	2.843	0.0024
Geographic Variable:					
Cost of living	+	0.0029	0.2141	5.289	0.0001

F statistic: 27.567; Probability > *F*: 0.0001; Adjusted R^2: 0.5175; Sample size: 323.

Control Variables

The results for the control variables are generally consistent with expectations. The size variable is significant at conventional levels and the coefficient has the expected sign. This result is consistent with the idea that larger funds pay higher audit fees. The activity variable of portfolio turnover had the expected sign, although the coefficient is not significant at conventional levels. This result was not in accord with the model's expectation that mutual funds with a higher level of activity would be charged a higher audit fee. The lack of significance for the turnover variable results may imply that the main focus of auditor attention is the existence and valuation of securities at year end, rather than changes in security holdings occurring during the period. Cullinan (1997) also found a lack of significance for a portfolio turnover measure in his sample of pension plans, which, like mutual funds, consist mainly of financial securities.

Three of the four complexity variables are in the expected direction and are significant at conventional levels. The number of mutual fund share classes and the percentage of foreign assets, with their translation requirements, are positively associated with mutual fund audit fees. These findings indicate that mutual funds of greater complexity pay higher audit fees than those funds with less complex operations. As expected, the percentage of cash held by the fund is negatively related to audit fees. However, no significant relationship was found between the Morningstar risk rating and audit fees.[14]

The coefficients for the CPA firm characteristic variables were both significant and in the predicted direction. These results indicate that, consistent with most previous audit fee literature, Big 6 firms charge higher fees than non-Big 6 CPA firms.[15] The findings also suggest that mutual funds which change auditors pay less for their audit than funds without an auditor change, which supports the finding of audit fee studies in other contexts.[16]

For the mutual fund market characteristics, the results indicate that the modified expense ratio (i.e. expense ratio less the effect of the audit fee) is positively associated with mutual fund audit fees. This finding implies that some mutual funds may be more cost conscious than others, and that this cost consciousness extends to the fund's audit fee.[17] Results also indicate that newer funds pay lower audit fees than older mutual funds, suggesting that auditors may discount their fees to obtain the new funds as audit clients.[18]

The cost of living variable is in the predicted direction and is significant. This finding indicates that cross-sectional differences in regional costs of living affect audit fees. CPA firm offices in cities with a high cost of living appear to charge more than CPA firm offices in cities with lower costs of living, which is supportive of the idea that hourly rates charged by auditing firms vary with the regional cost of living.

LIMITATIONS AND CONCLUSIONS

Limitations

This study is subject to a number of limitations. First, the R^2 associated with the audit fee model is lower than some other audit fee studies. The R^2 issue may be related to two different considerations: the potential for omitted variables, and the nature of the audit clients in the sample. There may be variables which were not measured in the current study which could influence audit fees. For example, the marketability of the securities held by the fund could affect audit cost because the valuation of securities with low liquidity may be difficult to audit. The marketability of securities (e.g. the percentage of private placement (i.e. 144A) securities) was not directly available for the current study. In addition, the strength of different fund's control structures could affect the audit fee. This variable was also not measurable in the current study.[19] Another part of the explanation for the R^2 in the current study may be that the sample used consisted entirely of mutual funds whose primary assets are financial instruments. Both Simunic (1980) and Maher et al. (1992) excluded banks from their audit fee studies because the audit fees of these financial service firms were inconsistent with the other firms in their sample. Cullinan (1998) examined the audit fees of pension plans, which consist primarily of financial assets. His R^2 was 0.42 suggesting that audit fees of firms with mainly financial assets may be less predictable than the fees of other types of audit clients.

An additional limitation is that the negative relationship between fund family size and audit fee is premised on cost savings resulting from the preparation of internal control reports on multiple funds with the same control system. An alternative explanation for these results could be that auditors costs may not vary based on fund family size, but that the auditors may offer "volume discounts" to obtain the audits of funds in large fund families. The available data does not allow separate testing of this alternative hypothesis. Finally, the results of this study may not be generalizable beyond the population of equity mutual funds from which the study's sample was drawn.

CONCLUSIONS

This paper developed a mutual fund audit fee model to examine the effects of mandated audit requirements on the audit fees of mutual funds. Results indicated that the SEC's requirement that auditors test the valuation of *all* the fund's security holdings increases audit fees, but not by a large amount (about $1 per additional security held, or $108 for the average fund in the sample). This finding suggests that the costs of the SEC requirement to audit the valuation of each security are fairly low. As such, meeting the cost/benefit criteria for government regulation in this area would require only a small benefit to accrue to fund investors. Evidence was also found which suggests that the cost of the SEC mandated internal control reporting may be lower for larger fund families. Future research efforts could focus on measuring the costs of new disclosure regulations in the mutual fund market, and developing models of other aspects of mutual fund disclosure costs.

NOTES

1. There are a number of studies investigating the effects *of* mutual fund fees *on* performance (e.g. Dellva & Olson, 1998), rather than what factors affect fund fees.

2. For funds that are sold with loads (i.e. buying and selling fees), the shares are bought and sold at NAV plus or minus the load. Nevertheless, the NAV is the basis for establishing the price at which the fund's share are bought and sold.

3. The total dollar size of the mutual fund is not an appropriate measure of the number of securities held by a fund. For example, in early 1998, The Gabelli Asset Fund had approximately $1.6 Billion in assets, and held 298 different securities. A fund of similar dollar size, Babson Value Fund, had assets of approximately $1.7 billion, but held only 46 different securities.

4. The N-SAR in a required SEC filing for all mutual funds.

5. Funds with multiple share classes (which have multiple listings in the Morningstar database) were counted as only one fund.

6. The AICPA professional standards address both audit risk (i.e. probability of a material misstatement), and the potential risk to the auditor's professional reputation (through lawsuits, etc.). This study focuses on audit risk because there is little evidence that mutual fund audits often result in legal action (except in an extreme case of auditor fraud (Emshwiller, 1996)).

7. These fee structure differences relate to sales commissions and marketing expenses, not to the basic operating costs of the fund such as the audit fee.

8. The one-year risk measure is used. Using three- or five-year ratings resulted in material decreases in sample size, but yielded similar results to those presented.

9. There is debate as to why big 6 firms charge higher fees. Some suggest that firms with larger market shares are perceived to be what Lindsay (1998) terms "market designated specialists" (e.g. DeFond et al., 2000), suggesting higher quality or expertise. Another possibility is that big 6 firms may use market power to obtain higher fees (Cullinan, 1998).

10. No opinion qualifications were noted in the sample.

11. Some mutual funds are a part of a trust. Some funds, therefore, did not have a matching N-SAR, because the trust had filed the N-SAR, not the individual fund. These funds were not included in this study because a preliminary analysis of these type of funds indicated large amounts of missing fund-specific data, and because of concern for measurement error arising from potential allocation of costs among funds within the trust.

12. The main issue causing elimination of funds from the sample was a lack of N-SAR disclosure of the audit fee. An examination of funds disclosing and not disclosing audit fees revealed no significant differences among the available variables except that funds with higher foreign security percentages and with lower modified expense ratios were more likely to disclose.

13. Approximately 42% of the funds in the sample were audited by CPA firm offices in New York or Boston.

14. This result may reflect the possibility that auditors measures audit risk differently than Morningstar, which focuses on investments returns.

15. Some studies have suggested that other variables may capture the difference in fee structures resulting from differences in perceived expertise. Alternative specifications to a big6/non-big6 dichotomy include a market share measure (Cullinan, 1998) or an ordinal

variable based on relative market share (e.g. Craswell et al., 1995). When each of these alternative specifications were substituted into the current audit fee model in place of the Big 6 variable, the models had a lower explained variance than with the inclusion of a dichotomous Big 6 variable.

16. This finding should be interpreted with caution due to the small number (8) of auditor changes in the sample.

17. An alternative explanation for the results presented may be that some unmeasured variable may be increasing both the audit fee and the modified expense ratio.

18. Simon and Francis (1988) suggest that the initial fee discount is likely to be eliminated by the fourth year of the auditor's tenure. Substituting a dichotomous variable indicating whether the fund is one to four years old, or greater than four years old, into the audit fee model yielded results which also indicate that the newer funds pay lower audit fees, ceteris paribus.

19. A review of internal control reports attached to the N-SARs revealed no disclosure of material auditor concerns regarding control, suggesting that there may be not be much variation in the strength of mutual fund control structures.

ACKNOWLEDGMENTS

The author gratefully acknowledges helpful comments received from the anonymous reviewers and participants at the 1999 AAA Northeast Regional Meeting.

REFERENCES

Abelson, R. (1997). A quandary for Fidelity. *New York Times*, September 28, Money and Business Section, p. 6.

ACCRA (1997). *ACCRA Cost of Living Index, Second Quarter 1997*. Louisville, KY: ACCRA.

AICPA (1997). *Audits of Investment Companies*. New York: American Institute of Certified Public Accountants.

Anderson, T., & Zhégal, D. (1994). The pricing of audit services: Further evidence from the Canadian Market. *Accounting and Business Research*, *24*(95), 195–207.

Brown, K. (2000). GAO urges funds to reveal fees – Shift could spur improved prices. *The Wall Street Journal*, (July 6), C1.

Chan, P., Ezzamel, M., & Gwilliam, D. (1993). Determinants of audit fees for quoted U.K. companies. *Journal of Business Finance and Accounting*, *20*(November), 765–786.

Craswell, A. T., Francis, J. R., & Taylor, S. L. (1995). Auditor brand name reputations and industry specialization. *Journal of Accounting and Economics*, *20*, 297–322.

Cullinan, C. P. (1998). Evidence of non-big 6 market specialization and pricing power in a niche assurance service market. *Auditing: A Journal of Practice and Theory*, *17*(Suppl.), 47–57.

Cullinan, C. P. (1997). Audit pricing in the pension plan audit market. *Accounting and Business Research*, *27*(2), 91–98.

DeAngelo, L. E. (1981). Auditor independence, "lowballing", and disclosure regulation. *Journal of Accounting and Economics*, *3*(August), 113–127.

DeFond, M. L., Francis, J. R., & Wong, T. J. (2000). Auditor industry specialization and market segmentation: Evidence from Hong Kong. *Auditing: A Journal of Practice and Theory*, *19*(Spring), 49–66.

Dellva, W. L., & Olson, G. T. (1998). The relationship between mutual fund fees and expenses and their effects on performance. *The Financial Review, 33*, 85–104.

Eaton, L. (1998). Hey, let's put on a fund, but why 8,000 of them? *New York Times*, April 5, 1998, Money and Business Section p. 35.

Emshwiller, J. R. (1996). SEC sues auditor of two mutual funds it deems bogus. *The Wall Street Journal*, (September 17), C22.

Francis, J. R., & Simon, D. T. (1987). A test of audit pricing in the small-client segment of the U.S. audit market. *The Accounting Review, 63*(January), 145–157.

Gist, W. E. (1992). Explaining variability in external audit fees. *Accounting and Business Research, 23*(89), 79–84.

Lindsay, D. (1998). Commentary on "Evidence on non-Big 6 market specialization and pricing power in a niche assurance service market." *Auditing: A Journal of Practice and Theory, 17*(Suppl.).

Maher, M. W., Tiessen, P., Colson, R., & Broman, A. J. (1992). Competition and audit fees. *The Accounting Review, 27*(January), 199–211.

Malhotra, D. K., & McLeod, R. W. (1997). An empirical analysis of mutual fund expenses. *The Journal of Financial Research 20*(Summer), 175–190.

Mulvihill, M. (1996). A question of trust. *Morningstar Mutual Funds, 28*(August 30), S1–S2.

Pearson, T., & Trompeter, G. (1994). Competition in the market for audit services: The effects of supplier concentration on audit fees. *Contemporary Accounting Research, 11*(Summer), 115–135.

Pearson, T. A., Brooks, R. C., & Neidermeyer, A. A. (1998). The determinants of monitoring costs in not-for-profit organizations. *Journal of Public Budgeting, Accounting, and Financial Management*, (Winter), 499–512.

Previts, G. J. (1996). The politics of disclosure: Accountants in the era of mutual fund investing. *Research in Accounting Regulation, 10*, 211–214.

Securities Exchange Commission (SEC) (2001). *Final Rule: Disclosure of Mutual Fund After Tax Returns*. http://www.sec.gov/rules/final/33-7941.htm

Securities Exchange Commissions (SEC) (1997). *Form N-SAR: Semi-Annual Report for Registered Investment Companies*. Washington: SEC.

Simon, D. T., & Francis, J. R. (1988). The effects of auditor change on audit fees: Tests of price cutting and audit fee recovery. *The Accounting Review*, (April), 255–269.

Simunic, D. A. (1980). The pricing of audit services: Theory and evidence. *Journal of Accounting Research, 18*(Spring), 161–190.

Simunic, D. A., & Stein, M. T. (1987). *Product Differentiation in Auditing: Auditor Choice in the Market for Unseasoned New Issues*. Vancouver, B.C.: The Canadian Certified General Accountants Research Foundation.

Tufano, P., & Sevcik, M. (1997). Board structure and fee setting in the U.S. mutual fund industry. *Journal of Financial Economics, 46*(December), 321–355.

Ward, D. D., Elder, R. J., & Kattelus, S. C. (1994). Further evidence on the determinants of municipal audit fees. *The Accounting Review, 69*(April), 399–411.

AUDIT COMMITTEE CHARACTERISTICS AND AUDITOR SWITCHES

Lawrence J. Abbott and Susan Parker

ABSTRACT

The role of the audit committee in corporate governance is the subject of increasing public and regulatory interest. We focus on the role of the audit committee in auditor selection at the time of an auditor switch. We argue that independent and active audit committee members demand a high level of audit quality because of concerns about monetary or reputational losses which may result from financial mis-statements. We find that audit committees which meet certain recommendations of the Blue Ribbon Committee with respect to composition and are at least minimally active are more likely to increase auditor quality at the time of an auditor switch. This study contributes to our understanding of audit committee functions and provides evidence that industry specialization is an important element of auditor selection.

INTRODUCTION

Although substantial prior research has addressed the question of why clients change auditors, researchers still cannot claim a complete understanding of the issue.[1] Moreover, although prior researchers acknowledge that audit commit-

Research in Accounting Regulation, Volume 15, pages 151–166.
ISBN: 0-7623-0841-9

tees are important stakeholders in the auditor selection process, few studies have actually examined the audit committee's influence over auditor selection. This paper investigates the role of audit committee characteristics in the auditor change/selection process.

We focus on the largely unexplored role of the audit committee for two reasons. First, auditor selection is a primary audit committee responsibility. Urbancic (1996) finds that 96% of audit committees providing audit committee reports in the annual report to shareholders disclose that the committee is responsible for auditor selection and retention. Parker (1997) notes that of a random sample of 500 publicly traded companies, 69% report that auditor selection is a primary audit committee responsibility. The lack of a comprehensive understanding of auditor change, combined with these findings, suggests a need to examine audit committee influence in the auditor change/selection process.

A second motivation for our study lies in the increased academic and regulatory scrutiny surrounding the audit committee. The Blue Ribbon Committee on Improving the Effectiveness of Corporate Audit Committees (the BRC) issued its report in February 1999 (BRC, 1999), recommending a stronger financial reporting oversight role for audit committees. The BRC recommends audit committee charters specify 'the outside auditor is ultimately accountable to the board of directors and the audit committee, which have the ultimate authority and responsibility to select, evaluate, and, where appropriate, replace the outside auditor', as well as recommending that the auditor and audit committee enter into significant discussions regarding the quality of financial reporting. Echoing the sentiments of the BRC, the Auditing Standards Board (ASB) proposed an amendment to Auditing Standards No. 61, "Communications with Audit Committees". The amendment requires external auditors to discuss with audit committees the clarity, consistency and completeness of the clients' accounting policies. Upon issuance, ASB chairman Deborah Lambert stated, "We fully support the BRC's recommendation for candid dialogue. We also recognize that the effectiveness of the amended Standard No. 61 depends upon everyone involved, including the auditor, management and the audit committee."

In this paper, we examine whether audit committees comprised solely of independent directors (consistent with the BRC's recommendation) and which exhibit a minimum level of activity have an incrementally higher demand for audit quality. This increased demand is expected to occur because outside audit committee directors view the directorate as a means of enhancing their reputations as experts in decision control (Fama & Jensen, 1983). Although audit committee service increases the reputational capital of these outside directors, it may also exacerbate the reputational damage should a financial misstatement occur. Since audit quality is generally defined as the joint probability of detecting and reporting a material financial misstatement (DeAngelo, 1981), we hypothesize that independent and active audit committees prefer higher quality external auditors during the auditor change/selection process.

We test our hypothesis in two different auditor switch samples from 1993–1995. The first is a 'name-brand' switch sample comprised of 78 firms switching to/from a Big 6 auditor from/to a non-Big 6 auditor.[2] The second is a 'specialist-switch' sample of 86 switches to/from a Big 6 industry specialist from/to a Big 6 industry nonspecialist auditor. Our tests indicate that the presence of an independent and active audit committee is significantly associated with increases in audit quality at the time of auditor change. Our results are consistent across both samples and are robust to alternate measures of our test variable. One caveat in interpreting our results is our reliance upon the Big 6/non-Big 6 dichotomy and industry market-shares as proxies for audit quality. While there is support from prior research for using these proxies to infer audit quality differences, we cannot observe nor demonstrate that such definitions actually result in higher audit quality.

Our study contributes to previous literature in two ways. First, we provide initial empirical evidence of the role of the audit committee in the auditor switching process. Our results suggest that active and independent audit committees are important stakeholders in the auditor choice process. Our evidence is also consistent with external auditors and audit committees functioning as complementary monitoring mechanisms.

Second, we provide time-series evidence on certain audit committee characteristics. Most notably, we find that of the 164 firms studied over a four-year sample period, 83 sample firms had audit committees that did not meet our independence and activity thresholds. Further, only eight of these 83 audit committees exhibited any improvement in our audit committee effectiveness proxy across the sample period. These results are consistent with a need to improve corporate governance in a manner recommended by the BRC. It also suggests that the BRC's recommendations will have a far-reaching impact on the structure of many companies' audit committees.

PREVIOUS LITERATURE AND HYPOTHESIS

The Demand for Audit Quality

Beatty and Fearnley (1995) provide a useful summary of the empirical literature on auditor selection. They identify two primary, but interlinked sources of audit quality demand: agency demand and information demand. Within the agency relationship, there are two aspects of the relationship that, in combination, create the agency problem: (1) the divergence in preferences of the management and shareholders with respect to management actions, and (2) the imperfect observability of managerial actions (DeFond, 1992). Variables that proxy for the first aspect of the agency relationship include managerial ownership and leverage. The primary proxy for the second agency relation aspect is client size. A *change* in variables related to the various types of agency costs is hypothesized to entail a change in the demand for audit quality (DeFond, 1992).

The information demand for auditor quality (Dopuch & Simunic, 1982) is closely related to agency demand. The selection of credible auditors is posited to signal the quality of management's representations regarding financial performance. The information demand is heightened by the presence of information asymmetry between management and market participants, especially when management seeks external financing for projects. As such, information demand is generally proxied by variables such as new funds received from external markets (Francis & Wilson, 1988).

As discussed above, prior research generally assumes that management selects the external auditor unassisted. However, Leddy (1982) argues that shareholders and the board of directors are important stakeholders in the auditor choice decision. In the following section, we outline the role of audit committees (who should serve as representatives of shareholder interests) in the auditor selection/change process.

Audit Committees and Auditor Selection

Fama and Jensen (1983) argue that the board of directors performs the important function of monitoring the actions of top management. The effectiveness of the monitoring function is increased by the inclusion of outside (i.e. nonmanagement) directors. Outside directors, who are presumably independent of management, reduce opportunities for the board to become an instrument of top management and limit management's ability to benefit themselves at the expense of shareholders. These directors are generally managers or important decision agents in other corporations, and the value of their human capital is directly linked to their reputations for high quality decision making. Negative outcomes, such as litigation or SEC investigation linked to the firm's financial reporting may adversely impact an outside director's reputation.

Menon and Williams (1994) provide a link between outside board directors and the audit committee. Menon and Williams (1994) find that as the proportion of outside directors on the board increases, firms are more likely to exclude insiders from the audit committees and that the audit committees of these firms are more active. Menon and Williams (1994) interpret these findings as evidence that independent and active audit committees are positively related to the liability concerns of outside directors.

Verschoor (1993) finds that audit committees generally review internal controls over financial reporting, review compliance with designated laws and regulations and serve as an intermediary between the board, management and the external and/or internal auditors. Therefore, audit committees may alleviate outside directors' liability concerns in two ways. First, if the audit committee effectively performs its assigned duties of reviewing the internal controls over financial reporting, this should significantly reduce the likelihood of financial misstatement (Beasley, et al., 1999).[3] Second, Reinstein et al. (1984) posit that outside, non-audit committee directors may demonstrate fulfillment of their fiduciary duties by asserting reliance upon the audit committee for issues such as the adequacy of the firm's financial reporting, internal control structure and relationship with its external auditor.[4] In cases of shareholder lawsuits alleging financial statement fraud, this strategy can subrogate outside director liability to audit committee members and also mitigate any reputational damage as well.[5]

In sum, we posit that outside audit committee directors possess a *unique*, two-factor audit quality demand function. The two factors are the preservation/enhancement of reputational capital and the avoidance of liability resulting from shareholder lawsuit. Both factors are a direct result of audit committee membership.

Hypothesis Development

Research on the influence of the audit committee on auditor selection is limited and has yielded only mixed results. For example, while Knapp (1991) finds audit committee members perceive a Big 8/non-Big 8 quality difference, Cottell and Rankin (1988) find that the voluntarily formation of an audit committee has no effect on the probability of a change in auditors or the selection of a Big 8 auditor. In contrast to Cottell and Rankin (1988), Eichenseher and Shields (1985) find a positive association between the existence of an audit committee and a change to a Big 8 auditor. Note that both Cottell and Rankin (1988) and Eichenseher and Shields (1985) only examine the relation between the *existence* of an audit committee and auditor selection. In the current study, we argue that it is the independence and activity of the audit committee, rather than its sheer existence, that leads to a demand for higher audit quality.

Given an independent and active audit committee, there are two reasons why the audit committee and management may have different incentives regarding audit quality. First, management may prefer to select an accommodating, compliant auditor who would allow management enough flexibility to attain earnings goals, while having sufficient credibility to allow management to appear to be a good steward of the shareholders' investment (DeFond & Subramanyam, 1998).

A second reason why management may prefer a lower quality auditor is to obtain a lower audit fee (Craswell, et al., 1995). Manager's may find less value in a higher audit quality and thus be less willing to pay a premium to obtain the potential advantages of a higher quality auditor, such as a lower cost of capital. We believe that even in non-financially distressed firms (such as those in our study), the desire to reduce audit fees is of greater concern to management than to active, independent audit committees.

To summarize, we expect an independent and active audit committee's audit quality demand function mitigates the attractiveness of lower audit fees offered by lower quality auditors and magnifies the consideration of audit quality during the auditor change/selection process, leading to our hypothesis:

> $H(a)$: Firms with independent and active audit committees are more likely to choose higher quality audit firms, during the auditor switching process.

Prior research on our hypothesis is limited to Abbott and Parker (2000), who find that audit committees comprised solely of outside directors and that meet at least twice annually are *associated* with the employment of industry specialist auditors. A weakness of Abbott and Parker (2000) lies in its cross-sectional design: the characteristics of the audit committee in the 1994 sample year are not necessarily indicative of its characteristics at the time the auditor was selected. The current study addresses this weakness by examining the monitoring characteristics of the audit committee at the time of the switch and also provides initial empirical evidence on the time-series behavior of audit committee activity and composition.[6]

RESEARCH DESIGN AND RESULTS

Research Design

Consistent with prior research, we use a regression framework that utilizes a dichotomous dependent variable. Our dichotomous dependent variable is coded 1 for an auditor switch resulting in an increase in auditor quality and 0 for those switches resulting in a decrease. We have two definitions for auditor quality increasing/decreasing switches. The first is a 'name-brand' switch coded 1 for switches to a Big 6 auditor from a non-Big 6 auditor and 0 for a switch in the opposite direction. The second definition is a 'specialist switch' coded 1 for switches to a Big 6 industry specialist auditor from a Big 6 industry non-specialist auditor and 0 for a switch in the opposite direction. Our definition of industry specialist auditor can be found in the appendix. Our independent variable of interest, labeled ACE, is also dichotomous. It is coded 1 for audit committees comprised entirely of outside, independent directors that meet at

Table 1. Sample Selection and Specialist Designations.

Panel A: Overall Sample Selection Results		
Criteria Description	Name-Brand Switch Sample	Specialist Switch Sample
Total non-financial services switches from 1993–1995	425	245
Less: switchers with unavailable proxy statement data	271	78
Less: switchers receiving going concern, adverse or qualified opinion from 1991–1997	2	6
Less: switchers changing auditors as a result of a merger	8	29
Less: switchers declaring bankruptcy	5	8
Less: switchers that are 20% owned subsidiary	45	22
Less: multiple switchers	16	16
Total switches	78	86

Panel B: Industry Distribution of Specialist Switches					
Focus Industry	Related Two-Digit SIC Codes	Specialist Auditor(s)	% of 1994 population	No. specialist switches	% specialist switches
Construction	15–17	AA, EY	1.3	2	2.3
Consumer product & food	20–33	PW	16.8	12	14.0
Energy	10–14, 46, 49	AA, DT	7.7	9	10.5
Financial Services	60–64, 67	PM, EY, DT	18.2	0	0
Information & Communication	78, 79, 84	CL	12.2	7	8.1
Manufacturing	34–39	DT	23.2	23	26.7
Personal services And healthcare	72, 80, 83	EY	2.6	5	5.8
Professional, commercial services, education	75, 76, 82, 87, 89	AA, CL, PM	2.3	9	10.5
Real Estate	65, 70	AA, EY	1.6	2	2.3
Retail and Wholesale	50–59	EY, DT	11.0	11	12.8
Transportation	40–42, 44, 45, 47	AA, EY	2.2	5	5.8
All other	1, 2,7, 8, 99	AA, EY	0.9	1	1.2
Totals			100	86	100

AA: Arthur Andersen, CL: Coopers & Lybrand (now PricewaterhouseCoopers), DT: Deloitte & Touche, PW: Price Waterhouse (now PricewaterhouseCoopers), EY: Ernst & Young, PM: KPMG Peat Marwick.

least twice annually, 0 otherwise. The other independent variables are derived from prior research and can also be found in the appendix section.

Sample Selection Results

Panel A of Table 1 summarizes sample selection results. There were 425 (245) non-financial services switches between Big 6 and non-Big 6 auditors (specialist and non-specialist auditors) in 1993-1995. Consistent with prior research, we deleted switching firms that received a going concern, adverse or qualified opinion; changed auditors as a result of a merger; declared bankruptcy; are over 20% owned by a parent corporation; or, switched auditors multiple times during the sample period. This resulted in 78 brand name switches and 86 specialist switches that had available proxy statement data. For the 78 brand name switches, the majority, 53, switched away from the Big 6. For the 86 specialist switchers firms, the majority, 50, moved from a specialist to a nonspecialist.

Panel B of Table 1 indicates the distribution of the 86 specialist switches appears consistent with the overall population industry distribution.

Descriptive Statistics

Panel A of Table 2 provides descriptive statistics. Not surprisingly, name brand switchers, with median total assets of $11.74 million, are smaller than specialist switchers, with median total assets of $64.48 million. Interestingly, only 32 (49) of the 78 (86) brand name (specialist) switchers have active and independent audit committees. In other words, over half of our 164 switching firms, or 83, did not have active and independent audit committees during year prior to the auditor switch.

Univariate Results

Panels B and C of Table 2 also provide Mann-Whitney tests for our two samples. We split the sample into those firms which switched to a brand name (specialist) auditor and those which switched away and test for differences between the two subsamples. For the name brand switchers, Panel B of Table 2 indicates that firms increasing auditor quality had a significantly higher incidence of independent and active audit committees. Switchers to the Big 6 also had significantly higher security issuance activity, growth rates and changes in leverage than switchers away from the Big 6. However, there were no significant differences between switches for size (at the time of switch) and inside ownership.

Table 2. Univariate Results.

Panel A: Descriptive Statistics for both samples

	Name-brand Switches			Specialist Switches		
Variable Name	Mean	Median	Standard Deviation	Mean	Median	Standard Deviation
ACE	0.4102	0.0000	0.4864	0.5698	1.0000	0.4981
GROW	0.2833	0.1755	0.5484	0.4438	0.4704	0.5431
INOWN	-0.0166	-0.0012	0.1048	-0.0027	-0.0028	0.0684
LEV	0.0263	0.0003	0.1784	0.0062	-0.0051	0.1602
ISSUE	0.1687	0.0457	0.3176	0.1876	0.0893	0.2785
SIZE (in millions)	68.7268	11.7375	200.5376	464.2312	64.4812	1312.3621

Panel B: Univariate Results for Name-brand switching sample

Variable Name	Mean for Switchers To Big 6 Auditor	Mean for Switchers from Big 6 Auditor	Mann-Whitney
ACE	0.5000	0.3076	2.7735*
GROW	0.4243	0.2133	2.7114*
INOWN	-0.0280	-0.0109	0.4541
LEV	0.0715	0.0036	2.6697*
ISSUE	0.3022	0.1019	7.4688***
SIZE (in millions)	123.8146	47.8335	1.3673

Panel C: Univariate Results for Specialist switching sample

Variable Name	Mean for Switchers To Big 6 Auditor	Mean for Switchers from Big 6 Auditor	Mann-Whitney
ACE	0.8333	0.4000	5.7992**
GROW	0.4637	0.4294	2.8797*
INOWN	-0.0078	-0.0009	0.7842
LEV	0.0326	-0.0126	3.1251*
ISSUE	0.2706	0.1278	5.810**
SIZE (in millions)	312.9389	573.1715	1.1125

*, **, *** = p-value < 0.10, 0.05, 0.01.

LEGEND

ACE = 1 if audit committee is comprised solely of non-employee directors and meets at least twice during the year preceding auditor switch; 0 otherwise. GROW = The percentage change in total assets, from two years before the auditor switch to two years after the auditor switch. INOWN = The change in ownership percentage of all managers and directors from two years before auditor switch to two years after auditor switch. LEV = The ratio of long-term debt to total assets is computed two years prior to the auditor switch and two years after the auditor switch. The difference between these two values equals LEV. ISSUE = The ratio of total proceeds from securities issues to total assets is computed for each of the two years after the auditor switch. ISSUE equals the average of those two ratios. SIZE = Total assets at beginning of switch year.

For specialist switchers, Panel C of Table 2 indicates a similar pattern. Firms switching to specialists have significantly higher growth rates, more post-switch issuance activity and greater increases in leverage compared to those firms switching away from specialists. Firms moving up in quality were generally smaller than those switching down, but this difference is not statistically significant. For specialist switchers, there is also a highly significant difference in the incidence of independent and active audit committees.

Table 3. Logit Regression Results.

$$AUDQUAL = \alpha + \beta_1 ACE + \beta_2 GROW + \beta_3 INOWN + \beta_4 LEV + \beta_5 ISSUE + \beta_6 SIZE + \varepsilon$$

	Panel A: Name-brand switching sample		
Independent Variable	Expected Sign	Parameter Estimate	Wald χ^2
Intercept		−2.9461	13.3699***
ACE	+	1.6117	5.6486**
GROW	+	1.0776	3.8152**
INOWN	−	−0.6744	0.0498
LEV	+	0.7748	3.1423*
ISSUE	+	3.7958	6.8512***
SIZE	+	0.2017	0.9608
Adjusted R^2 = 0.3098			Model χ^2 = 18.54**

	Panel B: Specialist switching sample		
Independent Variable	Expected Sign	Parameter Estimate	Wald χ^2
Intercept		−2.4663	8.2854***
ACE	+	3.0312	5.3722**
GROW	+	0.7787	3.3224*
INOWN	−	−1.5322	0.1080
LEV	+	3.0953	2.8832*
ISSUE	+	3.9687	5.9199**
SIZE	+	−0.1614	0.9713
Adjusted R^2 = 0.4270			Model χ^2 = 24.46***

*, **, *** = p-value < 0.10, 0.05, 0.01.

Note: For Name-brand switching sample, AUDQUAL is coded 1 for switches to Big 6 from non-Big 6; 0 for switches to non-Big 6 from Big 6. For Specialist switching sample, AUDQUAL is coded 1 from switches to Big 6 industry specialist auditor from Big 6 industry non-specialist; 0 for switches from Big 6 industry specialist auditor to Big 6 industry non-specialist auditor. Independent variables are defined in Table 2, with the exception of SIZE, which is in natural log form.

Multivariate Results

Panel A of Table 3 presents regression results for name brand switchers. The regression results support the hypothesis that independent and active audit committees are associated with the selection of a Big 6 auditor. Growth, the issuance of stock or debt, and higher levels of leverage are also associated with a switch to a Big 6 auditor, while size and inside ownership are not.

Panel B of Table 3 presents regression results for specialist switchers. Again, the engagement of a specialist at the time of a switch is associated with the presence of an independent and active audit committee. Results on control variables are similar to those related to brand name switchers.

Additional Tests

The BRC recommends that the audit committee include only independent directors for firms over a certain size. The basis of this recommendation is the belief that affiliated directors (those that may have economic or psychological dependence on current management) are thus more likely to be compliant with management. Examples of affiliated directors include relatives of management, attorneys whose law firm provides legal counsel, bankers or consultants (BRC 1999).

When we define audit committees without affiliated directors as independent, the number of name brand (specialist) switchers with independent and active audit committees is reduced from 32 to 22 (49 to 43). However, results (not reported) indicate that this more stringent version of our test variable remains significant at conventional levels. Interestingly, of the firms with affiliated audit committee directors, 75% had market capitalizations of less than $200 million at the time of the auditor switch. Recognizing the difficulty and cost of obtaining sufficient outside directors for smaller firms, (i.e. those with market capitalization of $200 million or less), the BRC specifically excludes them from meeting the more rigorous definition of audit committee director independence. This suggests that the appropriate measure of audit committee director independence is contingent upon firm size.

Finally, we performed similar tests to those described in Table 3 after: (1) deleting 16 over-the-counter firms, for which audit committees are not required as a condition of listing; (2) deleting 9 firms which exhibited a change in audit committee effectiveness over the four-year period (8 of which exhibited increases in audit committee effectiveness); and (3) 10 auditor switches resulting from auditor resignations. In all cases, our results remained robust after deletion of these observations.

CONCLUSION

Taken together, our results support the prediction that independent and active audit committees are associated with the selection of a higher quality auditor (either name brand or specialist auditor) at the time of an auditor switch. This is consistent with our argument that audit committee members influence the auditor selection process, with the objective of mitigating their risk of reputational or financial loss. This effect is incremental to agency-related and financial variables used in previous studies. However, our results suggest that the appropriateness of the more rigorous audit committee effectiveness variable is a function of firm size.

Our study has at least three limitations. First, our evidence does not preclude the possibility that the selection of both the auditor and the audit committee are related to unidentified characteristics of the firm or its management. We believe this is a fruitful area for future research. A second limitation is that since we cannot directly observe audit quality, we use proxies based upon the auditor's share of client revenues (derived from national market shares) within an industry. Neither conclusive evidence of a link between client-associated quality outcomes and industry specialization, nor a consensus measure of industry specialization has emerged. Until a consensus measure of industry specialization emerges, this issue will continue to be a concern for all studies in this area. A third limitation is that is the our study leaves open the question of why, if our hypothesis is accurate, we do not observe increases in audit committee effectiveness immediately preceding increases in auditor quality. One possibility is that audit committee incentives for increased quality are insufficient to *induce* an auditor change, but such incentives manifest themselves when the decision to switch has been made in response to other agency-cost related factors.

Despite these limitations, we believe our results are useful in exploring an area of corporate governance which has not been thoroughly studied. Our results provide new evidence on the influence of the audit committee in auditor selection and extend understanding of the importance of industry specialization as an indicator of auditor quality. Our findings have implications for both providers and consumers of audit services, as well as for academics in future auditor choice research.

Finally, while our results suggest a significant auditor selection role for independent and active audit committees, actions undertaken by recently departed SEC Chairman Levitt suggest an even larger and more important financial oversight role for audit committees in the near future. Upon his retirement, Chairman Levitt sent letters to audit committee members of publicly traded firms. In these letters, Levitt vigorously exhorted audit committee members to not only adhere to the recent BRC recommendations, but to also diligently pursue their corporate governance responsibilities. Levitt concluded in these letters: "There is no reason why every public company in America shouldn't have an audit committee made up of the right people, doing the right things, and asking the right questions."

NOTES

1. DeFond (1992) summarizes previous literature and notes the inconsistencies between prior studies. Francis and Wilson (1988) conclude their study by noting 'while agency costs appear, at the margin, to affect auditor choice above and beyond client size/growth, the auditor selection process seems to be more complex than modeled in this and related studies.'

2. The term Big 6 auditor is used as during our sample period of 1993–1996 there were six such firms. In 1998, the Big 6 became the Big 5.

3. In a comprehensive study of accounting fraud, Beasley et al. (1999) find that companies committing financial statement fraud overwhelmingly had weak, inactive audit committees comprised of insiders.

4. Audit committees are required by SEC disclosure rules to include a statement regarding their oversight responsibilities in the firm's proxy statement. This has the effect of bonding the committee to perform the indicated tasks and may effectively shift risk to audit committee members.

5. In the July 1998 issue of Directors Alert, Tom Dooley, PricewaterhouseCoopers audit partner, noted that 'audit committees are on the litigation hotseat' as more lawsuits are brought against audit committees.

6. Additionally, Abbott and Parker (2000) also do not examine quality differences between Big 6 and non-Big 6 auditors and thus cannot compare results when the quality measure differs. A final weakness of Abbott and Parker (2000) is the relatively low explanatory power of their regression models, combined with the lack of support for other control variables. We believe the auditor change setting provides a more powerful test of the audit committee's demand for audit quality.

7. Recent accounting mergers among Big 6 auditors (i.e. Price Waterhouse and Coopers & Lybrand) appear to be partially driven by a desire to be designated an 'industry leader.' "One way a Big 6 firm can differentiate itself, outside of size, price and independent client rating . . . is their industry specializations" (Novak, 1998).

8. In order to identify industry specialists, we follow a classification scheme which combines client firms into 12 groups of similar industries, based on two digit SIC code (Franz, et al., 1997). Following Palmrose (1986), we designate an industry specialist auditor as the auditor with the greatest percentage of client sales audited within that industry. Any other auditor within 15% of the leader's market share is also deemed an industry specialist; all other auditors are designated nonspecialists.

9. Because the number of meetings may be unusually high during the switch year, we use the number during the preceding year as our gauge of normal activity.

10. We do not examine changes in the ACE variable. While we initially expected changes in the audit committee to spur a change in the demand for audit quality, we

observe very little time-series variation in our test variable. Differences in ACE measure are not present in over 90% of our observations.

11. Francis and Wilson (1988) include another 'change' variable in their analyses: the adoption of an accounting-based bonus plan. Only two firms in our samples adopted accounting-based bonus plans (most firms already had established bonus plans before the auditor switch). Accordingly, we do not include this variable in our analyses.

ACKNOWLEDGMENTS

We would like to thank Steve Matsunaga, Neil Fargher, Reed Smith, Terry O'Keefe and Sam Tiras, for their assistance. We also thank Jeanne Werner for her capable research assistance

REFERENCES

Abbott, L. J., & Parker, S. (2000). Audit committee characteristics and auditor selection. *Auditing: A Journal of Practice and Theory*, *19*(Fall), 1–20.

American Bar Association (1978). *Corporate Director's Guidebook*. Chicago: American Press International.

Beasley, M. S., Carcello, J. V., & Hermanson, D. R. (1999). *Fraudulent Financial Reporting: 1987–1997 An Analysis of U.S. Public Companies*. Committee of Sponsoring Organizations of the Treadway Commission. Jersey City, NJ.

Beattie, V., & Fearnley, S. (1995). The importance of audit firm characteristics and the drivers of auditor change in U.K. listed companies. *Accounting and Business Research*, *26*(100), 227–239.

Blue Ribbon Committee (BRC) on Improving the Effectiveness of Corporate Audit Committees (1999). Securities and Exchange Commission. Stamford, CT.

Cottell P. G., & Rankin, L. J. (1988). Do audit committees bias auditor selection? *Akron Business and Economic Review*, *19*(4): 87–103.

Craswell A. T., Francis, J. R., & Taylor, S. L. (1995). Auditor brand name reputations and industry specializations. *Journal of Accounting and Economics*, *20*(December), 297–322.

DeAngelo, L. (1981). Auditor independence, low-balling and disclosure regulation. *Journal of Accounting and Economics*, *1*, 113–127.

DeFond, M. L. (1992). The association between changes in client firm agency costs and auditor switching. *Auditing: A Journal of Practice and Theory*, *11*(Spring), 16–31.

DeFond, M. L., & Subramanyam, K. R. (1998). Auditor changes and discretionary accruals. *Journal of Accounting and Economics*, *25*(1), 35–67.

Dopuch, N., & Simunic, D. (1982). Competition in auditing: An assessment. Fourth Symposium on Auditing Research. University of Illinois.

Eichenseher, J. W., & Shields, D. (1985). Corporate director liability and monitoring preferences. *Journal of Accounting and Public Policy*, *4*(1), 13–31.

Fama, E., & Jensen, M. (1983). Agency problems and residual claims. *Journal of Law and Economics*, *26*(2), 327–349.

Francis, J. R., & Wilson, E. R. (1988). Auditor changes: A joint test of theories relating to agency costs and auditor differentiation. *Accounting Review*, (October), 663–683.

Franz, D. R., Crawford, D., & Johnson, E. N. (1998). The impact of litigation against an audit firm on the market value of nonlitigating clients. *Journal of Accounting, Auditing and Finance, 13*(Spring), 117–134.

Hogan, C. E., & Jeter, D. C. (1999). Industry specialization by auditors. *Auditing: A Journal of Practice and Theory, 18*(1), 1–18.

Knapp, M. S. (1991). Factors that audit committee members use as surrogates for audit quality. *Auditing: A Journal of Practice & Theory, 10*(1), 35–52.

Leddy, T. (1982). The competition in auditing: an assessment. Fourth Symposium on Auditing Research (pp. 467–482). University of Illinois: Urbana.

Menon, K., & Williams, J. D. (1994). The use of audit committees for monitoring. *Journal of Accounting and Public Policy, 13*(Spring), 121–139.

Novak, G. (1998). Do clients care about the Big 6 mega-mergers? *Accounting Today,* (April 5), 7, 41.

Palmrose, Z. (1986). Audit fees and auditor size: Further evidence. *Journal of Accounting Research, 24*(Spring), 97–110.

Parker, S. (1997). The effect of audit committees on financial reporting. Unpublished dissertation, University of Oregon.

Reinstein, A., Callaghan, J., & Braiotta, L., Jr. (1984). Corporate audit committees: Reducing directors' legal liabilities. *Journal of Urban Law, 61*, 375–389.

Urbancic, F. (1996). A content analysis of audit committee reports. *Internal Auditing,* (Summer), 36–45.

Verschoor, C. (1993). Benchmarking the audit committee. *Journal of Accountancy,* (September), 15–22.

Walker, P., Casterella, J., & Moet, L. (1998). An investigation of audit failure in new audit engagements. *Research in Accounting Regulation, 12*, 61–75.

APPENDIX: RESEARCH DESIGN

The Model

Equation (1) summarizes our research design. Consistent with prior research, a logit regression framework is employed, with the dependent variable coded 1 for an auditor switch resulting in an increase in audit quality, 0 otherwise. The remaining independent variables follow and are defined subsequently.

$$
\begin{aligned}
\text{AUDQUAL} = b_0 + b_1\text{ACE} + b_2\text{GROW} + b_3\text{INOWN} \\
+ b_4\text{LEV} + b_5\text{ISSUE} + b_6\text{SIZE} + \varepsilon
\end{aligned}
\tag{1}
$$

Dependent variable

We measure auditor quality (AUDQUAL) in two ways. DeAngelo (1981) defines auditor quality as the joint probability of detecting and reporting a financial misstatement. This probability is assumed to be higher for Big 6 auditors than for non-Big 6 because the Big 6 firms have a greater reputational investment in delivering audit quality, as well as perhaps greater expertise. Consistent with prior research, we first code our change in auditor quality as 1 when moving to a Big 6 from a non-Big 6 auditor and 0 when moving in the opposite direction.

A second body of research suggests that industry specialization represents an additional level of audit quality beyond the Big 6/non-Big 6 dichotomy (Hogan & Jeter, 1999; Franz, et al., 1997).[7] Industry specialist auditors may provide higher quality audits due to: (1) better audit technologies (Dopuch & Simunic, 1982), or (2) superior knowledge through economies of scale (Walker et al., 1998). In this case, AUDQUAL is a dichotomous variable with a value of 1 for a switch to a Big 6 specialist from a Big 6 non-specialist, 0 for a switch in the opposite direction.[8]

Independent variables

Our measure of audit committee effectiveness (ACE) is based on the independence of the committee and its activity level. With regard to independence, consistent with BRC (1999) recommendations, we believe that nonemployee (current or former) directors are more likely to monitor management effectively. With regard to activity, we expect an outside audit committee director's level of monitoring commitment and reputational investment to be related to the audit committee's level of activity. We measure activity through the number of meetings. The Corporate Director's Guidelines (ABA, 1978) suggest the minimum number of meetings per year an audit committee should hold is two – one during the planning phase of an audit, the other after the audit's completion. Our test variable (ACE) is coded 1 if the committee does not include insiders (i.e. current or former employees of the firm) and meets at least twice during the year prior to the auditor switch, and 0 otherwise.[9] We use a combined threshold measure of both activity and independence because activity and independence are unlikely to result in effectiveness unless both elements are present (Menon and Williams, 1994).[10]

We also control for client-specific agency and information demand factors as discussed in prior sections of this paper. Changes (or anticipated changes) in client firm growth rates (GROW), inside ownership (INOWN) and leverage (LEV) have been shown to lead to changes in auditor quality (DeFond, 1992; Francis & Wilson, 1988).[11] Securities issuance (ISSUE) and firm size (SIZE) have also been shown to be associated with changes in auditor quality (Defond, 1992) and are also included in our analysis.

STAFF ACCOUNTING BULLETIN 101: TESTING STUDENTS' KNOWLEDGE OF REVENUE RECOGNITION PRINCIPLES

Jimmy W. Martin

ABSTRACT

Throughout the twentieth century, revenue transactions have presented challenges for accountants and auditors. Although the profession has devoted considerable efforts in defining the requisites for revenue recognition, the problems seem to proliferate. One plausible explanation for revenue recognition problems is that students are graduating with incorrect or incomplete concepts of revenue. To test this hypothesis, the author has utilized case situations developed by the Securities and Exchange Commission in Staff Accounting Bulletin No. 101 and structured responses to each case. These cases and possible responses were given to both undergraduate and graduate accounting students for the purpose of determining how they would make revenue decisions. The objective is to develop a test instrument that will identify revenue misconceptions and thereby allow instructors to modify their instruction techniques.

Research in Accounting Regulation, Volume 15, pages 167–189.
Copyright © 2002 by Elsevier Science Ltd.
All rights of reproduction in any form reserved.
ISBN: 0-7623-0841-9

INTRODUCTION

Accountants and auditors are having major difficulties in identifying revenue transactions and determining when revenue should be recognized. This is evidenced by many newspaper and journal articles publicizing audit failures in recent years (see references). In response, both the AICPA and the SEC have issued releases that provide guidance on revenue recognition practices, yet the problems continue. Why are we having such difficulty with revenue recognition? Do we not understand the basic underlying concepts that define revenue? Are our decision models used to identify revenue incorrect?

One plausible answer to the question, "Why are the revenue problems occurring?", is that students are graduating with imprecise concepts of the meaning of revenue. To test this hypothesis, the SEC's Staff Accounting Bulletin No. 101 is utilized in developing a series of short cases that capture information on how students make revenue decisions. The SEC identified several problem areas that have created major difficulties for accountants. In each case, the SEC described a set of facts concerning a transaction, and posed a question as to whether revenue recognition was proper.

I have used the SEC's fact situations (verbatim in some cases while modifications were made in other situations) and revenue recognition questions and provided answer choices for each question. Since the test subjects consisted solely of students, I tried to minimize the likelihood of misinterpreting the responses; thus, after each answer, I added a brief statement that emphasized the key issue underlying the response. In some of the situations, more than one correct response might be appropriate, and students could choose one or more answers. My purpose is to determine which revenue criteria are important to students.

Since a student might decide that more than one criteria is important, I also wanted to determine which criteria were deemed to be the most important. Thus, for each factual situation, I asked for a second response in which the student determined how much importance was placed on each possible answer. Here, the student circled a number from 1 to 5 that indicated the degree of importance placed on that particular response (5 being the highest degree of importance). Presumably, if one found that response A was not relevant to the revenue decision, the student would circle 1; meaning that this criterion was not important to the decision. However, if response A contained a criterion that was deemed to be critical to the decision, a 5 would be circled. Hopefully, from these responses, one can determine which criteria are heavily weighted and which ones are not deemed to be important.

The eleven cases were given to three undergraduate classes at the University of Montevallo: principles, intermediate II, and auditing II. The classes consisted of 28, 21 and 14 students respectively. Later, additional data was collected by a colleague at Case-Western Reserve University where the test instrument was used to elicit responses from an intermediate accounting class (16 students) and a graduate accounting class (19 students). Because of the small numbers, no statistical analysis was performed other than computing frequency percentages and mean scores for the students' evaluation of the importance of each revenue criterion (see Tables 1, 2 and 3).

Although the number of student participants was small and restricted to two universities, the results may provide tentative indications of types of misconceptions which lead to incorrect revenue decisions. It is likely that students' perceptions will be correct in some areas, but incorrect in others; thus, identifying weaknesses where more emphasis is needed. Finally, information on the degree of importance of each response should provide additional insights into whether students are placing enough emphasis on certain criteria. While these insights might be pertinent only to accounting instructors at these two universities, other educators can use the test to obtain information from their own students.

The test instructions and the test instrument are presented in the following section. The paper concludes with a brief discussion of the results of the test and teaching notes.

INSTRUCTIONS FOR REVENUE TEST

Eleven cases have been designed to elicit your ideas concerning revenue recognition. Some of these cases may present situations or transactions that you have not dealt with in the classroom. Use your best judgment in responding to each situation. In some of the cases, more than one answer may be appropriate. In part II of each case, you will be asked to indicate the degree of importance that you attached to each possible response. For those answer choices that you deem inappropriate, presumably you will circle the number 1 in part II, since this would indicate that you believe that answer is not important. In the comments section, briefly state why you believe those choices to be inappropriate. For those answers that you consider to be appropriate, carefully consider the key issues involved before indicating the degree of importance of a given criterion in making your decision. In the event that your revenue decision is determined by a criterion that is not mentioned in any of the answer choices, write your decision and state why you reached that decision in the comments section. Also, you are encouraged to use the comments section to make any observations regarding that particular case. For example, you may believe that some key piece of information needs to be provided in order for you to make a rational choice, or you may feel that a particular sentence is vague and needs to be clarified. Your comments could help to improve the testing instrument. Thank you for your participation.

Test Instrument

Use your best judgment in responding to the following cases.

(1) Regarding sales transactions, Company A's normal business practice is to enter into a written sales agreement that requires the signatures of authorized representatives of both buyer and seller before the agreement is considered binding. Near the end of the fiscal year, Customer B places a verbal order for merchandise with Company A. Company A's representatives sign the agreement, and A ships the merchandise to B. Company B has not signed as it is waiting for its legal department to approve the transaction; however, B's purchasing department has verbally committed to the sale and stated that it is very likely that the contract will be approved. Company A records the transaction as a sale. **Has Company A properly recognized this transaction as revenue?**

I. Select one or more appropriate answers from the following:

A. Company A may recognize the sale because of the high probability that Company B's legal department will approve the sale. [The key issue is the likelihood of consummation].

B. Company A may recognize the sale because the goods have been shipped. [The key issue is who has physical possession of the goods at year-end].

C. Company A may NOT recognize the sale because its normal policy requires the buyer's written authorization, and Company B has not signed the sales agreement. [The key issue is Company A's adherence to its normal business policies].

D. Company A may recognize the sale, if in fact, the customer's purchasing department has requested that the merchandise be shipped. [The key issue is whether the customerhas requested shipment].

II. Circle the appropriate response to indicate the importance that you placed on each issue in making the above decision.

	Very Important		Moderately Important		Not Important
Likelihood of consummating the transaction	5	4	3	2	1
Physical possession of the goods	5	4	3	2	1
Lack of adherence to normal policies	5	4	3	2	1
Customer's request that goods be shipped	5	4	3	2	1

Comments:

(2) Company A enters into an arrangement with Customer B to deliver A's products to B on a consignment basis. Pursuant to the terms of the arrangement, B is a consignee, and title to the products does not pass from A to B until B consumes the products in its operations. Company A ships the product to B; terms FOB Shipping Point. May Company A recognize revenue upon shipment of its product to Customer B?

I. Select one or more appropriate answers from the following:

A. No; products delivered on a consignment basis are not sales. [The key issue is that revenue should not be recorded on consignment transactions].

B. No; Title has not passed to the buyer. [The key issue is transfer of legal ownership].

C. Yes, assuming that the buyer has taken possession of the goods. [The key issue is physical possession].

D. Yes, because the goods are shipped FOB shipping point. [The key issue is the shipping term].

II. Circle the appropriate response to indicate the importance that you placed on each issue in making your decision.

	Very Important		Moderately Important		Not Important
Goods were shipped on consignment	5	4	3	2	1
Legal title not transferred	5	4	3	2	1
Physical possession of the goods	5	4	3	2	1
Shipping terms are FOB shipping point	5	4	3	2	1

Comments:

(3) Company X receives a purchase order from Company Y, and ships the merchandise to Y (legal title transfers to Y at the shipping point). Company X was able to obtain the order from Y when X's vice-president of sales entered into a side agreement wherein the following rights were granted to Y:

1. Y has the right to return the product.
2. Y does not have to pay for the product until it is resold.
3. Y's obligation to pay will be forgiven in the event of theft or physical damage to the product before it is resold.

May Company X record the transaction as a sale when the goods are shipped?

I. Select one or more appropriate answers from the following:

A. Yes, since legal title transfers when the goods are shipped. [The key issue is transfer of title].

B. No, since Y may return the product. [The key issue is the uncertainty created due to the right of return].

C. No, since X may not collect unless Y resells the product. [The key issue is the uncertainty resulting from the contingency of Y reselling the product].

D. No, since Y doesn't have to pay if the goods are stolen or damaged. [The key issue is that the risk of ownership has not passed to the buyer].

II. Circle the appropriate response to indicate the importance that you placed on each issue in making your decision.

	Very Important		Moderately Important		Not Important
Transfer of legal title	5	4	3	2	1
Uncertainty due to right of return	5	4	3	2	1
Contingent event – Y reselling the product	5	4	3	2	1
Risk of ownership not passing to buyer	5	4	3	2	1

Comments:

(4) On December 29, 1999, Co. A receives a purchase order from Co. B. The purchase order states a specific type, quantity, and price of a product that is manufactured by A and specifies a shipping date of January 18, 2000. A ascertains that the customer's request for a delay in shipment is due to a temporary lack of storage space. After conferring with B, A's controller decides to record the transaction as a December sale and immediately bills B for the goods. Payment is expected according to A's normal credit period of 30 days (January 28). Company A does not segregate the merchandise at this point in time, due to an ample supply of the product; i.e. there is no danger that A will be unable to ship the order on the 18th.

I. **Based on the facts given, which of the following would indicate that revenue should NOT be recorded in December?** As before, more than one answer may be appropriate.

A. The goods are not segregated and could be sold to other customers. [The key issue is that title cannot have transferred to the buyer if the goods are available to sell to other customers]

B. The goods are not shipped in December; therefore, there has been no sale. [The key issue is physical possession of the goods]

C. The customer might cancel the order. [The key issue is that contingent events could arise that would negate the transaction].

D. Payment is not expected before January 28 of the next year. [The key issue is that revenue should not be recorded until the cash is received].

II. Circle an appropriate response to indicate the importance that you placed on each issue in making your decision.

	Very Important		Moderately Important		Not Important
Failure to segregate merchandise	5	4	3	2	1
Physical possession of the goods	5	4	3	2	1
Uncertainty over finalizing the transaction	5	4	3	2	1
No cash receipt in December	5	4	3	2	1

Comments:

(5) On December 31, Company A accepts a purchase order from Customer C whereby C orders goods, but requests that shipment be made on February 1. There is nothing on the purchase order that indicates that C would bear the risk of loss in the event the goods were damaged. The apparent reason for ordering the goods in December is to allow C to "get inline" early to reduce the risk of not getting a February purchase (the supply of this good has been tight in recent months).

I. **Which of the following best explains why revenue recognition in December is not appropriate?**

A. Customer C has requested that shipment be delayed. [The key issue is that the customer is requesting the transaction to take place in the next year].

B. The requested shipping date is February 1. [The key issue is that a one-month shipping delay is too long for this to be considered a December transaction].

C. There is no indication that the customer would bear the risk of loss if the goods were lost or damaged during the January holding period. [The key issue is that the risks of ownership have not transferred].

D. The customer has no critical reason for ordering the goods early; thus, the order should not be considered a December transaction. [The key issue is that the customer must have a substantive business purpose for delaying the shipment].

II. Circle the appropriate response to indicate the importance that you placed on each issue in making your decision.

	Very Important		Moderately Important		Not Important
Customer is requesting a February shipment	5	4	3	2	1
One month shipping delay is too long	5	4	3	2	1
Risk of ownership has not transferred to buyer	5	4	3	2	1
Buyer has no substantial business purpose for requesting delay of shipment	5	4	3	2	1

Comments:

(6) Company R is a retailer that offers "layaway" sales to its customers. When a customer requests that an item be placed on "layaway," Co. R retains the merchandise, sets it aside from its main inventory, and collects a 20% cash deposit from the customer. Although Co. R requires the customer to remit the remaining 80% within 90 days, the customer does not sign an installment note or make any other fixed payment commitment. The customer understands that R will not release the product until the remaining amount is paid in full and that the deposit will be forfeited unless the remaining payment is made in 90 days. If the merchandise is lost, damaged or stolen, R bears the loss and must refund the deposit to the customer or provide replacement merchandise.

I. When may R recognize revenue for merchandise sold under its layaway program?

A. R can recognize revenue when it releases the product to the customer. [The key issue is physical possession of the inventory].

B. R can recognize 20% of the revenue when the deposit is received and 80% when the customer remits the remaining part. [The key issue is cash collection; revenue can only be recognized in proportion to the cash received].

C. R can recognize all of the revenue at the point when the customer commits to the purchase; i.e. asks that the item be placed on layaway. [The key issue is that the customer must initiate the transaction by requesting the purchase].

D. R can recognize revenue only after the customer has made some type of fixed commitment to purchase the goods. [The key issue is that revenue recognition is improper until R has an enforceable right to the remainder of the purchase price].

E. R can recognize revenue when the risks of ownership transfer to the customer. [The key issue is risks of ownership.]

II. Circle the appropriate response to indicate the importance that you placed on each issue in making your decision.

	Very Important		Moderately Important		Not Important
Phsyical possession of the product	5	4	3	2	1
Proportion of cash collected	5	4	3	2	1
Customer's initiating transaction	5	4	3	2	1
Customer's fixed commitment to purchase	5	4	3	2	1
Transfer of risk of ownership	5	4	3	2	1

Comments:

(7) Company G sells a one-year membership in its health club to Customer A. When A joins, G collects a non-refundable fee. A obtains the right to use the health club facilities as long as A pays an additional usage fee each month.

I. How should G account for the up-front fee?

A. Recognize the fee as revenue systematically over the expected period that the customer will use the facilities. [The issue is that G earns the fee over the period that services are provided].

B. G should recognize the fee as revenue immediately since the fee is earned by convincing customers to become club members. [The issue is that a separate transaction has occurred that deserves revenue recognition; this is separate from the future transactions of providing services to A].

C. Recognize the fee as revenue immediately since G keeps the cash regardless of how long A uses the facilities. [The key issue is that the fee is non-refundable and therefore has been earned.]

II. Circle the appropriate answer which best indicates the importance that you placed on each issue in making your decision.

	Very Important		Moderately Important		Not Important
Revenue recognized as services provided	5	4	3	2	1
Obtaining customer is a discrete earnings event	5	4	3	2	1
The fee is non-refundable	5	4	3	2	1

Comments:

(8) "Company M is a discount retailer. It generates revenue from annual membership fees it charges customers to shop at its stores and from the sale of products at a discount price to those customers. The membership arrangements with retail customers require the customer to pay the entire membership fee at the outset of the arrangement. However, the customer has the unilateral right to cancel the arrangement at any time during its term and receive a full refund of the initial fee. Based on historical data collected over time for a large number of homogeneous transactions, Co. M estimates that approximately 40% of the customers will request a refund before the end of the membership contract term. Co. M's data for the past five years indicates that significant variations between actual and estimated cancellations have not occurred, and Co. M does not expect significant variations to occur in the foreseeable future."

I. May Co. M recognize the revenue for the membership fees at the outset of the arrangement?

A. Yes, because the objective of originating a revenue-generating arrangement is achieved when the customer is convinced to join the shopping arrangement. [The key issue is selling a service arrangement to a new customer].

B. Yes, for the 60% that will be retained by Co. M; No for the 40% that experience indicates will be refunded. [The key issue is that the anticipated cash retention amount is the proper measure of revenue].

C. No, since Co. M has an unfulfilled obligation to sell products at a discounted price throughout the membership period. [The key issue is that the earnings process is not complete at the outset of the arrangement].

D. No, since the customer may cancel the contract and receive a cash refund. [The key issue is whether the sales price is fixed or determinable when the customer has the right to terminate the contract].

II. Circle the appropriate answer which best indicates the importance that you placed on each issue in making your decision.

	Very Important		Moderately Important		Not Important
Convincing customer to join	5	4	3	2	1
Anticipated cash retention amount	5	4	3	2	1
Existence of unfulfilled obligation by seller	5	4	3	2	1
Uncertainty as to whether customer will terminate contract	5	4	3	2	1

Comments:

(9) "Company A owns and leases retail space to retailers. Co. A (lessor) renews a lease with a customer (lessee) that is classified as an operating lease. The lease term is one year and specifies lease payments of $1.2 million, payable in equal monthly installments on the first day of each month, plus 1% of the lessee's net sales in excess of $25 million if the net sales exceed $25 million during the lease term (i.e. contingent rental). The lessee has historically experienced annual net sales in excess of $25 million in the particular space being leased, and it is probable that the lessee will generate in excess of $25 million net sales during the term of the lease."

I. Should Company A recognize any rental income attributable to the 1% of the retail store's net sales exceeding $25 million before the lessee actually achieves the $25 million net sales threshold?

A. Yes, since it is probable that sales will exceed $25 million during the lease term. [The key issue is the likelihood that the criteria for obtaining the additional revenue will be met].

B. No; since Co. A does not know the amount by which the store's net sales will exceed $25 million, no additional revenue can be recorded until year-end when the final sales figures are known. [The key issue is the inability to quantify the amount of additional revenue, if any, that should be accrued].

C. No; Co. A cannot recognize additional revenue until the $25 million sales figure is achieved; at which time, it could begin to accrue additional revenue. [The key issue is that contingent revenue can be accrued only when the factor on which the contingency is based is achieved].

D. No, because contingent revenue should not be recorded until the retail store remits the cash. [The key issue is that due to the uncertainty of receiving contingent revenue, recognition must await the cash receipt].

E. Yes; the revenue should be recognized systematically (accrued) over the period of time in which the leased property is employed. [The key issue is that Co. A earns revenue as the leased asset is used].

II. Circle the appropriate answer which best indicates the importance that you placed on each issue in making your decision.

	Very Important		Moderately Important		Not Important
Likelihood that the required sales amount would be met	5	4	3	2	1
Inability to quantify the additional revnue	5	4	3	2	1
Recording revenue before contingency is resolved	5	4	3	2	1
Recognizing revenue before cash received	5	4	3	2	1
Recognizing revenue as leased asset is used	5	4	3	2	1

Comments:

(10) P Co., a manufacturer of laser surgical equipment, sells its product to doctors and hospitals. The customers have a right to return the product, if for any reason, they become dissatisfied within six months of purchase. P has recently started selling a new product that is a "first-of-its-kind", but which may well revolutionize cosmetic surgery. While initial sales have been brisk, it is difficult to determine the degree of ultimate acceptance among doctors.

I. May Co. P recognize revenue when the product is shipped to the customer?

A. Yes, assuming title transfers at the shipping date. [The key issue is transfer of legal title to the buyer].

B. No; in situations where a right of return exists, revenue cannot be recognized until the return period expires. [The key issue is that a right to return the product creates a contingency which negates revenue recognition until the contingency is resolved.]

C. No; because this is a new unique product, it is difficult to estimate the number of returns. [The key issue is not that a right of return exists, but rather the inability to reasonably estimate the number of returns.]

D. Yes; where a right of return exists, revenue can be recognized to the extent of the cost of the product; however, recognition of any profit margin should be deferred until the return period expires. [The key issue is that since the product is removed from inventory, only the profit should be deferred until the right of return expires.]

E. Yes, since customers often have a right to return the product, the revenue should be recorded when the product is sold; however, if the product is returned, the seller must promptly record the return in Sales Returns and Allowances in the period of the return. [The key issue is that the sale and any future return are two separate transactions and are recorded appropriately when each is incurred].

II. Circle the appropriate answer which best indicates the importance that you placed on each issue in making your decision.

	Very Important		Moderately Important		Not Important
Transfer of legal title to buyer	5	4	3	2	1
Uncertainty over returns negates revenue	5	4	3	2	1
Difficulty in estimating extent of returns negates revenue	5	4	3	2	1
Appropriateness of recognizing some revenue since product was removed from inventory	5	4	3	2	1
Returns are separate transactions, and are recorded if and when they occur	5	4	3	2	1

Comments:

(11) "Co. A operates an Internet site from which it will sell Co. T's products. Customers place their orders for the product by making a product selection directly from the Internet site and providing a credit card number for the payment. Co. A receives the order and authorization from the credit card company, and passes the order on to Co. T. Company T ships the product directly to the customer. Company A does not take title to the product and has no risk of loss or other responsibility for the product. Co. T is responsible for all product returns, defects, and disputed credit card charges. The product is typically sold for $175 of which Co. A receives $25. In the event a credit card transaction is rejected, Co. A loses its margin on the sale (i.e. $25)."

I. Should Co. A report revenue on a gross basis as $175 along with cost of sales of $150 or on a net basis of $25?

A. Gross basis, since A makes a customer sale for $175 – not $25. [The key issue is the sale must be recorded at the actual amount which the customer remits].

B. Gross basis, since recording only the net amount makes it impossible for one to determine the gross margin on the sale. [The key issue is providing full disclosure of a revenue transaction.]

C. Net basis; since A does not take title to the product, A is making the sale for Co. T rather than for itself. [The key issue is that A serves as T's agent and can only record the agent's commission – not the entire amount of the sale.]

D. Net basis, since A does not bear the risk of not collecting. [The key issue is that the risk of loss is borne by Co. T; since A bears no risk, the gross revenue is earned by T, rather than A].

II. Circle the appropriate answer which best indicates the importance that you placed on each issue in making your decision.

	Very Important		Moderately Important		Not Important
Revenue recorded at amount remitted by customer	5	4	3	2	1
Full disclosure of pertinent details of transaction	5	4	3	2	1
As an agent, A should only record the commission	5	4	3	2	1
The firm bearing the risk should record the gross revenue	5	4	3	2	1

Comments:

RESULTS OF TEST

Tables 1, 2 and 3 summarize the responses to each case. (The author has compiled similar tables that focus on each class that took the test. These are available upon request). Table 1 reflects the responses of University of Montevallo (UM) students; all of these are undergraduate students. Table 2 reveals the responses of the Case Western Reserve (CW) intermediate accounting class, and Table 3 shows the results of the Case Western Reserve graduate accounting class. A study of the data reveals insights into each case. Case No. 1 deals with the importance of following a company's normal business policies in recording revenue. The majority of students from both universities correctly focused on this important criterion. In weighing the importance of the criteria, UM and CW graduate students considered the normal policies factor (answer choice C) as the most important of the criteria, both groups giving it a mean score of 3.8. CW intermediate students also weighed "normal policies" heavily with a mean of 3.7. Surprisingly, among the UM students, the principles class focused more heavily on this factor than the upper level classes. SAB 101 clearly states that a firm's normal business policies will be a key factor in determining whether revenue should be recognized. In addition, the intermediate students from both UM and CW believed that revenue could be recognized because of the high probability of the sales transaction

Table 1. Combined Responses of UM Students to Revenue Cases.

Case	Response Frequency Percentages					Mean Weighting				
	A	B	C	D	E	A	B	C	D	E
1	25	35	57	18	NA	2.9	3.1	3.8	2.7	NA
2	40	66	13	19	NA	3.5	4.2	2.3	2.2	NA
3	52	17	48	33	NA	3.8	2.6	3.5	3.0	NA
4	56	61	36	39	NA	3.3	3.5	2.9	2.7	NA
5	65	23	52	6	NA	3.8	2.3	3.3	1.7	NA
6	48	49	13	22	29	3.5	3.4	2.1	2.6	2.8
7	13	52	89	NA	NA	2.3	3.3	4.6	NA	NA
8	40	48	15	17	NA	2.9	3.3	2.3	2.7	NA
9	7	56	69	25	13	2.3	3.8	3.6	2.6	2.1
10	35	19	17	17	81	3.2	2.4	2.5	2.7	4.3
11	6	6	84	37	NA	2.0	2.0	4.3	3.1	NA

Table 2. Responses of CW Intermediate Students to Revenue Cases.

Case	Response Frequency Percentages					Mean Weighting				
	A	B	C	D	E	A	B	C	D	E
1	38	25	44	19	NA	3.8	3.3	3.7	2.6	NA
2	53	40	7	7	NA	3.6	3.7	2.4	2.4	NA
3	38	31	56	13	NA	3.5	3.1	3.7	2.2	NA
4	50	44	31	19	NA	3.5	3.4	3.5	2.4	NA
5	50	31	38	0	NA	3.5	2.7	3.5	1.6	NA
6	31	38	6	13	44	3.1	3.1	2.5	2.9	3.5
7	27	40	60	NA	NA	3.7	3.2	3.9	NA	NA
8	6	44	19	31	NA	2.9	3.5	3.5	3.5	NA
9	13	25	56	0	25	3.1	4.0	3.9	2.9	3.6
10	19	6	13	13	69	3.3	2.5	3.0	2.8	4.0
11	6	6	81	25	NA	2.6	2.7	4.2	3.8	NA

Table 3. Responses of CW Graduate Students to Revenue Cases.

Case	Response Frequency Percentages					Mean Weighting				
	A	B	C	D	E	A	B	C	D	E
1	11	21	63	21	NA	3.4	3.3	3.8	3.0	NA
2	63	58	0	5	NA	4.2	4.4	2.1	2.1	NA
3	21	32	79	47	NA	3.4	3.2	4.4	3.6	NA
4	42	53	26	26	NA	3.3	3.7	3.5	2.4	NA
5	37	21	68	21	NA	3.2	2.7	4.2	2.7	NA
6	26	32	16	53	21	3.2	3.4	2.7	3.8	3.4
7	47	26	47	NA	NA	3.7	3.3	3.5	NA	NA
8	42	47	21	21	NA	2.8	3.6	3.2	3.3	NA
9	0	53	63	16	5	2.3	4.2	4.2	2.7	2.4
10	26	16	16	21	47	3.7	2.7	2.7	2.4	3.9
11	5	5	90	26	NA	2.0	2.4	4.6	3.7	NA

being approved and also because the goods had been shipped to the customer. Intermediate students may be prone to focus on the probability of a transaction occurring due to the emphasis given to contingent liabilities and SFAS No. 5 in most intermediate courses. Case No. 2 presents a consignment transaction, and the student is queried as to whether revenue recognition is appropriate. Most students correctly rejected the idea of recognizing revenue, citing that legal title had not transferred and that the transaction was only a consignment. All classes concentrated heavily on the lack of transfer of legal title. The UM auditing students and the CW graduate students concentrated more on the consignment issue than did the other groups.

Case No. 3 involved a purported sale that was obtained when the seller entered a side agreement giving the purchaser the right to return the merchandise; specifying that payment was contingent on the customer's reselling the product; and stating that the purchaser is not liable for damages or theft while the product is awaiting resale. Despite the side agreement, a majority (52%) of the UM students focused on who had legal title; however, a significant percentage (48%), comprised mainly of upper level students, realized that the contingency of customer resale negated immediate recognition of revenue. As with case 2, the combined UM students decided that legal title was the most important of the criteria (mean of 3.8), although UM auditing students focused most heavily on the contingent resale situation and on the fact that ownership risks did not transfer to the buyer. While CW intermediate students concentrated heavily on the contingent resale factor, and on the issue of legal title, they failed to recognize the importance of the failure to transfer ownership risks. The CW graduate students weighted all decision factors at a mean of 3 or higher; however, they correctly concentrated most heavily on the contingency issue and the "ownership risks" factor. It appears that, in this side agreement scenario, the more mature students are able to analyze the factors more effectively. The author believes that side agreement issues should be given more emphasis in the lower level classes.

The fourth case presented a bill and hold situation where the purchaser requested, due to a temporary lack of storage space, that shipment be delayed for 20 days. However, the seller did not segregate the purchased goods from other inventories, thus allowing these particular goods to be sold to other customers. The answer choices provided several possible reasons why the transaction should not be recorded as revenue. In justifying nonrecognition of revenue, the UM students were closely split between two key issues: (1) the goods were not shipped (61%); (2) the goods were not segregated (56%). Again, the more advanced students focused more heavily on the failure to segregate the merchandise as being the best reason why revenue should not be recognized immediately. The combined UM students considered the fact that the seller still had physical possession (not shipped) to be slightly more important (3.5 mean) than the failure to segregate the merchandise (3.3 mean). The CW students were also focusing on the shipment and segregation factors, with the CW graduate students focusing more heavily on the fact that the goods had not been shipped. The CW intermediate students considered the failure to segregate the goods to be slightly more important than the shipment issue.

Case 5 involves another bill and hold transaction where the customer submits a December 31 purchase order, but requests shipment on February 1. Here, the customer's reason for ordering the goods is to "get in line" early to reduce the risk of not getting a February purchase of a good that is in tight supply. As with Case 4, the student is asked to choose a reason why revenue recognition in December is not appropriate. Most students believed that the customer's request of a delayed shipment was the critical issue. Again, the UM advanced auditing students and the CW graduate students were more on target, as they emphasized the failure to transfer ownership risks to the buyer as being the primary reason why revenue should not be recorded immediately. Unfortunately, only 6% of the combined UM students, and none of the CW intermediate students, correctly viewed the customer's lack of a critical reason for requesting a delayed shipment to be important. The SEC states that the customer must have a substantive business purpose for delaying the shipment before revenue recognition can be considered; only 21% of the CW graduate students focused on the customer's reason for the delayed shipment. These results may indicate the need for more emphasis on bill and hold transactions, perhaps at the intermediate level, in the accounting curriculum.

In case 6, a customer makes a 20% downpayment and requests that the item be placed on layaway. The customer knows that the deposit will be forfeited unless full payment is made within 90 days. The transaction does not involve a note or any other fixed commitment to pay, nor does risk of ownership transfer to the customer while the merchandise is on layaway. The students were asked when revenue should be recognized. The UM responses were closely split between two choices: when the product was released to the customer and the proportion of the cash received; i.e. recognize 20% of the revenue when the downpayment is made. The majority of UM students failed to focus on the two critical issues; namely, there was no fixed commitment to purchase nor were the risks of ownership transferred. Both of these latter issues are emphasized in the SEC's discussion of layaway transactions in SAB No. 101. In contrast, 44% of the CW intermediate students correctly selected the failure to transfer ownership risks as a key factor; however, they did not focus on the fixed commitment factor. A majority of the CW graduate students emphasized the fixed commitment factor and weighted it most heavily among the five choices with a mean of 3.8. The graduate class also considered the ownership risk factor to be important and weighted it at 3.4.

In case 7, a customer joins a health club and pays a non-refundable up-front fee to join the club. The customer will pay additional usage fees each month. How should the club account for the up-front fee? The majority (89%) of the UM students believed that the up-front fee could be recognized immediately as revenue because it was non-refundable. The refundability criterion also received the highest importance weighting of 4.6. Unfortunately, only a small minority of UM students believed that revenue should be recognized as services were provided to the customer. A majority of the CW intermediate students also focused on "non-refundability" and weighted this factor at 3.9. In contrast, 47% of the graduate students correctly opted to recognize revenue over the period that the services would be provided. They also gave this choice their highest weighting of 3.7. Unfortunately, 47% of the graduate class also dwelled on the non-refundability issue and weighted this factor at 3.5; thus, all of the classes believed that "non-refundability" of up-front fees was a critical issue. The SEC staff's position is clear; when a company sells a service that will be provided over time, revenue recognition should occur over the period that the services are provided.

Case 8 involves a discount retailer who, for an up-front membership fee, enters into an agreement whereby customers can buy merchandise at discount prices. While the entire fee is paid in advance, the customer has the right to cancel and request a full refund at any time during the term of the agreement. The retailer has reliable historical data indicating that 40% of the customers terminate the agreement and request a refund. Students were asked whether the membership fee may be recognized as revenue at the outset of the arrangement. Most students from all three groups believed that immediate revenue recognition was proper. The most common response was that the anticipated 60% retention amount warranted immediate revenue recognition. In addition, a significant number of students believed that all of the membership fee could be recorded as revenue immediately since a new customer had been convinced to join the shopping arrangement. Notably, 43% of the UM auditing students preferred to defer revenue recognition, questioning whether the sales price is fixed when the customer has the right to terminate the contract and receive a cash refund. This view is more in line with the SEC position in SAB 101, although the SEC will permit immediate revenue recognition in certain situations.

In case 9, a lessor is confronted with the question of whether to recognize rental revenue where an additional 1% will be received if the lessee (a retailer) exceeds $25 million in sales. The retailer will probably exceed the $25 million figure. The students' predominant view was that revenue recognition was premature until the contingent event, meeting the minimum sales figure, had occurred. A significant number of students, however, believed that immediate revenue recognition was improper due to the inability to quantify the additional revenue that might be earned. While these views prevailed among all three groups, SAB 101 states that contingent rentals should not be recognized until the customer's net sales actually exceed $25 million. The SEC staff concluded that it was inappropriate to recognize revenue based upon the probability of an event being achieved.

In case 10, a manufacturer is selling a unique, "first-of-its-kind" medical device to doctors and hospitals. Customers may return the device for any reason within six months, and because of the new and unique device, acceptance of the product is difficult to determine. The students must decide if revenue may be recognized when the product is shipped. A huge majority from all three groups believed that immediate revenue recognition was proper as long as any returns were promptly recorded. A lesser, but significant (35%), number concluded that immediate recognition was warranted because legal title transferred at the shipping date. Only a small minority of students, equally distributed among the three groups, correctly focused on the new, unique nature of the product and the difficulty in estimating the extent of the returns. These tentative results indicate that instructors should give more emphasis to return transactions and accounting guidance provided by SFAS No. 48.

Case 11 describes a company that sells goods on its Internet site that belong to another firm. The product was sold for $175, of which the Internet firm received $25. The Internet firm took the order and authorization from a credit card company and passed the order on to the other firm, who shipped the goods to the customer. The Internet firm did not take title to the goods or assume any ownership risks. The students were asked whether the Internet firm should record revenue on a gross basis of $175 or on a net basis of $25. A huge majority of the students believed that the Internet firm should only recognize the net amount of the revenue. Most students focused on the seller's role as an agent although many upper level students also believed that only the firm bearing the risk of loss could record revenue on a gross basis.

TEACHING NOTES

Administration of Test

After handing out the test, I read the instructions aloud to the students. I wanted to be as certain as possible that they understood that I wanted their choice or choices of the most appropriate answers. I also wanted them to understand the purpose of Section II of each case; namely, to determine the student's perception of the importance of each criterion.

One of my main concerns involved the content of the exam. The majority of these cases involve transactions that students have not been exposed to in the classroom. For this reason, I did not choose to grade the test as a regular examination. Instead, I informed the students that I was interested in learning more about their conceptions of revenue, and would give them a maximum of ten bonus points if they took this "special revenue exam".

My next concern was motivation. I wanted the students to give their best effort, and not quickly go through the cases in a perfunctory manner. To reduce this risk, I added a comments section. Several days before the exam, I informed the students that I wanted them to explain why particular answers were not appropriate. I told them that their grade of 1 to 10 bonus points would depend, not so much on their answer choices, but rather on my perception of the effort put into the examination. I emphasized that I would be examining the discussion section closely to determine this effort, and therefore, their grade.

I gave the students the entire class period of 75 minutes to complete the examination. This appears to be ample time to read, consider, and respond to the eleven cases. Many of the intermediate and advanced auditing students took the entire class period, and discussed their answers thoroughly. The principles students took less time. I would estimate that the typical principles student took about 50 minutes to complete the exam. Nevertheless, I was pleased with the effort given as reflected in their discussion; only two or three students seem to short-change the discussion section.

I also encouraged the students to ask any questions that they might have concerning the facts of the case. Only a few students, mostly in the principles class, had questions, and these were mainly to request verification of their interpretation of the case facts. I concluded that the lack of questions meant that the cases were presented clearly. In addition, my examination of the students' comments indicated that they understood the case situation.

Implications for Instruction

The answer choices in Part I of each case focus on certain themes. For example, should revenue recognition hinge on the cash receipt, on physical possession of the product, or on transfer of legal title to the product? A summary of the conceptual themes and the cases in which they are included are as follows:

Cash receipts: Cases 4, 6, 8 and 9
Physical possession: Cases 1, 2, 4, and 6
Transfer of legal title: Cases 2, 3, and 10
Transfer of risk of ownership: Cases 3, 5, 6, and 11
Presence of uncertainties/contingencies: Cases 1, 3, 4, 8, 9 and 10

I have observed that some principles students cling to the idea that revenue recognition depends on whether the cash has been received; thus, four of the cases used the cash receipts factor as a possible answer. As suspected, many of the principles students and even a disturbing number of UM intermediate students focused on this issue. Even worse, in cases 6 (layaway sales) and 8 (up-front membership fee to a discount retailer), the upper level auditing students believed that the cash receipt was a key decision criterion. Case Western students also placed a surprising amount of emphasis on the cash receipt factor, although not to the extent of the UM students. For example, in the layaway (case 6) and up-front fee (case 8) situations, significant percentages of both CW intermediate and graduate students focused heavily on the cash receipt issue.

Four of the cases cited physical possession as a critical criterion. As with cash receipts, students focused heavily on this issue. The UM students disregarded physical possession as a key factor only in the consignment situation (case 2). In the layaway (case 6) and bill and hold situations (cases 4 and 5), many UM students from all three classes focused on physical possession in making their revenue decisions. While not placing as much emphasis on physical possession as UM students, both CW classes placed significant emphasis on the "possession" factor. This was evident especially in case 4 (bill and hold) where large percentages of both intermediate and graduate classes based their revenue decision on physical possession of the merchandise.

Distinguishing between substance and form has always been a difficult area for accountants in analyzing transactions. Thus, I included the transfer of legal title as a possible answer choice in three of the case scenarios. In the consignment situation (case 2), the students correctly identified legal title as a key issue; however, in cases 3 and 10 (a side agreement and a return situation), many students from all of the classes focused on the transfer of legal title which led them to incorrect revenue decisions.

In a purported sales transaction, one of the critical factors to be evaluated is the extent to which risks of ownership have transferred from the seller to the buyer. The transfer of ownership risks was involved in four cases. The UM principles students consistently under-emphasized this factor in making their revenue decisions, thus sending a strong signal that more emphasis should be placed on the risk transfer issue in principles classes. The intermediate students, both from UM and CW, emphasized this issue to a considerable degree in almost every case; only in case 3 (the side agreement) did the CW intermediate students fail to focus on the risk transfer. As for the upper level students, both the UM auditing class and the CW graduate class consistently focused on the transfer of ownership risks. Thus, based on these limited results, it appears that most upperlevel students do correctly consider the transfer of risks when making revenue decisions.

Six of the cases included some type of major uncertainty, such as a contingent event, which enveloped the revenue decision. An analysis of the student responses reflects a "mixed bag" with some prudent decisions and yet some major errors in judgment. My main concerns are with cases 8 and 10 (the upfront fee and sales return cases). In case 8, the UM principles students did not focus on the contingency issue, although the UM auditing students placed heavy emphasis on the contingency factor. In case 10, all student groups failed to focus adequately on the uncertainty surrounding the task of estimating customer returns on the new, unique product. Instead of emphasizing the contingency, all of the groups were concentrating on the legal title issue.

In conclusion, I believe this revenue test provides valuable feedback concerning the conceptual framework that students, at various levels, use in making revenue decisions. Students clearly have a tendency to allow cash receipt information to influence their decisions. In addition, the test results indicate that physical possession of inventory and possession of legal title are two factors that students often emphasize; yet these criteria should be used with caution in making revenue decisions. Instructors must develop pedagogical methods that instill skepticism in the student so that, on learning that legal title has transferred, they don't automatically jump to the conclusion that revenue should be recognized. We must emphasize the importance of analyzing the economic substance of a transaction. In other situations, unfamiliarity with specific SEC guidelines undermined student decisions. For example, students fared poorly on the bill and hold cases where knowledge of SEC pronouncements would have been beneficial. This latter finding may reflect a need for increased classroom attention to critical SEC releases and staff bulletins. With extra attention to these areas of indicated misperceptions, future students will hopefully obtain a stronger grasp of revenue concepts.

REFERENCES

American Institute of Certified Public Accountants (1999). *Audit Issues in Revenue Recognition*. www.aicpa.org
Carmichael, D. R. (1999). Hocus Pocus Accounting. *Journal of Accountancy*, (October), 59–65.
Feroz, E. H., Park, K., & Pastena, V. S. (1991). The Financial and Market Effects of the SEC's Accounting and Auditing Enforcement Releases. *Journal of Accounting Research*, 29(Suppl.), 107–148.
Levitt, A. (1998). The Numbers Game. *The CPA Journal*, (December), 14–19.
Moody, L. (2000). SAB 101's Requirements for Revenue Recognition. *The CPA Journal*, (May), 68–72.
Phillips, Jr., T. J., Luehlfing, M. S., & Daily, C. M. (2001). The Right Way to Recognize Revenue. *Journal of Accountancy*, (June), 39–46.

Sack, R. J. (1987). The SEC and the Profession: An Exercise in Balance. *Research in Accounting Regulation, 1*, 167–175.

Securities and Exchange Commission (1999). *SEC Staff Accounting Bulletin: No. 101 – Revenue Recognition in Financial Statements.* www.sec.gov

Securities and Exchange Commission (2000). *Staff Accounting Bulletin No. 101: Revenue Recognition in Financial Statements – Frequently Asked Questions and Answers.* www.sec.gov

Steinberg, R., & Van Brunt, R. (2000). 1999 AICPA National Conference on SEC Developments. *The CPA Journal*, (March), 32–38.

Turner, L. E., & Godwin, J. H. (1999). Auditing, Earnings Management and International Accounting Issues at the Securities and Exchange Commission. *Accounting Horizons*, (September), 281–297.

THE LEGALITY OF THE SEC'S AUTHORITY TO REGULATE THE SCOPE OF SERVICES FOR CPA FIRMS

Mark A. Segal and Frank R. Urbancic

ABSTRACT

On June 27, 2000 the SEC proposed a rule to address auditor indepen-dence requirements and impose restrictions on the scope of non-audit services offered by CPA firms. The restrictions, as initially proposed by the SEC, had the potential to greatly impact the public accounting profes-sion, especially the Big-Five CPA firms. However, following an extensive public hearing process, the SEC reached a compromise agreement with the accounting profession on November 15, 2000 and approved a modi-fied version of its original proposal.

The purpose of this study is to assess whether the SEC has the legal authority to regulate the scope of services offered by CPA firms. The assess-ment considers whether there is either a clear set of directives or prior court case(s) that empowers the SEC to establish regulations in the area of services offered by CPAs. An understanding of the parameters of the SEC's authority is important as the Commission may revisit the issue of independence in the foreseeable future.

Research in Accounting Regulation, Volume 15, pages 191–202.
ISBN: 0-7623-0841-9

INTRODUCTION

Since the end of World War II, CPA firms have realized a significant growth in revenue by increasing the scope of non-audit services (NAS) which they provide. This growth has been accompanied by persistent questions concerning auditor independence for CPA firms that perform NAS for their audit clients. According to Magill and Previts (1991), "the belief that a firm should not audit and at the same time provide other services to the same client is a concern when and if, in fact or in public perception, a loss of independence occurs." Nevertheless, in 2000 the Securities Exchange Commission (SEC) proposed Rule S7-13-00, *Revision of the Commission's Auditor Independence Requirements*, to establish restrictions on the scope of NAS offered by CPA firms that audit publicly regulated corporations. Specifically, the proposed rule identified certain NAS that, if provided to an audit client, the SEC believed would impair an auditor's independence. The restrictions on scope of services, as initially proposed by the SEC, had the potential to greatly impact the public accounting profession, especially the Big-Five CPA firms. However, following an extensive public hearing process, the SEC reached a compromise agreement with the accounting profession and approved a modified version of its original proposal.

The purpose of this study is to assess whether the SEC has the legal authority to regulate the scope of services offered by CPA firms. The assessment considers whether there is either a clear set of directives or prior court case(s) that empowers the SEC to establish regulations in the area of services offered by CPAs. It is not the purpose of the study to determine whether the rule is needed, nor to evaluate the merits of the rule with regard to NAS. The study is organized in four sections. First, an overview of the initial rule proposed by the SEC and a discussion of the circumstances surrounding the NAS controversy that preceded the SEC's action is presented. The second section identifies key differences approved in the final rule in comparison to the proposed rule. Next, the legal issues regarding the SEC rule are reviewed in the third section. The final section presents relevant concluding observations and comments.

RULE PROPOSED BY THE SEC

On June 27, 2000 the SEC voted unanimously to issue a proposed rule to address auditor independence requirements, Rule S7-13-00. The proposal described certain relationships that have the potential to impair the independence of an accountant with respect to an audit client. The rule addressed financial and employment relationships between auditors, including members of their family, and audit clients, as well as, relationships between auditors and their audit clients where the auditor provides certain NAS. The provisions of the rule pertaining to NAS resulted from an increasing concern by the SEC for the dramatic growth in the nature, number, and monetary value of NAS provided by audit firms. According to Arthur Levitt (2000), Chairman of the SEC:

> Where management consulting services for traditional audit firms once represented just a small portion of their total revenue, today it accounts for *one-half*. Meanwhile, revenues from auditing services have dropped to only a *third* of total revenues. As a result, auditors who also provide consulting services for their audit clients must now serve *two* masters: a public obligation to shareholders, and a professional duty to management. And when the two come into conflict, the independent audit – dwarfed by the more lucrative consulting businesses – too often may be compromised (p. 2).

Therefore, though not intended to represent an all-inclusive list, the SEC's proposed rule identified ten different types of NAS that cause independence to be impaired for audit purposes.The SEC proposed the rule as an amendment to Rule 2.01 of Regulation S-X and Item 9 of Schedule 14A under the Securities Exchange Act of 1934. Proposed paragraph (b) of Rule 2.01 gave clarification to the general standard for auditor independence which recognizes that an auditor must be independent in fact and appearance, and that appearance is measured by reference to reasonable investors knowing all the relevant circumstances. To make the general standard more specific in paragraph (b), the SEC identified four governing principles for determining when an auditor is not independent. The principles prescribe that a lack of independence results when an auditor: has a mutual or conflicting interest with the audit client; audits the accountant's own work; functions as management or an employee of the audit client, or; acts as an advocate for the audit client.

Though the SEC proposal stated that independence in fact is inseparable from the appearance of independence, the aforementioned principles serve primarily as a framework for evaluating the appearance of independence. Appearance and perception are at the very core of the NAS controversy since, according to Barry Melancon (2000), President and CEO of the AICPA, there has never actually been a proven instance where the provision of NAS to an audit client has resulted in an audit failure. The concern with the impact of NAS on the appearance of independence first gained prominent attention in the late 1970s during Congressional hearing investigations into the accounting profession. The Metcalf Senate Subcommittee in 1976 and the Moss House of Representatives Subcommittee in 1978 expressed serious reservations about the propriety of providing NAS to audit clients. Though an actual case of impaired audit independence in relation to providing NAS was never produced during the hearings, the Congressional committees expressed an opinion that it would be best if the practice of rendering NAS for audit clients were to be discontinued. However, at that time no federal regulations were enacted to restrict NAS. Instead, the SEC responded by promulgating Accounting Series Release 250 in 1978 to require that proxy statements of public corporations disclose fees paid for NAS expressed as a percent of total fees paid to their audit firms. Later, in 1981, the SEC withdrew its requirements for proxy statement disclosures relative to NAS fees.

Research concerning perceptions about audit independence relative to NAS, at best, has yielded mixed results. Kinney (1999) states that he reviewed 20 years of empirical research on investors' attitudes and concerns about independence and found virtually no evidence that investors share the NAS concerns of regulators. Conversely, as discussed in Pany and Reckers (1984), several previous surveys have indicated that financial statement users question CPA independence when NAS are performed for audit clients. Instead of a conventional survey approach, Pany and Reckers (1984), McKinley, Pany and Reckers (1985), and Pany and Reckers (1988), relied on a controlled experiment methodology to assess the impact of NAS on audit independence and from the results concluded that auditor provided NAS exerts little, if any, effect on perceptions of auditor independence.

In 1994 the staff of the SEC reconsidered the effects of NAS relative to independence and issued a *Staff Report on Auditor Independence*. The 1994 *Report* noted that most of the growth in NAS until then was attributable to services provided to parties other than audit clients. The staff concluded that no regulatory changes were necessary at that time, but added that the SEC would continue to remain alert to the possible development of an independence problem relative to NAS. However, in 1997 and continuing through 1999, corporations began to restate their audited annual financial reports at an accelerating pace. According to McNamee, Dwyer and Schmitt (2000) this alarming trend served to convince the SEC that auditors had relaxed their vigilance and grown "cozier with management." Thus, the SEC concluded it was time for regulatory action and, as a result, Rule S7-13-00 was proposed.

RULE APPROVED BY THE SEC

On November 15, 2000 the SEC approved a modified version of its proposed rule on auditor independence. The approved rule is generally similar to the proposed rule in terms of the provisions related to investments in audit clients by auditors or their family members, as well as, employment relationships between auditors or their family members and audit clients. However, the SEC revised its restrictions on NAS in its final version of the rule.

As discussed in the previous section, the SEC had proposed four governing principles for determining when an auditor is not independent. However, since these principles could be broadly misconstrued so as to affect services that do not impair audit independence, the SEC decided to leave the principles out of the rule and incorporate them only as a preliminary note. Another important change concerns the SEC's original proposal to establish as an inseparable principle that an auditor must be independent in fact and appearance. Following public hearings on its proposed rule the SEC concluded that an application of standards for assessing the appearance of independence would most likely be very subjective. Therefore, the Commission's final rule separates the two concepts to recognize that independence is impaired *either* when an auditor is not independent in fact, *or* when, in light of all relevant facts and circumstances, a reasonable investor would conclude that an auditor would not be capable of acting without bias.

The approved rule can also be differentiated from the proposed rule in terms of the types of NAS that are subject to restriction. Seven of the services identified in the proposed rule are already restricted by existing regulations. Therefore, the approved rule codifies the restrictions. These seven services are: (1) bookkeeping or other services related to the audit client's accounting records or financial statements, (2) appraisal or valuation services or fairness opinions, (3) actuarial services, (4) management functions, (5) human resources, (6) broker dealer services, and (7) legal services. In contrast, the approved rule omits the restriction that was originally proposed with respect to expert services. In the proposed rule the SEC had expressed that an accountant's independence would be regarded as impaired if an accountant renders or supports expert opinions for the audit client in legal, administrative or regulatory filings or proceedings. The SEC had held that the appearance of client advocacy and corresponding appearance of mutual interest created by providing expert services were sufficient basis for a belief that audit independence was impaired. However, as a result of separating independence in fact from appearance as set forth in the final rule the restriction pertaining to expert service was not adopted.

In its approved rule the SEC took a compromise position compared to its proposed position with regard to two types of NAS. First, concerning services related to financial information systems design and implementation, originally the SEC had proposed that an accountant is not independent if the accountant designs or implements a system that generates information that is significant to an audit client's financial statements taken as a whole. However, the SEC's final rule allows an accountant to provide such services when criteria are met by audit client management to establish that management is primarily responsible for the internal control system, making significant decisions related to the project, and determining the adequacy of the financial reporting system. Also, the total amount of fees paid for such services must be disclosed in the annual proxy statement.

The second type of service for which the approved rule is less restrictive than the proposed rule concerns internal audit services. In the original proposal the SEC declared that independence is impaired when an auditor performs certain internal audit services for an audit client. By contrast, the final rule allows an audit firm to perform up to 40%, measured in terms of hours, of an audit client's internal audit work. The aforementioned restriction does not apply to internal audit services that are unrelated to accounting controls, financial systems, financial statements or operational auditing. Also, the rule established an exception for providing internal audit services to smaller businesses by excluding companies with less than $200 million in assets.

Another key difference between the proposed rule and the final rule concerns the definition of an affiliate of an accounting firm. In the proposed rule an affiliate includes any person controlling, controlled by, or under common control with the accounting firm, shareholders of more than 5% of the firm's voting securities, and entities 5% or more of whose securities are owned by the accounting firm. The rule also includes any officer, director, partner, or co-partner of any of the foregoing entities or persons. Thus, this broad definition would prohibit virtually all business associations or relationships for accounting firms. For example, accounting firms could not have alliances with each other, and joint ventures with non-audit clients would also be limited. However, in reaching its compromise with the accounting profession the SEC omitted the overly broad definition of affiliate from the final rule. Instead, the Commission will continue to scrutinize these situations by reference to existing regulations.

The approved rule also establishes disclosure requirements for providing additional information about NAS in the annual proxy statements filed by publicly regulated corporations. First, the amount of fees paid for audit services, information/technology services, and all other services provided to a corporation by its audit firm must be disclosed. Second, the proxy statement must include a statement to indicate that the corporate audit committee has considered whether the provision of NAS is compatible with maintaining the auditor's independence. Finally, corporations must disclose the percentage hours worked on the audit engagement by persons other than the audit firm's full time employees, if that figure is in excess of 50%. Though the SEC is empowered to establish standards of reporting by publicly regulated corporations, including the aforementioned disclosure requirements, the question that remains for examination in the next section is whether the SEC has legal authority to regulate the scope of services offered by CPA firms to their audit clients.

LEGAL ISSUES REGARDING THE SEC RULE

Despite the compromise reached between the accounting profession and the SEC there remains concern over the extent of the SEC's authority to define independence and establish rules pursuant to which a lack of independence may be found. The importance of resolving the parameters of the SEC's authority in this regard continues to be important as the Commission may revisit the issue of independence in the foreseeable future. Legal issues raised by the SEC's issuance of the rule in need of address are:

(1) The authority of the SEC to issue the rule concerning independence.
(2) If such authority exists, whether the language of the rule exceeds the SEC's authority.
(3) Whether the SEC followed appropriate procedure in developing the rule.
(4) Whether the language of the rule satisfies constitutional due process requirements.

Authority to Define Independence

The SEC has broad general authority to promulgate rules and regulations necessary to carry out the provisions of the Securities Act, the Exchange Act, Public Utility Act and the Trust Indenture Act. According to Section 23(a) of the Exchange Act (15 USCS No. 78w(a)) in carrying out this role the SEC is required to consider the impact of any rule or regulation on competition, and no rule or regulation is to be promulgated which would impose a burden on capital, not necessary or appropriate in furtherance of the provisions of the Act. While the SEC has broad general authority to issue rules and regulations in furtherance of the Acts, such authority is not unbridled. One inherent limitation is that any such rule or regulation must be based upon the language of the statute. Thus, it is believed that the SEC has the general authority to issue rules or regulations that define the term "independent" with respect to accountants who certify financial statements filed with the Commission. The setting of such definition must, however, be consistent with the relevant Act and within the sphere of the SEC's authority. Historically the expression has been construed by the Commission and accounting profession to mean that the accountant must be independent in fact and appearance. While after the facts findings of a violation relate to whether the accountant was factually independent, the appearance of independence has been largely defined in terms of financial relationships with the client or holding of a position with the client.

Language of the Rule

If one accepts the fact that the Commission has general authority to define "independent" consistent with its powers under the Securities Acts, the question then must be addressed as to whether the Commission acted and rendered such definition under the final rule consistent with its authority. Questions as to the SEC's authority in this regard relate to the SEC's jurisdictional authority, its ability to restrict multidisciplinary practice, and its ability to define terms which appear to have already been well defined by Congress.

(1) Jurisdictional Authority – The SEC lacks authority to issue rules governing the accounting profession. Its authority extends only to the independent audit function for companies which file financial statements with the Commission. In many respects the rule as issued suggests a policing effort that goes well beyond this audit function and impacts aspects of the public accounting profession not involved in the rendering of such audits. If the rule only applies to the audit function under the purview of the SEC's authority, the question arises as to whether the Commission has the authority to restrict the NAS that may be rendered by accountants under its authority, while other accountants, e.g. those rendering audit services for non-SEC registrants, are not subject to such restriction. For such other accountants to be subject to similar regulation it may be necessary for other regulatory bodies to adopt similar rules.

(2) Multidisciplinary Practice – Does the SEC have authority to largely restrict the ability to engage in multidisciplinary practice (MDP)? In this regard the SEC's proposal listed legal services as one of the types of business relationships that may impair independence where ". . . the accounting firm, or a covered person in the firm has a direct or material indirect business relationship with an audit client, an affiliate of an audit client, or either of their officers, directors or shareholders holding a 5% or more interest of the audit client's equity securities." Problematic is a catch-all phrase, however, which leaves open the question of whether the accountant may still be vulnerable to challenge notwithstanding this provision. Legal services under the SEC rules involve the rendering of any service in the jurisdiction which could only be provided by someone licensed to practice law. This provision directly bars the use of certain MDPs. The question therefore being, does the SEC have such authority? At present the question of whether an MDP can be utilized is a question being examined by both the accounting and legal professions. Oversight of each profession has been largely accomplished through self regulation and relevant state agency. If one assumes that the federal government has the authority to regulate MDPs, then a question arises over which agency, if any, has such

authority. In a comment letter to the Commission, former SEC Chairperson Roberta Karmel indicated that regulation of MDPs should be considered a competitive practice issue and, as such, governed by antitrust laws rather than securities laws. Pursuant to this approach, MDPs would not generally be subject to the SEC's regulatory authority.

(3) Terms Defined by Congress – Does the SEC have authority to set forth certain definitions of terms where the meaning of such terms have already been established by Congress? The definition of the term "affiliate" in the proposed rule raised such a question. The term "affiliate" has been previously defined by Congress as applying to reach any person that directly or indirectly controls or holds with the power to vote, 5% or more of the outstanding voting securities of another company, or whose executive leadership overlaps (see Public Utility Act of 1935, Trust Indenture Act of 1939, and Investment Company Act of 1940). According to McKee, in his comment letter to the Commission, the meaning of "affiliate" is expanded by the proposed rule to include:

(a) Any entity that participates in any undertaking in which an accounting firm participates and the parties agree to any shared benefit.
(b) Any entity that provides non-audit services or professional services to an audit client of the accounting firm, if the accounting firm has any equity interest in the entity; has loaned the entity money, shares revenue with the entity; or any covered person in the firm has any direct business relationship with the entity.
(c) Any entity with which the accounting firm is publicly associated by cobranding; using the accounting firm's name, initials or logo; cross selling services; or co-management.

As noted by McKee previously in *American Bankers Association v. SEC*, (1986) the Court held that the SEC lacked authority to deny banks the ability to engage in brokerage services for nonbanking customers based upon the already existent definition of a bank set forth in the 1934 Act. According to the Court the SEC could not use its definitional authority to expand its jurisdiction beyond that accorded it by Congress.

Procedure

In response to the initially proposed rules the AICPA questioned whether the Commission had followed appropriate procedures. In this regard the AICPA expressed the following concerns:

(1) The period for making comments being limited to 75 days; whereas, it was alleged that proposed rules of such magnitude typically are accorded a longer comment period, e.g. 120 days.
(2) There being 400 questions raised by the SEC in its proposal.
(3) The lack of any empirical evidence in support of the proposed rule.
(4) The lack of any cost/benefit analysis concerning the proposed rule.

The success of a challenge to the SEC should it engage in this type rule making procedure is uncertain. The SEC is recognized as a regulatory agency. In this regard it has the authority to issue rules, make adjudications and render sanctions so long as acting within the scope of its authority. Case law indicates that an agency is accorded broad discretion in establishing and applying rules for public participation (*Cities of Stateville v. Atomic Energy Commission*, 1969).

Procedure which should be followed by federal agencies, e.g. the SEC, are set forth in the Administrative Procedures Act (APA) (5 U.S.C. Section 553). The purpose of this procedure is to assure fairness and due consideration of the proposed rule. The APA provides the following general procedural rules:

Pursuant to Section 553 (b), "General notice of proposed rule making shall be published in the Federal Register . . ."

The notice shall include:

(a) A statement of the time, place and nature of the public rule making proceeding
(b) Reference shall be made to legal authority under which the rule is proposed; and
(c) Either terms or the substance of the proposed rule or a description of the subjects and issues involved.

According to Section 553 (c), "After notice is provided the agency shall give interested parties an opportunity to participate in rule making though the submission of written data, views or arguments, with or without an opportunity for an oral hearing."

Section 553(d) provides that notice of the proposed rule shall be made not less than 30 days before the effective date of the proposed rule.

Based upon the broad discretion granted a regulatory agency in determining the manner of public participation, and the SEC appearing to meet the requirements set forth in the Administrative Procedures Act with regard to the proposed rule, a challenge of a rule enacted in such manner based upon procedure would appear difficult to sustain.

Due Process

Did the SEC propose a rule that was susceptible to being considered void for vagueness? According to the Supreme Court a law that is so indeterminate that ordinary individuals must guess at its meaning or application may be held void for vagueness (*Connally v. General Construction Co.*, (1926). Similarly, a statute may be challenged where it lacks sufficient definiteness for enforcement in a nonarbitrary manner (*Big Mama Rag, Inc. v. United States*, (DC Cir. 1980). Certain aspects of the proposed rule are potentially too vague to enable good faith compliance, e.g. the definition of "affiliate" and the language of the "catch-all provision."

CONCLUDING COMMENTS

In the relatively brief period of time between release of the SEC's proposed rule on independence and its approved rule there were continual negotiations with members of the public accounting profession, thousands of written comments, and several days of hearings. Then shortly before its final vote on the rule, the SEC reached an agreement with four of the Big Five accounting firms (KPMG was the exception) and the AICPA. Several key provisions of the approved rule are primarily the result of that compromise.

The independence controversy may very well have signaled a new era of heightened vigilance by the SEC with regard to accountants. A characteristic of this era could be highly aggressive and confrontational tactics by the SEC. Thus, there is cause for concern by the accounting profession that the independence issue of 2,000 may have been an important first battle as prelude to a war between the regulated and the regulators. The arrival of this era is untimely for an accounting profession that is already experiencing other difficulties, especially with regard to attracting a sufficient number of competent qualified new entrants to the profession.

REFERENCES

Administrative Procedures Act, 5 USCS Section 553.
American Bankers Association v. SEC, 804 F.2d 739, (DC Cir., 1986).
Big Mama Rag, Inc. v. United States, 631 F.2d 1030, (DC Cir., 1980).
Cities of Stateville v. Atomic Energy Commission, 441 F.2d 759, (1969).
Connally v. General Construction Co., 269 U.S. 385, (1926).
Kinney, W. (March 1999). Auditor Independence: A Burdensome Constraint or Core Value? *Accounting Horizons, 13*, 69–75.

Levitt, A. (September 18, 2000). A Profession at the Crossroads, A Speech to the National Association of State Boards of Accountancy, Boston Massachusetts.

Magill, H., & Previts, G. (1991). *CPA Professional Responsibilities: An Introduction*. Cincinnati, Ohio: South-Western Publishing Company.

McKinley, S., Pany, K., & Reckers, P. (Autumn 1985). An Examination of the Influence of CPA Firm Type, Size, and MAS Provision on Loan Officer Decisions and Perceptions. *Journal of Accounting Research*, 887–896.

McNamee, M., Dwyer, P., & Schmitt, C. (September 25, 2000). Accounting Wars. *Business Week*, 156–166.

Melancon, B. (September 13, 2000). Testimony On Auditor Independence Before the Securities and Exchange Commission.

Metcalf Committee (1976). *U.S. Senate. Subcommittee on Reports, Accounting and Management of the Committee on Government Operations. The Accounting Establishment: A Staff Study*. Washington, D.C.: Government Printing Office.

Moss Committee (1978). *U.S. House of Representatives. Subcommittee on Oversight and Investigation of the Committee on Interstate and Foreign Commerce. Reform and Self-Regulation Efforts of the Accounting Profession*. Washington, D.C.: Government Printing Office.

Pany, K., & Reckers, P. (Spring 1984). Non-Audit Services and Auditor Independence: A Continuing Problem. *Auditing: A Journal of Practice and Theory, 3*, 89–97.

Pany, K. (June 1988). Auditor Performance of MAS: A Study of Its Effects on Decisions and Perceptions. *Accounting Horizons, 2*, 31–38.

Section 23(a) of the *Exchange Act* (15 USCS No. 78w(a)).

Securities and Exchange Commission (June 1978). Disclosure of Relationships with Independent Public Accountants. *Accounting Series Release*, Number 250.

Securities and Exchange Commission (1994). Staff Report on Auditor Independence.

PART III:
PERSPECTIVES

EBITDA!

Julia Grant and Larry Parker

ABSTRACT

This paper presents definitions and explanations of a popular non-GAAP alternative performance measure, EBITDA. The authors provide a consideration and review of several instances where the measure has been employed in recent years. Also they identify several issues and concerns, especially as related to limitations of EBTIDA when used by individual investors. They conclude by identifying the importance of relating EBITDA to GAAP-derived cash flow measures.

EBITDA: 1. {acronym} Earnings Before Interest, Taxes, Depreciation, and Amortization; 2. for some companies, depending on the quarter being reported, Earnings Before Interest, Taxes, Depreciation, Amortization, Preopening/startup Costs, and Extraordinary Items;[1] OR Earnings Before Interest, Taxes, Depreciation, Amortization, CRDA, Indiana regulatory costs, and non-operating expenses;[2] OR other alternatives as desired; 3. an extraction from an accrual accounting income statement, essentially a 'subtotal' from that statement, chosen by the reporting company, and not specified in current GAAP; *pronunciation-e-bit-DUH*

[1] From www.trump.com, Trump Hotels & Casino Resorts, Inc. Reports Fourth-Quarter and Year-end Results, February 14, 1997

[2] From www.trump.com, Trump Hotels & Casino Resorts, Inc. Reports First Quarter 2000 Results, May 12, 2000

There is nothing new about the desire of companies, even industries, to attempt to provide more positive views of earnings than allowed by GAAP. While the right to free speech for business entities permits management to issue pro forma numbers, the determination of reported income in annual reports and filings to governmental agencies must conform to GAAP. Rule 203 of the AICPA's

Research in Accounting Regulation, Volume 15, pages 205–211.

Professional Code of Conduct permits non-GAAP presentation for an individual company *if* GAAP presentation would be misleading. Real estate investment trusts commonly report Funds From Operations (net income plus depreciation) in an effort to make themselves more comparable to other businesses. But currently companies in other industries are using EBITDA and other *pro forma* versions of earnings to present themselves as having more future earning power than is reasonable under GAAP. And companies with real estate operations are moving beyond the basic depreciation adjustment.

There are many reasons why companies are turning to alternative earnings presentations. One is that mergers and acquisitions are extremely important for companies that believe they must continue to grow to attract favorable investor attention. Depreciation of assets marked up to fair value from book value and amortization of goodwill (often more than 50% of assets acquired) hurt profitability of such companies. Pooling has been a method for some companies to avoid such depreciation and amortization expenses, but at the time of this writing, it appears, the pooling option will be eliminated. Perhaps one of the most important reasons EBITDA is used is the difficult economic position of many companies. The financial problems of the technology industry, including dotcoms and telecommunications, are of particular note. Many technology companies are highly leveraged (sometimes at junk bond rates), and hence require high cash flow levels to service interest expense. There is often very large capital investment in long-term technology, creating depreciation expense – and sometimes write-downs. Perhaps the most frustrating aspect of GAAP financial reporting for technology companies is the perceived inability to express the value and importance of intangibles such as their networks, investments in human capital, marketing expenditures, and R&D. Lack of clear guidance by the SEC, FASB and AICPA, combined with attention to alternative performance measures and an expanded Business Reporting Model, probably have exacerbated the use of non-GAAP performance metrics.

The uses of EBITDA and other manipulations of GAAP earnings are problematic for two main reasons. First, there is no standardization for such calculations. Companies may choose as they see fit. For example, EBITDA may include one-time cash charges and write-downs, or not. But the most important difficulty is that there is no additional information provided in the *pro forma* earnings, and such presentations are generally very misleading to investors. All relevant information needed to make the fundamental calculations for EBITDA is already in GAAP financial reports – balance sheet, income statement, cash flow statement, and related notes to the statements.

The measure EBITDA is one estimation of pre-tax, pre-interest operating cash flows under the assumption that changes in working capital accounts are immaterial. In the stable operating company, the receivables, payables, and inventory can reach a steady state, in which the balances vary around some typical operations level. In this situation EBITDA allows the interested investor or analyst to do a quick estimate of what operating cash flow would look like if these assumptions hold. However, such a steady state is very rarely the case, and EBITDA also excludes any measure of capital asset usage. The non-GAAP earnings measures are misleading to current or potential shareholders because they do not represent what will be available to shareholders, since payments to lenders (interest) and governments (taxes), both of whom have priority over shareholders, are disregarded. These earnings calculations provide no information concerning the cost of using current capital assets (or, more to the point, the need for reinvestment in these long term earning assets). EBITDA is merely a sum of selected parts of the income statement, where the selection is at the discretion of the reporting firm. These *pro forma* earnings statements provide no more information than already exists, and such statements are usually misleading. They should not be used.

Accrual accounting net income, from the income statement, automatically incorporates a measure of usage of capital assets in the form of depreciation and amortization. The income statement does not include the working capital change, but that can be determined from the operating cash flow measure in the cash flow statement, or from examining the balance sheets. Operating cash flow reflects any changes in working capital levels, while removing from net income noncash items including depreciation and amortization. Additionally the investing activities section of the cash flow statement provides more details on the acquisition or disposal of capital assets by the firm. These already-mandated disclosures give a more complete picture to the user of the financial information generated within the firm during the reporting period.

EBITDA calculations can be useful within the analysis function when applying detailed financial valuation models that use projected future cash flows if the underlying assumptions make sense as a starting point for this projection exercise. In applying these sorts of models, if there is a planned change in investment in working capital, those plans will be incorporated explicitly as part of the future cash flow projections. Additionally, these models will also incorporate projections of cash outflows needed to maintain or increase the capital assets as required to operate the business under the assumed conditions. So the intermediate calculation, EBITDA, is only one step in applying a valuation model if a firm plans to change investments in working capital and/or capital assets.

The fact that EBITDA is really an intermediate computational component makes it an inappropriate measure to be reported in a stand-alone manner as some firms are doing. The St. Joe Company provides an example of increased use of this measure. The 1997 GAAP financial statements within the St. Joe Company annual report include no EDITDA measure, and incidentally, the company also notes in the Chairman's letter that this company has no debt. In the 1998 annual report, the company indicates its primary focus is now on real estate, has taken on some long-term debt on the balance sheet, and introduces the use of EBITDA as an important measure that appears several places: in the financial highlights with the CEO's Letter, including EBITDA per share figures; and included as a measure in the Management Discussion pages of the operating segments of the company. By 1999 this company does not present the full set of GAAP financial statements within the printed annual report, but rather has adopted the practice of providing printed summary financial information with the 10-K included on CD. The summary financial information provided focuses heavily on EBITDA, with one page providing a report that appears to be an income statement at first glance. However, the entire bottom half of the page is devoted to alternative income measures, several of them EBITDA based, with per share counterparts.

EBITDA may be useful as an internal measure, and some consultants advertise using it as an internal measure of effectiveness of line activities. This may be appropriate if the firm does not want to hold line managers responsible for capital investment, financing, and tax management decisions. But this is purely an internal communication and motivation situation. To report EBITDA externally, particularly with discretionary adjustments included, can be materially misleading. To report EBITDA per share is inappropriate and incomplete because interest and taxes are relevant to stockholders. Capital investment is required to maintain the firm's operating capacity. And discretionary adjustments to EBITDA only further increase the lack of comparability in this measure. One example of this can be found in the quarterly earnings announcements of Trump Hotels and Casino Resorts Inc. on its website. EBITDA is reported each time, but its definition and the adjustments made to earnings vary from quarter to quarter in the earnings announcements.

As the SEC points out in Financial Reporting Release (FRR) 1, section 202.04, "Net income, as a measure of ultimate result, may reasonably be interpreted on a per share basis since no significant claims stand between it and the common stock owner." The same cannot be said for EBITDA and other cash flow numbers. Therefore, the SEC concludes, ". . . per share data other than that relating to net income, net assets, and dividends should be avoided in reporting financial results." FRR 1, section 202.02, also states ". . . the presentation of measures of performance other than net income should be approached with extreme caution. Such measures should not be presented in a manner which gives them greater authority or prominence than conventionally computed earnings."

When the informed analyst or informed investor calculates EBITDA for making cash flow projections, that person will know that a careful projection must include measures of working capital needs and capital investment needs. When the firm itself calculates and reports EBITDA publicly, several problems arise. First, the less informed users of the information may fail to make adequate allowance for the rest of the story. Perhaps more importantly, since EBITDA is non-GAAP, firms are free to define it as best suits their opinion of their position. Without GAAP guidance, companies may be tempted to abuse their discretion thus reporting whatever set of adjustments suits them. The company that reports such measures surely chooses its adjustments for a particular reporting period, using the particular lens that provides a rosier glow than others.

Some critics of net income note that the add-back of goodwill amortization is appropriate because this is not an asset that the firm will necessarily be using cash for in the future. But the cautious analyst might see the existence of a goodwill asset related to an acquisition as signaling the need for future advertising or other sorts of maintenance and development costs to ensure that the company does not waste the value of the purchased goodwill. Any user is free to make such adjustments as needed and depending on the user's opinion of the firm's prospects. But allowing the firms to make the adjustments on an ad hoc basis only creates an opportunity for manipulation. While the informed market will quickly see through such manipulation, less informed investors could be hurt in the process.

EBITDA is appearing regularly in the press, lending undeserved credibility to this ill-defined and inconsistently-used measure. One interesting recent example of the misuse of EBITDA concerns the Philip Morris initial public offering of Kraft, it's wholly-owned subsidiary. The *New York Times* News Service article reporting on this IPO discusses the valuation as a function of EBITDA.[1] Presumably the analysts who worked on this valuation incorporated into their models future needs for working capital and capital asset replacement. It is likely that the experts did assess traditional GAAP measures of earnings, but the article did not report these. In a *Wall Street Journal* article about the telecommunications industry on May 11, 2001,[2] EBITDA is reported and defined as "cash flow." These are only some examples that illustrate the casual use and acceptance of an inferior and possibly misleading measure.

The expanded Business Reporting Model calls for increased and enhanced disclosures that will let the information user understand the business's operations more fully. Firms that report EBITDA under this guise miss the point. EBITDA may be a useful measure to include within the context of an expanded discussion of, say, the existence of intangibles; but what would make that meaningful is the expanded discussion of intangibles, not EBITDA.

If firms are to be allowed to report EBITDA, then the inherent lack of comparability or consistency that is created by allowing them to include the measure or not as they see fit must be addressed. The important goal of a point of comparison is essential for any measure, but there are two ways to create a basis for that comparison. One is cross-sectional, i.e. comparing one company to other similar ones. This goal will be met only if the profession wants to write new standards mandating how EBITDA should be calculated. That is the same thing as determining where other subtotals can appear in the income statement.

The other way to provide a basis for comparison is to compare a company to itself over time. This currently is made difficult by a firm's ability to include or exclude these optional measures as it sees fit. An easier way for the profession to mandate a degree of comparability is to require that if a firm wishes to include a quantitative measure derived from the financial statements, it must be able to include the same measure for the previous reporting period, and it must commit to continuing to report the measure for a specified number of years following. Such an approach will mitigate the inclusion of extra measures only when they provide a favorable appearance.

The potential need for alternative measures of financial performance has been specifically acknowledged in FRR 1, section 202.02, which states that

> If accounting net income computed in conformity with generally accepted accounting principles is not an accurate reflection of economic performance for a company or an industry, it is not an appropriate solution to have each company independently decide what the best measure of its performance should be and present that figure to its shareholders as Truth . . .
>
> Where management believes that the existing conventional income model does not present the results of operations realistically or fully, an explanation of the reasons and a description of possible alternatives which might be used to measure results may be presented . . . accompanied by a careful explanation of the data presented. The adding together of figures derived by different measurement techniques . . . should be avoided as should per share data relating to measures other than net income . . .

For the investing public, given the current lack of consistency, if a firm discloses an EBITDA measure, the best use of that is to compare it with the GAAP-mandated cash from operating activities on the cash flow statement. *If a material difference exists, that is a signal to search for the reason for the difference, either by looking at what is going on in working capital or by determining what the firm has chosen to adjust out of the numbers.* These analyses are made possible by the mandated GAAP financial statements. The careful use of these will provide the investor with the information needed to make an informed decision.

Notwithstanding recent efforts by the Committee on Corporate Reporting of Financial Executives International [FEI] to provide voluntary guidelines, the reliance on custom-crafted measures such as EBITDA, and others currently appearing in the financial press and in financial reports, places an unacceptable burden on information users to recreate any semblance of comparability.

NOTES

1. Schultz, Abby. "Does Big Offering Put Kraft in Company of Giants," *New York Times News Service*, June 9, 2001.
2. Zuckerman, Gregory and Deborah Solomon. "Telecom Debt Debacle Could Lead to Losses of Historic Proportions," *Wall Street Journal*, May 11, 2001, p. A1.

ACKNOWLEDGMENTS

The authors acknowledge the valuable commentary and assistance received during the editorial review process.

DISCLOSURE AND ACCOUNTING IN A GLOBAL MARKET: LOOKING TO THE FUTURE

Lynn E. Turner[1]

ABSTRACT

In today's global economy, many businesses of all sizes operate and conduct business on an international basis. World trade has grown as businesses have extended their operations beyond their own national borders, aided by technological advances in communication and data transmission, and the reduction of national barriers to commerce, trade and travel. Companies have learned that to be successful, they must be able to compete in international markets for both customers and capital.

Quality financial reporting is critical to the efficient operations of the world's capital markets. With the increasing expansion of all market participants beyond their national borders, the challenges of continuing to maintain quality and transparency in financial reporting has increased. Those challenges include protecting investors and international capital markets in an environment of exploding technology and fierce global competition.

These challenges require the coordinated effort of public companies, auditors, standard setters, regulators and governments. They cannot be met by just one or two of these groups. They cannot be met by a rush to "short-term convergence" just for the sake of getting a "quick fix" that

Research in Accounting Regulation, Volume 15, pages 213–237.
© 2002 Published by Elsevier Science Ltd.
ISBN: 0-7623-0841-9

ultimately could cause incredible damage to the markets. Instead, it is critically important that everyone closely coordinate their efforts and devise and execute the changes needed for future success. These are changes that need to be made in a timely fashion, with input from the public, and with appropriate due process. With such an approach, it is hopeful that a quality product will be developed that ensures the continued success of the world's capital markets. That success in turn should result in companies having access to capital that is so important to the global economy.

THE GROWTH IN INTERNATIONAL BUSINESS

In today's global economy, many businesses of all sizes operate and conduct business on an international basis. World trade has grown as businesses have extended their operations beyond their own national borders, aided by technological advances in communication and data transmission, and the reduction of national barriers to commerce, trade and travel. Companies have learned that to be successful, they must be able to compete in international markets for both customers and capital.

During the last decade we also saw the privatization of large sectors of governments, such as telecommunication, utilities and transportation. In less developed countries, such industries and infrastructure within their economies continue to require further development.

Globalization and privatization have created an enormous need and appetite for the capital necessary to fund these undertakings. They have also created, when the risks were appropriate, an eagerness on the part of investors to take part in the resulting global investing opportunities.

At the same time businesses were expanding internationally, the global financial landscape has been undergoing a significant transformation. The world's financial markets have become increasing tied to one another. Financial service firms as well as the capital markets have been building the infrastructure necessary to link the capital markets on a global basis. Events since 1996 such as the Asian and Russian financial crisis, Long Term Capital Management, and the recent events of September 11th, have all shown that our economies have become increasingly interdependent. A major event affecting the financial markets in one part of the world, may very likely affect the markets and investors around the globe. This has caused some to criticize the quality of international financial reporting and the role a lack of transparency played in some of the crisis involving the international markets.

The ability for markets to be efficient and thereby attract capital sufficient to provide the necessary liquidity and depth is dependent in part on their ability to provide investors with high quality transparent information on a consistent and timely basis. That information must be sufficiently credible to investors that they believe it is reliable and are willing to invest based on it. Markets that have experienced events where the credibility of financial information was in question have experienced a flight of capital to safer havens. In addition, as was recently experienced by the Neuer Market, companies may leave or avoid markets where their reputation is affected by a lack of credible financial reporting.[2]

THE INCREASING IMPORTANCE OF THE U.S. MARKETS TO INTERNATIONAL BUSINESS AND ECONOMIES

The public capital markets in the United States have been the largest source of equity capital for funding economic growth in business in the U.S. and internationally and for privatization of governmental entities. At the end of 2000, the total global market capitalization of domestic listed companies on all exchanges was an aggregate of $28 trillion dollars. $14.3 trillion of this or 51% of the worldwide capitalization was invested in companies listed on either the New York Stock Exchange or the Nasdaq Stock Market. The Tokyo, London and Germany exchanges accounted for an aggregate market capitalization of $6.1 trillion of the remaining capitalization.[3]

As corporations and borrowers have expanded into new international markets for their products, they have looked beyond their home country borders for capital. An increasing number of foreign companies routinely raise or borrow capital in U.S. financial markets, and U.S. investors have shown interest in investing in foreign enterprises.

Over the last fifteen years, the number of foreign companies listing in the U.S. capital markets has increased steadily. In 1986 there were 322 foreign registrants. In subsequent years, the number has grown as follows:

1990:   434
1995:   744
2000:   1310

At the end of 2000, these foreign registrants included companies incorporated in 59 countries throughout the world. The U.S. capital markets and investors have provided capital for a wide variety of companies, in many industries and in many countries. The summary of foreign companies registered and reporting with the Securities and Exchange Commission (SEC) as of December 31, 2000 are as follows:[4]

	Number of Companies	Percentage Of Total
Canada	481	36.7
United Kingdom	143	10.9
Israel	101	7.7
Mexico	42	3.2
Netherlands	42	3.2
France	35	2.7
Brazil	34	2.6
Australia	32	2.4
Bermuda	32	2.4
Japan	27	2.1
Chile	26	2.0
Germany	26	2.0
Other countries (9) with 10 To 25 companies	142	10.9
Other countries with 9 or Fewer companies	147	11.2
Total	1310	100.0

The above companies are listed on the New York Stock Exchange (417), the American Stock Exchange (48), the Nasdaq Stock Market-National Market System (360), the NASDAQ Stock market-Small Cap Market (64) and the Over-the-Counter Market (421). An analysis of the accounting principles followed in the financial statements the companies file with the SEC shows that approximately 872 use home country generally accepted accounting principles (GAAP), 365 use U.S. GAAP, 49 use standards promulgated by the International Accounting Standards Committee (IASC) standards, and the remaining 24 use some other type of accounting principles (e.g. those of another country).[5]

The growth in foreign company listings has been indicative of the strength and attractiveness of the U.S. capital market to those companies. It is also indicative of the desire of foreign issuers to compete for access to the capital of those markets, as well as investors desire to provide them with the capital. Without a doubt, the U.S. capital markets provide foreign companies many benefits such as capital at a lower cost, a higher level of liquidity, and a source of stock that can be readily used in acquisitions.

MEETING THE CHALLENGES AND OPPORTUNITIES FOR THE MARKETS AND INVESTORS

The SEC has explored ways to permit foreign issuers to compete with U.S. domiciled companies for access to the U.S. capital markets. At the same time the SEC has worked to ensure U.S. investors will continue to have access to high quality financial information. As a result, the SEC has taken a number of steps to further facilitate the access of foreign companies to the U.S. capital markets including among other activities:

- Chairmen and members of the Commission have actively worked with the stock exchanges to encourage foreign companies to access the U.S. capital markets and list with the exchanges.
- The SEC has adopted international disclosure standards endorsed by the International Organization of Securities Commissions (IOSCO).[6]
- The SEC has also permitted companies to register with the SEC using accounting principles accepted in their home country in their basic financial statements provided they disclose in the footnotes to those financial statements an audited reconciliation of those numbers to what the numbers would be using U.S. GAAP with a few limited exceptions.
- The SEC has permitted foreign companies to undertake initial public offerings with fewer years of audited financial statements or with financial statements audited by an auditor whose independence must be established for only the most recent years. Both of these positions have eased the public requirements for foreign registrants that would otherwise be applied to their U.S. counterparts.
- The SEC has permitted foreign filers to provide less current and timely information by exempting them from having to comply with requirements that U.S. companies must meet for filing on a quarterly basis, financial statements and Management's Discussion and Analysis (MD&A) as well as certain annual proxy disclosures such as those related to audit committees.[7]
- The SEC staff often work closely with foreign companies in preparing for a registration allowing them to file "drafts" of their registrations on a "private" basis and receive the staff's comments on the drafts before more formal filings are made that become public. U.S. companies are not afforded this accommodation.

Notwithstanding the above efforts of the SEC to make it easier for foreign companies to raise capital in the U.S. markets, other significant issues may result in companies choosing other venues for sources of capital. Some of these may also cause private companies in the U.S. to avoid going public. They include a desire to:

- Avoid the transparent disclosures required by public markets including financial statement disclosures, proxy disclosures such as those about officer's compensation, and discussions about trends in the business and its operating results.

- Keep information from competitors that may otherwise have to be disclosed if a company were to trade publicly.
- Avoid the potential for securities litigation.
- Avoid the short term earnings focus of analysts and the markets.
- Maintain corporate governance structures that are not conducive to attracting capital in the public markets.

ENSURING INVESTOR PROTECTION

The SEC has taken reasonable steps to ensure investors receive reliable, transparent financial information while providing the types of accommodations cited above. The SEC has required that audits be conducted in accordance with U.S. Generally Accepted Auditing Standards (GAAS). The SEC has also continued to require auditors to comply with the applicable SEC independence requirements for auditors.[8] The result has been that foreign issuers may list in the U.S. exchange market while submitting financial statements prepared in accordance with accounting standards permitted in their home country, IASC accounting standards, or U.S. GAAP, so long as a reconciliation is made to U.S. GAAP, and so long as the financial statement audits are conducted according to U.S. auditing standards, including auditor independence standards. Thus U.S. disclosure standards and enforcement of those standards has centered on high quality accounting standards, audit performance, and acceptable auditor independence standards. This is consistent with the following statement of the SEC on April 11, 1996:

> The Commission supports the IASC's objective to develop, as expeditiously as possible, accounting standards that could be used for preparing financial statements used in cross-border offerings. From the Commission's perspective, there are *three* key elements to this program and the Commission's acceptance of its results:
>
> - The standards must include a core set of accounting pronouncements that constitutes a comprehensive, generally accepted basis of accounting;
> - The standards must be of high quality – they must result in comparability and transparency, and they must provide for full disclosure; and
> - The standards *must be* rigorously interpreted and applied (emphasis supplied).[9]

In the SEC's Concept Release on International Accounting Standards, the SEC noted that accounting standards need to be of high quality, but as noted above and equally important, they must be rigorously interpreted and applied. Standards that are not followed in essence do not result in standards at all. As a result, the SEC went on to set forth the elements that need to exist in the global accounting infrastructure to ensure standards are followed as written and intended.[10]

As international financing activities have grown, the SEC has ensured the quality of information provided to investors by foreign registrants. This has been accomplished to a great extent through its review and comment process. That process results in the SEC staff identifying circumstances when it believes filers have not complied with the applicable home country or IASB pronouncements.[11] At the same time the accounting profession has also taken steps to improve the quality of the enforcement of the standards. For example, at the urging of the SEC staff, the SEC Practice Section (SECPS) of the American Institute of Certified Public Accountants (AICPA) adopted membership rules enhancing the quality controls over reviews of filings by foreign companies with the SEC.

However, the SEC will in all likelihood not be capable of being the sole regulator who enforces the implementation of international accounting and auditing standards. The ultimate acceptance of such international standards by their ultimate customer, the investing public and capital markets, will be dependent on their rigorous implementation and application on a global basis. That will take, without a question, the cooperation among:

- The regulator's of the world's capital markets, including the SEC.
- The international and national accounting standard setters working in close cooperation with the regulators.
- The international and national auditing standard setters working in close cooperation with the regulators.
- The support of major international financial institutions such as the World Bank and International Monetary Fund who are stakeholders in quality financial reporting and enhanced international transparency.
- The support of governments around the globe who may well have to adopt changes in laws and regulations to support enhanced accounting standards, rigorous audits, and provide the regulators of the capital markets and accounting profession, appropriate enforcement capabilities.

Enforcement capabilities and actions of regulators and governments around the world differ significantly. The self discipline and regulation by the accounting profession also varies greatly on a global basis. Some regulators review filings for compliance with the applicable disclosure and accounting standards. Others do not and in fact may not have the statutory authority to do so. The SEC has an enforcement division that undertakes to enforce the applicable rules and regulations. Other organizations such as the European Commission (EC) and national securities regulators do not currently have such capabilities and/or the requisite statutory authority. For example, during his tenure as Chief Accountant, the author was asked by a G-7 country accounting standard setter if the SEC would be willing to enforce their accounting standards as there were no other substantive enforcement mechanisms in place for these standards.

THE CHALLENGE OF ACHIEVING HIGH QUALITY FINANCIAL REPORTING ON AN INTERNATIONAL BASIS

Many have stated the need for achieving convergence on an international basis on a single set of high quality accounting standards for use in cross-border filings.[12] The SEC has worked in close cooperation with other members of IOSCO to achieve this goal. However, to actually achieve high quality standards that result in transparent standards that consistently reflect the economics of the reporting enterprise, whose principles are applied in spirit as well as written, and that are enforced so as to provide investors and the markets with confidence in the financial information, it will take more than just the development of quality accounting standards. It will also require that preparers, accounting and auditing standard setters, regulators and governments focus on the following issues:

- Interpretation as well as development and implementation of accounting standards based on a goal of achieving transparency for investors and the world's capital markets.
- Performance of independent audits which will require:

  - The development of high quality international auditing standards in sufficient detail to provide guidance that will result in rigorous audits and reasonable assurance with respect to the reported results;
  - Timely training and education on the applicable accounting and auditing standards.
  - Quality control standards and processes within accounting firms that audit foreign companies who do cross-border filings;
  - Active monitoring, oversight and discipline of audit firms and their personnel; and
  - Independence standards for auditors that prescribe and prevent conflicts that reasonable investors would believe impair the auditor's independence.

- Effective regulatory schemes by securities regulators and/or governments that provide enforcement of the applicable accounting, disclosure and auditing standards and discipline for those market participants who chose to not to comply with the appropriate standards, laws and regulations.[13]

It is critical that all market participants cooperate in working on the objectives outlined above. For example, if a country's laws require auditors to follow national standards that are of lower quality, or result in lower quality audits, the goals outlined above cannot be achieved without the government changing its laws and regulations. Likewise, audit firms and the accounting profession must adopt standards that are developed based on a mission of how can the investing public and capital markets best be served. Firms can take steps to upgrade the quality of their audits to a more consistent and higher quality approach on a global basis so that investors clearly understand the quality of the product they are receiving when they read the auditors report on a set of financial statements, regardless of the jurisdiction in which they are prepared. Likewise, regulators must come to grips with issues they face in ensuring compliance with standards applicable to cross-border offerings. Failure to do so in a timely fashion can only result in either a lack of investor confidence in the financial information they receive, which in turn increases the cost of capital and decreases efficiency in the markets, or a delay in the adoption on a global basis of international accounting standards for cross-border filings.

TOWARDS CONVERGENCE OF INTERNATIONAL ACCOUNTING STANDARDS

The SEC was given the authority by Congress to establish generally accepted accounting principles to be used by all companies, both foreign and domestic, who register with it and trade their securities in the U.S. capital markets. However, the Commission early on decided to look to the private sector accounting standard setting bodies for the development of accounting standards. Since1938, the Financial Accounting Standards Board (FASB), an independent private organization, and its predecessors have created the GAAP that are accepted by the SEC for use in corporate financial statements filed with it.[14] But the SEC has retained its authority to establish accounting standards when it believes private sector standards did not provide adequate protection for investors.[15]

The growth in the number of foreign issuers seeking access to the U.S. capital markets has raised the interest in the use of international accounting standards for cross-border filings with the SEC. The acceptance by the SEC of such standards would lessen the burden of those foreign companies who use international accounting standards from having to obtain the information necessary for preparing the reconciliation from IASB standards to U.S. GAAP. It is also important to note that the EC has presented a proposal for a regulation that would require all European Union (EU) companies listed on a regulated market to prepare consolidated accounts in accordance with International Accounting Standards (IAS).[16]

The IASC was formed in 1973 by the International Federation of Accountants (IFAC), a group of private accounting organizations, for the purpose of promulgating IAS.[17] Until 2001, the IASC's business was conducted by a board of sixteen voting delegations and five non-voting observers with the privilege of the floor. The delegations were drawn from the accounting profession and preparers of financial statements, were part-time volunteers and met approximately four times a year.

In 1990, IOSCO endorsed the development of internationally acceptable accounting standards for use in cross-border filings. By 1994, IOSCO had completed a review of the IASC standards and through this process identified a number of standards that required improvement before IOSCO would consider endorsement of IASC standards for use in cross-border filings. In 1995, the IASC and IOSCO agreed to a work program, commonly referred to as the "core standards" project.[18] Upon completion of the core standards project in 1999 by the IASC, IOSCO undertook another review of those standards. As a result of that review, in May 2000, IOSCO recommended that its members accept the IAS, as supplemented by additional requirements for reconciliation, interpretation, or disclosures where necessary to address any outstanding issues. The SEC's current rules and reconciliation process is totally consistent with IOSCO's resolution.

During the late 1990s, a Strategy Working Party (SWP) undertook to restructure the IASC into an improved and new structure for creating accounting standards. A number of interested parties, including the SEC and other securities regulators, worked closely with the SWP to develop a more effective board whose members were to be chosen based on their technical competence as opposed to geographical location. In addition, the structure that emerged also ensured the board members would be independent and free of potential conflicts with their serving the public interests. The new structure also provided for a new Standards Advisory Council (SAC) and the continuation of the boards interpretive body, the Standing Interpretations Committee (SIC). The new International Accounting Standards Board (IASB) held its first technical session in April, 2001. One of the key features of the new IASB is that it emphasizes cooperation with national accounting standard setters in creating "International Financial Reporting Standards" (IFRS).

Convergence was one of the crucial aspects of the SWP's proposal. In its December 1998 Discussion Paper, the SWP stated that it believed that "IASC's short-term aim should be for national accounting standards and International Accounting Standards to converge around high-quality solutions" and that: "IASC's aim in the longer term should be for global uniformity – a single set of high-quality accounting standards for all listed and other economically significant business enterprises around the world."[19]

The SWP's December 1998 Discussion Paper emphasized the need for convergence of accounting standards. By working closely with the national standard setters, it is hoped that the efforts of the IASB and those national standard setters will result in a "best of breed" set of standards and common viewpoints on what constitutes standards that will provide consistent, transparent financial reporting to investors that reflects the economic reality of the financial transactions. In turn this may very well increase the likelihood that national standard setters and the IASB would adopt similar, if not the same, accounting standards. Of course, there may be some countries where the national standard setter must appropriately reflect laws and business practices in their final standards.

A lot of attention has been paid to whether the SEC would accept IASB standards in lieu of its reconciliation to U.S. GAAP requirements. The comment letters the SEC received on its Concept Release were, quite expectedly, divided as to their response based on where the respondent was located. U.S respondents in general believed that IASB standards are not yet of sufficient quality and effective enforcement mechanism does not exist to ensure their proper implementation and application. For example, IBM stated:

> We do not believe that IAS ensure the same *quality* reporting that U.S. GAAP ensures, and strongly believe that IAS are not acceptable accounting standards for companies filing on the U.S. exchanges . . . IAS lack an enforcement mechanism. At times, certain enterprises that have asserted that their financial statements are in compliance with IAS have been found not to be in compliance.[20]

McDonald's Corporation stated:

> . . . we do not believe that foreign private issuers should be allowed to file financial statements prepared solely under IAS as they exist today because we do not believe current IAS are of a high enough quality to ensure that U.S. investors have the appropriate information to making proper investing decisions. Therefore, if financial statements were allowed to be prepared under current IAS, it may place more investors at risk and create a competitive disadvantage to companies who file financial statements prepared under U.S. GAAP.

The vast majority of U.S. respondents expressed concerns related to the IAS permitting the use of alternative accounting principles, a lack of the necessary supporting infrastructure and a lack of effective discipline. However, most European respondents expressed a belief that the SEC should withdraw its reconciliation requirement and permit the use of IAS standards in filings with the SEC.

A notable comment was made by the AICPA which has been an active participant and supporter of the IASC. In its comment letter the AICPA stated "With the convergence of IAS and national regimes around high quality standards, fewer reconciling items will exist over time and, at a future date, reconciliation will become unnecessary. By convergence, we mean a movement toward higher quality standards from all jurisdictions, not simply a movement toward IAS or only toward U.S. GAAP or some other existing regime." With the new IASB establishing liaisons with the major national accounting standard setters, it appears that the accounting profession is moving in the direction suggested by the AICPA. A continuation of these efforts will result in the elimination of differences in accounting principles through a private sector initiative of the IASB and national standard setters. This in turn would eliminate the need for reconciliation for filings with the SEC.

One recent hurdle that has been placed in front of the IASB gaining acceptance of its standards is the newly formed European Commission European Financial Reporting Advisory Group of its Technical Expert Group.[21] The EC has stated: The establishment of an endorsement mechanism at the EU level is necessary because it is not possible politically, nor legally, to delegate accounting standard setting unconditionally and irrevocably to a private organization over which the EU has no influence . . . The endorsement mechanism will also examine whether the standards adopted by the IASC conform with EU public policy concerns."[22] However, other jurisdictions have established statutory structures that accept the use of accounting standards without each and everyone being "legally validated" and ruled on by a separate oversight body. It is interesting the EC wants the U.S. to accept the use of IASB standards but is not willing to do so itself without first "blessing" them.

It is widely known that the staff of the EC preferred a restructured IASB whose members were chosen based on geography. This endorsement mechanism allows the EC to gain input from its member states and use that information in deciding whether to accept IASB standards, and apparently influence the IASB decision-making. However, the EC has not published any criteria by which it will evaluate prospective standards of the IASB. If the EC uses this endorsement mechanism in a heavy-handed fashion or to sway the deliberations and final standards of the IASB, it likely will result in other regulators considering how they will interact with the IASB.

ISSUE: Are the IASB and national standard setters likely to be successful in achieving convergence around a set of high quality, "best of breed" International Financial Reporting Standards? Should the private standard setters or SEC undertake to eliminate reconciling differences? Should each regulator, including IOSCO, adopt an endorsement mechanism?

INTERPRETATION OF INTERNATIONAL ACCOUNTING STANDARDS

It is one thing to write an accounting standard. It is quite another thing to have to interpret it and apply the guidance in the standard to the billions of actual transactions that occur in the business world. This is especially true if the standard provides "broad general principles" to be followed without further implementation guidance.[23] Accordingly, companies who follow IFRS's standards, as well as their auditors and regulators, will have to interpret them.

In the United States, the FASB and its Emerging Issues Task Force (EITF) interprets U.S. GAAP. The FASB does not approve the guidance adopted by the EITF and the EITF is not required to adopt the most transparent accounting from among the alternatives considered. However, the FASB may take formal action and reverse a consensus of the EITF but has only done so once.[24] The SEC Chief Accountant is an observer to the EITF and has the right of the floor. Periodically when the staff has considered it appropriate, the Chief Accountant has objected to a proposed or final consensus of the EITF being applicable to public companies. The SEC and its staff also exercise their statutory authority when necessary and interpret GAAP. Often registrants may request the staff's interpretation of an accounting standard, especially if they are trying to expedite a filing.

At the IASB, the IFRS are interpreted by the SIC. A SIC interpretation must be approved by the IASB prior to its adoption; a process some believe is superior to that of the FASB. In addition, as the IFRS are expected to be broader principles based standards with less interpretive guidance than is typically provided in U.S. GAAP, interpretations of the standards will also be done by preparers and their auditors.

The SEC and banking regulators will also be interpreting international accounting standards. The SEC has the statutory authority and mandate to ensure investors are adequately protected through the disclosures and financials information they receive. The International Accounting Standards Survey 2000 written by David Cairns, the former Secretary General of the IASC, cites numerous examples of companies who disclose they are using IAS but who are not in compliance with the standards.[25] Accordingly, it is expected the SEC staff will review the financial statements filed with it in order to make sure that the accounting standards used have been properly applied

ISSUE: With interpretations being made by at various interpretative bodies, preparers, auditors and regulators, a challenge exists with respect to ensuring convergence with interpretation of the standards. High quality standards require consistent, comparable financial reporting by companies for similar types of transactions. Accordingly, the issue arises with respect to what appropriate steps can and should be taken to ensure that interpretive bodies, preparers, auditors and securities regulators will interpret and apply IFRS and U.S. GAAP in a consistent and effective manner.

PERFORMANCE OF EFFECTIVE AUDITS

Performance of an effective audit that provides investors with reasonable assurance that the financial statements *and* disclosures have been prepared in compliance with the applicable accounting standards requires the establishment of a supporting infrastructure. Elements of such an infrastructure must include:

- Effective, independent and high quality accounting and auditing standard setters;
- High quality auditing standards;
- Audit firms with effective quality controls worldwide;
- Profession-wide quality assurance; and
- Active regulatory oversight.[26]

EFFECTIVE AUDITING PROCEDURES ARE NECESSARY FOR ENFORCEMENT OF ACCOUNTING STANDARDS

Audits are considered an integral part of the capital markets system, including for foreign registrants, as they provide investors confidence that an independent third party, separate and distinct from management who prepares the financial statements, has examined the numbers and found them to be presented in accordance with the accounting principles applied. Accordingly, auditing is an important and critical part of ensuring effective financial disclosure.

The international audit firms are composed of national firms that have entered into international affiliations and have typically created an international entity that shares costs in marketing the firm on a global basis, as well as working to ensure consistency in the delivery of services to the firms' global clients. However, these structures also affect the governance of the firms, as well as their ability to establish and enforce global auditing, quality control and independence standards.

Auditing has a critical role in minimizing the risk of fraudulent financial reports. Competent and rigorous auditing is also needed to prevent a lack of comparability in financial reporting. As noted above in the 1999 and 2000 were surveys conducted by David Cairns, former Secretary-General of the IASC, numerous instances of companies purporting to follow international accounting standards but in fact not complying fully with such standards, while at the same time receiving a "clean" report from their auditor.[27] The Commission staff's own review of foreign issuer filings has indicated that many interpretation and compliance problems exist, necessitating restatement of primary financial statements even before reconciliation to U.S. GAAP.[28]

TRAINING AND EDUCATION

As set forth above, the number of companies utilizing IASB standards in the U.S. capital markets, as compared to those using home country or U.S. GAAP are relatively small. Many of the core standards developed by the former IASC have effective dates that are also fairly recent.[29] As a result, many preparers, auditors and regulators lack the knowledge of these standards that may be required to implement them in a quality fashion. As a result, the major international accounting firms have been building up their technical resources in Europe, in anticipation of the EC's move to international standards. However, the conversion of thousands of European companies to these standards, which entails a tremendous learning curve, changes in information systems and training of accounting staff in companies and auditing staff in accounting firms is without a doubt, a daunting task.

ISSUE: What steps have been taken and what must yet be done to educate preparers, auditors and regulators with respect to IASs and IFRSs? Are sufficient resources available to accomplish the education and training necessary to ensure these standards are properly implemented when first applied?

DEVELOPMENT OF GLOBAL AUDIT QUALITY CONTROL AND MONITORING SYSTEMS

At the urging of Congress and the SEC, the AICPA and U.S. auditing firms established the Public Oversight Board (POB), the AICPA Division for Firms, the SECPS and SECPS Executive Committee in approximately 1977. Within the structure of the SECPS, the accounting profession has established membership requirements and quality control and monitoring systems for the performance of audits. In the 1980s, the AICPA created the Quality Control

Inquiry Committee to consider if in cases of alleged audit failures, there is information that would suggest the audit process should be improved. The SEC actively oversees the work of the SECPS and the POB.

However, these quality control and monitoring systems have been mainly focused on the audit procedures and work performed in the United States. As large international companies such as IBM, Coca Cola and General Motors have become more global, an increasing percentage of the audit has been performed by affiliates of the U.S audit firm. This has resulted in an increasing part of the audit being outside the reach of the quality controls established here in the U.S.[30] In some instances, a question has been raised as to whether inappropriate financial reporting has been directed to that segment of the business outside the U.S. In addition, the growth in the number of foreign registrants has also increased the number of audits that are not subject to the type of quality controls and monitoring systems that ensure the quality of audits performed in the U.S.

The Panel on Audit Effectiveness issued its report on August 31, 2000.[31] Staff of the Panel met with the members of IOSCO's Working Party (WP) No. 1 and subsequent to the issuance of the report, an auditing subcommittee of WP No. 1 has been formed. That report made a number of important recommendations including:

- Establishment of a global-self-regulatory structure to monitor and report on the activities of individual country self-regulatory organizations. The report notes the primary goal of this oversight body is to serve the public interest and that it should be established through a mechanism that "ensures its independence and viability."
- There should be comprehensive annual reports by the oversight body to the public.
- Audit firms should "Implement uniform audit methodologies throughout the world that use international auditing standards as the base *minimum*" (emphasis supplied and footnote omitted).
- A key element of quality assurance should be external reviews of the quality controls of audit firms over their accounting and auditing practices.

The accounting profession has initiated projects to respond to concerns about the quality of international audits. Perhaps the most progressive action taken to date has been that taken in the United Kingdom. The U.K. Department of Trade and Industry has established a regulatory system for audits that includes: (1) an oversight body (The Foundation), (2) an audit review board, (3) an auditing practices board to set auditing standards, (4) an ethics standards board, and (5) an investigations and discipline board.[32] This proposal is currently in the process of being implemented in the U.K.

IFAC and audit firms performing international audits have undertaken projects to improve the quality of audits. These projects include the improvement of international auditing standards through IFAC's International Auditing Practice Committee (IAPC), the establishment of a proposed Forum of Firms (the Forum) and the Transnational Auditors Committee of the Forum (its executive committee), and a proposed Public Oversight Board (IFAC POB).[33] These projects are still under development and the ultimate impact they will have on the quality of international audits remains to be seen. One proposal, that a firm on firm peer review system be established, is proposed for completion on an international basis, including engagement reviews, by no later than 2005.[34]

IFAC proposes to establish the operating procedures for the IFAC Public Oversight Board (IFAC POB) in its proposed charter. The draft charter notes the IFAC POB will be a seven member Board of independent highly respected individuals charged with the responsibility of overseeing the public interest activities of IFAC, particularly the setting of auditing standards, compliance by member bodies, and the quality assurance, compliance and other self-regulatory processes of IFAC, including oversight of the system of Quality Assurance Review under TAC. The charter establishes a system of self regulation that is missing several of the components of the system proposed by the Panel on Audit Effectiveness and that are part of both the U.S. and U.K. systems. These include the rights of the proposed POB to carry out investigations it deems necessary, to discipline members and to appoint members or chairs of those committees of the profession under its oversight. In addition, the proposed funding for the IFAC POB is *significantly* less than that provided to the U.S. POB which raises questions regarding its future ability to function in a meaningful manner.[35] Finally, while the IFAC POB is to operate independently of IFAC, the final decision on the POB's initial members rests with IFAC.

The SEC's 2000 Annual Report sets forth critical elements and characteristics that are needed for an international public oversight organization to be effective. It states that, "Among these elements are the following:

- The selection of the initial members of the oversight organization, including a chairman, should only be finalized after seeking and receiving consideration from international organizations representing the public interest, including securities regulators;
- The members of the oversight organization should be public interest representatives without ties to the accounting profession;
- The funding for the organization's operations should be structured in such a manner that the organization can be independent in fact and in appearance; and

• Other characteristics noted by the staff include details relating to membership and review processes, reporting to the public and other matters."[36]

It will be important that the securities regulators and accounting profession around the globe reach an agreement on an appropriate and meaningful structure for the establishment of quality control systems, monitoring and discipline. The accounting profession has taken initial steps which are an improvement over the current system in many countries, but which are of lesser quality than those in some of the more developed countries. In addition, the proposed system does not provide for active ongoing oversight by the respective securities regulators, a key component of the U.S. system.

ISSUE: What should be the role of the profession, the role of the public and the role of regulators in the development of the necessary quality controls and monitoring systems for the performance of international audits?

ENHANCEMENTS TO THE AUDITING STANDARDS-SETTER

Over the last fifteen years, developments toward the improvement of auditing practices have also been occurring in the area of international auditing standards, though not with the same resources and level of intensity that has been devoted to accounting standards. Since the 1970s, IFAC has developed and issued a body of International Auditing Standards (ISAs). However, much of the content in these standards is in the form of guidelines and general principles for consideration, rather than in the form of specific requirements.

On July 27, 1987, the staff of the SEC issued a report to Congress on "Internationalization of the Securities Markets". This report included coverage of the standards and status pertaining to audits of foreign issuers in the U.S. securities markets, noted that auditing standards differed among nations, and stated that "while accounting principles can be reconciled, auditing standards cannot."[37] The report further went on to state that, for foreign issuers registering in the U.S. capital markets, steps are taken by the SEC "to provide assurance that the examinations of financial statements by foreign auditors are as extensive and complete as those conducted by U.S. auditors."[38]

Harmonization of international auditing practices was also recognized as an issue in the 1987 Report. The report noted that, "by July 1, 1987, the International Audit Practices Committee of the International Federation of Accountants had issued guidelines on professional ethics, pre-qualification education and training and twenty-four auditing guidelines plus three exposure drafts. Although the IFAC's auditing guidelines are impressive, they are not coordinated in the manner of the auditing standards generally accepted in the United States." In particular, it was noted that "IFAC international auditing standards cite audit procedures as examples of what an auditor may do, while, in contrast, they are required procedures under U.S. GAAS in appropriate circumstances."[39]

IFAC has recently established an International Auditing Practices Committee (IAPC) Review Task Force for the purpose of conducting a comprehensive review of the membership, organization, and processes of the IPAC. That Task Force published a proposal with recommendations for changes in the IPAC on July 18, 2001,[40] and recommends IFAC and the IAPC adopt a number of changes, including:

(1) Selection of members on based on professional competence.
(2) Enlargement of the committee from 14 to 15 members, and including one public interest representative.
(3) Greater interaction with national standard-setting bodies.
(4) Improved due process with open meetings and published drafts
(5) Strengthen the role of the Planning Committee
(6) Removing ambiguity created by the IAPC's "black lettering."

The accounting profession should reach out to securities regulators, including IOSCO and the SEC, and enable them to participate in a meaningful and effective manner in the oversight of audit standard setting. While the Task Force recommendations note they do not intend the IFAC POB or securities regulators to manage the process, they must both be given unrestricted oversight of the audit standard setting process and the resulting product if it is to gain market acceptance. Audit and quality control standards that do not provide sufficient detail to ensure effective audits that protect investors, will result in a lack of market credibility in the auditing process.

ISSUE: In light of concerns over the quality of international audits, should the SEC continue to require the use of U.S. GAAS until further improvements are made to international auditing standards?

ACTIVE REGULATORY ENFORCEMENT MECHANISM

The SEC is one of the few, if not the only securities regulator, whose staff reviews filings on a selected basis to ensure compliance with the applicable disclosure standards, and that has an enforcement division that can undertake legal actions when necessary. In many countries such regulatory oversight does not exist and the securities regulator may not have the statutory legal authority to take enforcement actions when a company or its auditors violate financial reporting or auditing rules.[41] During the Asian markets crisis of 1997–1998, it was noted that some of the Asian market regulators had very limited, if any real enforcement powers with respect to the performance of audits.

The SEC has also acknowledged the limitations of its own ability to gain access to necessary files and information when cases under investigation involve a registrant with foreign operations that have been audited by a foreign affiliate of a U.S. firm.[42] For example the SEC has noted the difficulty it has had in obtaining access to the work papers of foreign auditors or foreign affiliates of U.S. auditors. This has also been an issue for banking regulators. In such cases, the SEC has the potential to use a domestic compulsory mechanism, or memorandum of understandings or similar arrangements with non-U.S. regulators.

The U.K.'s new framework for the regulation of the accounting profession includes a proposed Investigations and Discipline Board. In the United States, the SEC and AICPA Ethics Executive Committee fill such a role. However, the SEC has noted in its annual report that the AICPA may not always take disciplinary action when the SEC has determined to do so.

ISSUE: What should and can be done to improve the regulatory oversight of international securities regulators and disciplinary mechanisms?

AUDITOR INDEPENDENCE

The SEC's new auditor independence requirements were adopted in November of 2000 after much public debate, numerous public hearings, and over 3000 comment letters from investors, the accounting profession, foreign and domestic regulators and many others.[43] The final rules that were adopted mirrored in many instances, previously existing rules of the AICPA and SECPS.[44]

Other countries also have requirements that establish rules governing the independence of auditors. In some of these countries, consulting services permitted in the U.S. are prescribed while other services prescribed by the SEC's rules may be permitted. In some foreign countries, accounting firms have established affiliated entities that provide services, such as legal services, that might be otherwise prescribed if they are performed directly by the auditing firm. There may also be varying degrees with respect to the actual enforcement of the rules. The SEC and its staff have expressed reservations with respect to the existence or effectiveness of quality controls that ensure the foreign affiliates of U.S. audit firms are complying with the applicable independence audit requirements.

In April of 2001 the Ethics Committee of IFAC proposed a draft entitled: "Independence – Proposed Changes to the Code of Ethics for Professional Accountants."[45] In contrast to the SEC's independence rules, the draft in many cases relies upon the auditing firm to assess whether a particular threat to the auditor's independence based on the auditors determination (rather than the investors) calls for an action to preserve independence. Accordingly, the auditor serves as one's own enforcer of the rules, rather than utilizing a separate enforcement mechanism.

Some securities regulators have expressed concern over the IFAC proposal. The President of the Commission des Operations de Bourse in a letter to IFAC stated:

> However, we are particularly concerned with what seems to be a fundamental flaw in the basis of the argument: the proposed code is based on the assumption that a very wide range of non-assurance services can be provided by accountants to their clients . . .. This conveys the impression that the audit of financial statements is just an ordinary business service as any other engagement . . ..
>
> We hold a different view. We believe that public accountants should make a clear choice with respect to their role to a given client: they should either elect to be the company's auditor or to be a multi-disciplinary consultant. To mingle the two roles would only lead to confusion in the public mind and weaken the confidence placed in the function of the independent auditor, the very foundation of reliable capital markets.[46]

Many U.S. investor's who testified at the SEC's public hearings or commented on the SEC's rule proposal on auditor's independence, felt the SEC should have taken a far more aggressive approach in the final rule. In the area of independence, the SEC faces substantial differences in practice elsewhere. It will have to decide whether to accept independence attitudes in other countries or continue with its recently adopted standards.

ISSUE: The basic issue that arises is whether securities regulators should accept international auditor independence requirements based on a standard of the appearance of independence to the reasonable investor or based on a determination by the auditor.

CONCLUSION

Quality financial reporting is critical to the efficient operations of the world's capital markets. Since its inception, the SEC has been a leader in ensuring investors have been provided with such information in the past.

But with the increasing expansion of all market participants beyond their national borders, the challenges of continuing to maintain quality and transparency in financial reporting has increased. Those challenges include protecting investors and international capital markets in an environment of exploding technology and fierce global competition.

These challenges require the coordinated effort of public companies, auditors, standard setters, regulators and governments. They cannot be met by just one or two of these groups. They cannot be met by a rush to "short-term convergence" just for the sake of getting a "quick fix" that ultimately could cause incredible damage to the markets. Instead, it is critically important that everyone closely coordinate their efforts and devise and execute the changes needed for future success. These are changes that need to be made in a timely fashion, with input from the public, and with appropriate due process. With such an approach, it is hopeful that a quality product will be developed that ensures the continued success of the world's capital markets. That success in turn should result in companies having access to capital that is so important to the global economy.

NOTES

1. An issues paper prepared by Lynn E. Turner, Professor and Director of The Center for Quality Financial Reporting, College of Business, Colorado State University and former Chief Accountant, U.S. Securities and Exchange Commission, for a Major Issues Conference: "Securities Regulation in the Global Internet Economy, presented by the Securities and Exchange Commission Historical Society in cooperation with the United States Securities and Exchange Commission, November 14–15, 2001. Professor David S. Ruder, former Chairman of the Securities and Exchange Commission has written a companion article entitled: "Worldwide Convergence in Accounting, Auditing, and Independence Standards."

2. See *The Financial Times*, June 14, 2001, *Anglo-Saxons help reluctant German groups to open up: Changes in accounting methods alter results disclosure says Uta Harnsichfeger.*

3. New York Stock Exchange Quick Facts at: http://www.nyse.com.marketinfo/marketcapitalization.html

4. U.S. Securities and Exchange Commission, Foreign Companies Registered and Reporting with the U.S. Securities and Exchange Commission, December 31, 2000. Office of International Corporate Finance, Division of Corporation Finance.

5. The International Accounting Standards Committee was restructured during 1998 to 2000 and commenced operations as the International Accounting Standards Board (IASB) in 2001. Standards of the IASC are commonly referred to as International Accounting Standards (IAS) and those of the IASB are referred to as International Financial Reporting Standards (IFRS).

6. Securities and Exchange Commission Release Nos. 33-7745: 34-41936: International Series Release No. 1205, International Disclosure Standards, published in the Federal Register October 5, 1999.

7. See for example Securities and Exchange Commission Release Nos. 34-422266; File No. 7-22-99, Audit Committee Disclosure, December 22, 1999 in which the Commission stated:

A. Foreign Private Issuers.

We proposed to exclude from the new requirements foreign private issuers with a class of securities registered under Section 12 of the Exchange Act or that file reports under Section 15(d) of the Exchange Act. Foreign private issuers currently are exempt from the proxy rules, are not required to file Quarterly Reports on Form 10-Q or 10-QSB, and are subject to different corporate governance regimes in their home countries. Accordingly, we do not believe it is appropriate to extend the new requirements to foreign private issuers at this time. The Commission, however, is continuing to consider how the periodic reporting requirements for domestic companies should apply to foreign private issuers. (footnotes omitted).

8. Securities and Exchange Commission Release Nos. 33-7919; 34-43602; IC-24744; IA-1911; FR-56; File No. S7-AH91; Revision of the Commission's Auditor Independence Requirements; November 21,2000. In this release the Commission noted that some encouraged it to adopt a "conceptual approach" put forward by the European accounting profession but in deciding to continue to require auditors of foreign registrants to comply with the SEC's rules noted:

We understand that many regulators do not agree with the conceptual approach, and several foreign countries prohibit certain non-audit services though standards vary from country to country. Standards vary for a number of reasons, including that in some countries, audits are conducted by statutory auditors who are directly responsible to shareholders and in some cases audits may be conducted for other than financial reporting purposes.

We believe that our final rules combine important and useful elements of both approaches ... The four factors provide guiding principles for the Commission, similar to what a 'conceptual approach' would provide (footnotes omitted).

The release also references a letter from Phillipe Danjou, Chief Accountant of the COB, to Lynn Turner in which he states "I can assure you that many regulators in Europe (mainly continental Europe) do not agree with the FEE's [conceptual] approach and have made their views known to the European Commission . . .." See also Letter from Michael Prada. President, COB, to Marilyn Pendergast, Chairman, Ethics Committee, IFAC (September 15, 2000) stating "The proposed change from a prescriptive approach to a framework approach is flawed by the absence of a clear definition of an auditor's unique role and position." These letters are available at the SEC website.

9. SEC Statement Regarding International Accounting Standards, April 11, 1996.

10. Securities and Exchange Commission Release Nos 33-7801;34-42430; International Series Release No. 1215; File No. S7-04-00, International Accounting Standards (Hereafter, "Concept Relase").

11. See speeches of the staff for examples of situations in which foreign registrants were not in compliance with applicable GAAP and were required to correct their accounting including International Reporting Issues, Craig C. Olinger, Deputy Chief Accountant, Division of Corporation Finance, December 6, 2000; International Reporting Issues, Travis Gilmer, Professional Accounting Fellow, Office of the Chief Accountant, December 6, 2000; and International Reporting Issues, Donald J. Gannon, Professional Accounting Fellow, Office of the Chief Accountant, December 8, 1999. In the speech by Mr. Olinger, he notes that there had been at least 40 restatements of financial statements or U.S. GAAP reconciliations in just the previous two years. It has been the SEC staff practice that when such issues arise, they do periodically consult on a no-name basis with the FASB or its staff and national offices of major accounting firms to obtain

their viewpoints. The author's experience has been that often the FASB staff and/or the national office views are consistent with those of the SEC staff.

12. For example see the May 23, 2000 comment letter of the European Commission Director General to the SEC responding to the SEC Concept Release on International Accounting Standards.

13. See also SEC Concept Release, Supra n. 10, p. 6.

14. See Securities and Exchange Commission Accounting Series Release No. 4, Administrative Policy on Financial Statements, April 25, 1938; Securities and Exchange Commission Release No. 150, Statement of Policy on the Establishment and Improvement of Accounting Principles and Standards, December 20, 1973.

15. For example, the SEC has issued amendments to its Regulation S-X, Accounting Series and Financial Reporting Releases over the years providing guidance on such issues as consolidated financial statements, redeemable preferred stock, income taxes, lease accounting and disclosure, capitalization of interest and software development costs, and accounting by oil and gas producers. In addition, the SEC staff periodically issues Staff Accounting Bulletins (SABs) that are not rules of the Commission, but which do provide companies and their auditors, especially smaller firms, with the staff's interpretations of the accounting standards and rules.

16. See http://europa.eu.int/comm/internal_market/en/company/account/news/ias.htm for "Financial reporting; Commission proposes requirement for listed companies to use International Accounting Standards by 2005."

17. IFAC is a private accounting organization of 153 professional institutes in 113 countries.

18. For a discussion of the IASC and IOSCO development of the work program as set forth in two June 17, 1994 letters from IOSCO to the Chairman of the IASC, Mr. Eiichi Shiratori, see the *October 1997 Report on Promoting Global Preeminence of American Securities Markets* in the public filing room of the Securities and Exchange Commission.

19. *Shaping IASC for the Future*, A Discussion Paper issued for comment by the Strategy Working Party of the International Accounting Standards Committee, p. 57 (International Accounting Standards Committee, December, 1998).

20. Others expressing similar viewpoints included the Business Round Table and Pfizer.

21. For additional information concerning this organization, see http://europa.eu.int/comm/internal_market/en/company/account/news/creationeteg.htm

22. Proposal for a Regulation of the European Parliament and of the Council on the application of International Accounting Standards, Commission of the European Communities, COM(2001) 80 final, Explanatory Memorandum p. 4 (February 13, 2001) (hereafter EC Proposal) see also EU Press Release IP/01/ . . . at: www.iasc.org.uk (26 June 2001).

23. It has not been uncommon in the U.S. that a preparer would insist on an accounting treatment while noting there is nothing in an accounting standard that expressly prohibits the proposed accounting. The SEC staff has also observed similar explanations by foreign registrants. This makes enforcement of principle based standards much more difficult for an auditor. It has also resulted in diversity in practice and a lack of comparability in reporting for similar transactions by registrants.

24. The FASB staff issued FASB Technical Bulletin No. 90-1, Accounting for Separately Priced Extended Warranty and Product Maintenance Contracts which nullified the EITF's consensus on Issue No. 89-17.

25. International Accounting Standards Survey 2000, David Cairns at www.cairns.co.uk/survey-introduction.asp

26. SEC Concept Release, p. 3.

27. Cairns, supra, n. 25.

28. SEC Staff, Supra n. 11.

29. SEC Concept Release, see Appendix B for the effective date of the standards issued as part of the core project. Thirteen of the 31 standards had effective dates of January 1999 through January 2001.

30. The U.S. Quality controls and peer review procedures related to international audits typically focus on the instructions the U.S. firm provides to its international affiliates.

31. The Panel on Audit Effectiveness, Report and Recommendations, August 31, 2000. The report is available at www.pobauditpanel.org

32. Department of Trade and Industry, *A Framework of Independent Regulation for the Accountancy Profession*, November, 1998 available at http://www.dti.gov.uk/cld/framework/index.htm

33. See http://www.ifac.org/News/LatestReleases for IFAC's Request for Comment on Proposals for Establishment of the IFAC Public Oversight Board and IFA Forum of firms. This includes links to the draft constitution and operating procedures of the Forum of Firms.

34. Request for Comment on Proposals for Establishment of the IFAC Public Oversight Board and IFAC Forum of Firms, IFAC News and Events, October 18, 2001, www.ifac.org

35. The initial annual budget for 2001 as proposed is not to exceed $1 million and increase to $2.5 million for 2004 and subsequent years. The U.S. POB has a budget of approximately $5 million.

36. Securities and Exchange Commission Annual Report 2000, pp. 89–90.

37. SEC Report to Congress on Internationalization of the Securities Markets, July 27, 1987.

38. Id.

39. Id.

40. Review of the Operations of the IFAC International Auditing Practice Committee, IAPC Review Task Force, International Federation of Accountants, www.IASC.org (July 18, 2001).

41. For example, the EC does not have the regulatory oversight and enforcement mechanisms the SEC does and the securities commissions in its member states do not all have such enforcement authority or oversight of the accounting profession.

42. SEC Concept Release, Supra n. 10, pp. 17–18.

43. Revision of the Commission's Auditor Independence Requirements, Release Nos. 33-7919 and 34-40602, Nov. 21, 2000 at p. 2.

44. The question is often referred to as to the "appearance" of an auditor's independence and has been a cornerstone of the accounting profession's and SEC's rules and interpretations for many years.

45. www.ifac.org, hereafter "the IFAC Independence Code."

46. Letter dated September 15, 2000 from Michel PRADA, President of the French Commission des Operations de Bourse to the Chairman of the IFAC Ethics Committee.

THE DEVELOPMENT OF FINANCIAL REPORTING, THE STOCK EXCHANGE AND CORPORATE DISCLOSURE IN THAILAND

Aim-orn Jaikengkit

ABSTRACT

After enjoying a decade of economic growth, Thailand was suddenly hit by the crisis of 1997. This crisis brought with it not only a reformation in monetary and fiscal policies, but also a fundamental change in the Thai financial structure. The Thai financial structure switched from depending on funds from banks or financial institutions, to using money markets, both in Thailand and overseas. The new era, the era of appreciation for better disclosure by Thai firms, was ushered in. This study discusses the development of financial reporting, the stock exchange and corporate disclosure in Thailand from the period before 1974 to 2000.

INTRODUCTION

We cannot deny that each country has its own history that has made it what it is now. Thailand is no exception. It has a unique history, and culture, and is endowed with its own special resources. It also faces a unique set of opportunities and threats that have developed in the post-World War II period.

Research in Accounting Regulation, Volume 15, pages 239–258.
© 2002 Published by Elsevier Science Ltd.
ISBN: 0-7623-0841-9

However, unlike most other developing countries, Thailand has never been colonized and has retained a long history of bureaucratic centralism. Furthermore, as a result of its strong relationships with western countries, particularly the U.S., Thailand possesses the unusual status of being a major food exporter and was once called the "fifth tiger" (Muscat, 1994). All of these characteristics have played a significant role in shaping Thailand's economy, institutions such as the Stock Exchange of Thailand, and professions, including accountancy.

The modern development of Thailand has been strongly influenced by the country's intellectual, economic, and security relationships with the industrialized world. The major contribution of foreign aid to Thailand's development after World War II has been in the creation of the institutional capacities required to develop and manage a modern state and in the education and training of Thai elite's and professionals to lead and staff these institutions.

As a "soft" state in which government has a limited ability to impose its policy decisions on its citizen's economic behavior, the Thai government usually reacts to the logic and pressure of economic conditions (Muscat, 1994). However, it does establish policies, which are relatively stable and powerful. For example, policies exist with regard to major determinants respecting the role of government and the private sector; public-sector performance in the provision of public goods and services; the extent and efficiency of market determination of prices and resources allocation decisions; government policies affecting the overall monetary and fiscal condition of the economy; the general price level, the exchange value of the currency; and the climate for domestic and foreign investment (Muscat, 1994).

Until recently, Thailand enjoyed a decade of the fastest growing in economy in the world (Warr, 1999), but the crisis of 1997 changed Thailand in many and different ways. Several financial institutions were closed by the Bank of Thailand due to deficiency problems (BOT, 1997). Output and investment contracted, the incidence of poverty began to rise, and the exchange rate collapsed. All these led to a significant shift in the foundation of the Thai economy.

In the aftermath of the 1997 crisis, the Thai financial market structure switched from depending on funds from banks or financial institutions, to using money markets, both in Thailand and overseas. This drew attention to the concept of good corporate governance, more specifically, transparent disclosure, was established within the principal criteria for lenders, creditors and investors (Jelatianranat, 2000).

The brief profile about Thailand provided below is necessary background for the paper which follows. The development of financial reporting and the stock exchange in Thailand are presented in chronological order, starting from the period before 1974, proceeding to the period between 1974 and 1997, and closing with the period from 1998 to 2000. Demand and supply of stocks are also discussed. GAAP, disclosure requirements and the emergence of a transparency concept in Thailand are then presented, followed by a discussion of the role of audit committees and boards of directors in Thailand. The concluding remarks are drawn in the final section.

PROFILE

History

The Thai people are believed to have migrated from Southern China in the early Christian era when they formed the cities of Chiang Saen, Chiang Rai and Chiang Mai, which today represent the northern part of Thailand. They then moved further down to populate the entire Indochina Peninsular. Recent discoveries have revealed that the northeast hamlet of Thailand's Ban Chiang is the world's oldest Bronze Age civilization.

Sukhothai became the first independent city of Thailand when Khun Bang Klang Tao and Khun Pha Muaang defeated the Khom regime and declared Thailand's independence. Even though Sukhothai was the kingdom of Thailand for only a short period of time, its culture and history were assimilated during the Ayutthaya period. During the Sukhothai reign, the Thai people gradually expanded through the riverside of the Chao Phra Ya River and later established Theravada Buddhism as their main religion. It is also the place where distinctive evidence of both Thai architecture and literature were found.

Sukhothai was absorbed by the Ayutthaya kingdom, which lasted through the reign of thirty-four kings for more than 417 years. During this age of culture and prosperity the Ayutthaya gradually developed good relationships with Arabian, Indian, Chinese, Japanese and European nations. Thailand established a good and firm relation with the western world during the reign of King Narai the Great (1656–1688) who decided to send an envoy to visit France and build foreign diplomacy. Ayutthaya remained the Thai capital until it was overturned and burned by the Burmese.

Thailand was revived once again by King Taksin, the founder of a new capital, Thonburi. Then, in 1782, King Rama I started the Chakri Dynasty by establishing the new capital on the riverside hamlet called "Ban Kok", the village of wild plums.

During the Rattanakosin Era, from 1851 to 1868, King Mongkut (Rama IV) reigned, and was followed from 1868–1910, by King Chulalongkorn (Rama V) their successive reigns saved Thailand from the Western colonialism through adroit diplomacy and selective modernization. Thailand has been a constitutional monarchy since 1932. The King exercises his legislative rights through a national assembly and his judicial power through the courts of law.

Geography

Thailand, with an area of 514,000 square kilometers, is located in the center of the continent of Southeast Asia. The neighboring countries are Laos at the Northeast, Myanmar at the North and West, Cambodia at the east and Malaysia at the South.

Climate

The overall weather is humid and tropical, interrupted by a prolonged monsoon season. Thailand is marked by its rainy season which lasts from May to September. The highest temperature is in March or April while the lowest is in December or January. The average temperature is about 23.7 to 32.5 degree Celsius.

Population

The population of Thailand is approximately 61.7 millions. The most important ethic minority group is Chinese.

Religion

The Thai national religion is Theravada Buddhism which comprises 95% of the nation. The Thai people have the freedom to choose which religion to believe in, therefore, all major religions can be found in practice.

People

The majority of the population, sixty-one million, consists of Thai Buddhists who live together peacefully with the other minority groups. In the city, Chinese people are the most familiar minority ethnic group, followed by Khmer and Lao in the Northeast and Eastern part of Thailand, while most Muslims live in the South. Other minorities can also be found, such as the hill tribes in the far north, and the Hindus and Sikhs in Bangkok.

Government

At present, Thailand is governed by a constitutional monarchy with His Majesty King Bhumibol Adulyadej as the head of the state, while the Prime Minister empowers the government. Currently, the Thai Prime Minister is gaining personal power more and more, partly because it is a cultural tradition of the

Thai people to prefer a single high authority to make decisions. The Thai constitution is the highest law and governs Thailand through a centralized system.

Legislative power is exercised through a bicameral National Assembly in the Parliament. The parliament must approve all matters before passing to the King for his approval to become the law of Thailand.

Judicial power is exercised through three courts of law including the court of the first instance, the court of Appeal, and the Supreme Court.

Executive power is exercised through a cabinet headed by a Prime Minister. The government includes the Prime Minister and a Council of Ministers who control fifteen ministries.

THE DEVELOPMENT OF FINANCIAL REPORTING AND THE STOCK EXCHANGE IN THAILAND

The period before 1974

Banks and financial institutions have long played a leading role in the Thai financial system by serving both household and corporate sectors. The history of commercial banks in Thailand began with the establishment of foreign bank branches in Hong Kong and Shanghai in 1888 (Skully, 1984). At that time there were no other types of financial institutions and only commercial banks operated for both money and capital markets. The first Thai bank, Siam Commercial Bank, was set up in 1906. Nevertheless, domestic banks had a very minor role relative to that of the foreign banks during those years.

All commercial banking business in Thailand has long been regulated and supervised by the Bank of Thailand (BOT), the country's central bank, which started its operation on December 10, 1942, under the Commercial Banking Act 1962 (amended in 1970 and 1992). According to the Commercial Banking Act, commercial banking business traditionally consisted of funds accepted from deposits, purchasing and selling, or collecting bills of exchange, or other transferable instruments, and purchasing and selling foreign exchange, gold, or silver.

Finance companies, which consequently became ranked only second to commercial banks in terms of their aggregate volume of business, began operations in 1969. The bulk of their business is in personal consumption, hire purchase, and leasing. They obtain funds mostly through issuing promissory notes in the domestic market and overseas and by borrowing from commercial banks. Only deposits in the form of bills of exchange and certificates of deposits are permitted. Since the branching regulations for finance companies were more restricted than those for commercial banks, they concentrated their business only in Bangkok and nearby provinces.

In 1961, influenced by foreign aid and recognizing the significance of having a concrete plan for long-run improvement, the government launched the first Thailand National Economic and Social Development Plan (NESD), and subsequently, established a series of subsequent plans defining the new direction and the growth objectives of the country. A new stock exchange was incorporated in the Second NESD plan (1967–1971) (SET, 2001).

As mentioned earlier, Thailand has been viewed as a soft state because the government usually reacts to situations rather than being proactive. The first phase in the development of the stock exchange and capital market in Thailand was initiated by the private sector without the involvement of state officials. The Bangkok Stock Exchange Co. Ltd. (BSE), the first organized stock exchange in Thailand, was established in 1962 as a partnership. During the early years, however, rather than providing a place for trading, BSE primarily served as a vehicle to signal or indicate current share prices (Priebjrivat, 1992).

The Thai government anticipated potential growth in the BSE, and when the BSE annual turnover reached baht 160 million in 1969, put the BSE under consideration. An outside consultant, Professor Sidney M. Robbins of Columbia University, a former chief economist of the U.S. Securities and Exchange Commission, was hired to study and report on the existing financial markets, and to make suggestions for the reorganization of the BSE. Professor Robbins provided some influential recommendations that were consequently incorporated in the Securities Exchange of Thailand Act, which was passed in May 1974. Such recommendations included changes in Civil and Commercial Laws, which provided tax benefits for listed companies and for investors to in order to encourage supply and demand respectively, as well as the development of accounting and auditing standards, and projects to increase demand and supply (Priebjrivat, 1992).

The Securities Exchange of Thailand Act 1974 established a new exchange entity, the Securities Exchange of Thailand (SET). The SET focused mainly on mobilizing capital from both domestic and overseas sources to finance the growth and development of manufacturing sectors as well as the country's economy (SET, 2001).

The Period 1975–1997

The extent to which the capital market contributes to economic growth hinges on its role as the main external source of capital. Firms can resort to their own savings, that is, reserves and retained earnings. When internally generated funds are insufficient, firms can obtain additional finance by borrowing from domestic financial institutions and, for larger firms, from aboard, by receiving trade credit, issuing shares and bonds directly or via the Stock Exchange of Thailand (SET), and through various other means.

Table 1 highlights the rapid growth of the stock market in the 1980s. On April 30, 1975, SET began operations with 14 quoted securities with an opening-day index of 100. However, because of political instability in neighboring Indochina and the impact of a worldwide recession on the Thai economy, there was no active participation in the market from either private or institutional investors during SET's first years of operation, 1975 and 1976. At the end of 1976, the SET index dropped to 76.44, below its opening day index of 100.

However, between 1977 and 1978, Indochina's political environment improved significantly. Foreign investment capital flowed increasingly to the Thai capital market, helping to build a positive attitude toward investment in the Thai market. Although suffering from the increase in oil and commodity prices during the end of 1978, the SET index rose to 257.7.

Table 1.   Market Statistics.

Year	The Stock Exchange of Thailand			The U.S. Stock Exchange	
	Number of Securities	Market Capitalization ($ Billion)	SET index	NYSE Index	DJIA
1975	27	0.3	84.1	47.64	852.41
1980	85	1.3	124.7	77.86	962.03
1983	88	1.4	134.5	95.18	1258.63
1984	96	1.7	142.3	95.89	1211.57
1985	100	1.8	135	121.59	1546.67
1986	98	3	207.3	138.58	1895.11
1987	125	5.5	284.9	138.23	1938.82
1988	165	8.7	386.7	156.26	2168.57
1989	218	25.8	879.2	195.04	2753.2
1990	261	24	612.9	180.49	2633.66
1991	318	35.1	711.4	229.44	3167.71
1992	359	58.5	893.4	240.21	3301.11
1993	408	130.8	1682.9	259.08	3754.09
1994	494	131.7	1360.1	250.94	3834.44
1995	538	141.5	1280.8	329.51	5117.12
1996	579	100.81	831.57	392.3	6448.27
1997	529	36.00	372.69	511.19	7908.25
1998	494	30.50	355.81	595.81	9181.43
1999	450	57.77	481.92	650.3	11501.85
2000	438	31.77	269.19	656.87	10786.85

Sources: The Stock Exchange of Thailand and The New York Stock Exchange.

The oil crisis had a significant negative impact on Thai economy during 1979. This resulted in the liquidation of Raja Finance Co, Ltd., a listed company that had provided margin financing services. The condition of the market was seriously weakened. The situation worsened in 1980 and 1981. High interest rates, tight money, and reduced profitability in the business sector contributed to a continuously decreasing capital market. In August 1981, the SET index was 103.19.

The market began to recover during the second half of 1982. Falling oil prices, declining interest rates, and favorable government policies were factors that helped the market to recover through the first half of 1984. Moreover, to establish penalties for stock manipulation and insider trading, an amended Securities Exchange of Thailand Act was enacted in 1984. Also about this time direct foreign investment in Thai securities increased significantly to the level of 29 million shares or 13.8% of total shares traded in the SET due to the relatively cheaper securities and products of Thailand, which was the result of the devaluation of Thai currency during this period. All these factors helped to speed up the recovery of the market.

Lower interest rates, lower oil prices, and new tax incentives encouraged more investment from both domestic and foreign sources. The Thai economy continued to recover through the last quarter of 1985 when a downturn took place as a result of the limits of major agricultural exports and a U.S. quota on textiles.

On October 19, 1987, the Thai market was infected by the U.S. "Black Monday" experience. The crisis brought with it a decline in the SET index to 243.97, a 48% drop from it's peak, and the decline on the daily average trading value from baht 760 million before Black Monday to almost baht 570 million after the crisis.

In 1988, because of its strong economy, the SET demonstrated one of the world's best post-crash recoveries. Both the index and average trading volume rose sharply. In 1989, the SET reached a recorded high, with average daily turnover of more than baht 1,500 million and the SET index of 879.2, an increase of 127% from 1988.

During 1990 to 1996, the Thai economy was claimed to be the fastest growing in the World (Warr, 1999). Thailand was called "the fifth tiger" of Asian. Investors held optimistic view about SET. The remarkable stability of its growth played a significant role in boosting the capital market. In 1993, the SET index hit its record at 1650.

To improve the Thai capital market, the regulatory body of the Stock Exchange of Thailand (SET), the Securities Exchange Commission (SEC), was established in 1992, followed by a credit rating agency, the Thai Rating and Information Service (TRIS), in 1993.

The first domestic government bond was issued by the Ministry of Finance in 1933, and the Thai bond market was dominated by government bonds for many decades until 1990. However, before 1979 there was no bond trading in the secondary markets. Due to budget surpluses since 1987, there was a lack of supply of government issues, with the last series of government bonds issued in 1990. Hence, the amount of government bonds outstanding has been declining steadily with the result that no treasury bills were left outstanding in 1996. Trading in government bonds was also very thin as commercial banks and finance companies were required by the Bank of Thailand to hold them as part of legal reserves and branch-opening requirements (Vichyanond, 1994).

Compared to its neighbors, the bond market in Thailand is relatively small. At the end of 1994, its total size was 344.6 billion baht ($13.7 billion), or 10% of GDP. Of this amount, 56% were government bond issues, followed by corporate issues of 26%, and state enterprise issues of 18%. When bonds in foreign currencies are also included, the total value of bonds outstanding in 1994 was 435.7 billion baht ($17.4 billion), which amounted to only 10.4% of the equity market. After the Securities and Exchange Act was enacted in 1992, the proportion of corporate issues in the bond market grew from 3% to 26% between 1993 and 1994. Prior to 1992, corporate bond issues were limited as a consequence of the Public Company Act which permitted listed companies to issue only debt instruments on a restrictive basis and prohibited private companies from offering bonds to the public.

Although the significance of the SET as the market of funds supply to Thai economic has increased since its establishment, until 1997, domestic commercial banks and financial companies still played a leading role in the Thai financial system by serving both household and corporate sectors. Besides lending for personal consumption, they specialized in financing trade and manufacturing sectors. As can be seen from Table 2, at the end of 1996, outstanding credits of commercial banks and outstanding loans of finance companies were 4,911 and 1,488 million baht, which together was about 2.22 times of market capitalization of the stock exchange (2,599 million baht) and about 2.08 times of market capitalization of the stock exchange and the outstanding value of domestic bonds (513 million baht) together (Bank of Thailand). These factors indicated that commercial banks and finance companies were the key players in the financial system.

However, a recession hit the Thai economy in 1997, after the growth of the 1990s, changing the degree of the significance of the bank sector on the sources of finance in Thailand. The Thai economy collapsed during 1997 largely due to the announced free-fall in the value of baht relative to the U.S. dollar. Unlike the situation in 1984, this devaluation of Thai baht did not bring with

Table 2. Loans and Capital Market Funds as of 31 December 1996.

Items	Amount (Billion)
Outstanding Credits of Commercial Banks	4,911
Outstanding Loans of Finance Companies	1,488
Outstanding Value of Domestic Bonds	513
Market Capitalization of the Stock Exchange	2,559
Mutual Fund Assets	217
Pension Fund Assets	89

Sources: Bank of Thailand, Thai Bond Dealing Centre.

it a favorable increase in inflow to the capital market. The economy was in disarray. Output and investment contracted, poverty increased, and the exchange rate collapsed. The banking sector in Thailand has been severely affected by this crisis. A numbers of banks and financial institutions, which were highly leveraged and had a number of debt obligations which had to be paid in currency other than Thai currency, faced difficulty in continuing their operations. Notwithstanding this situation, the SET index went down significantly from 850 in 1996 to 372.69 in 1997. This collapse had significant effects not only on the Thai economy, but also on the world economy (Warr, 1999).

The period 1998–2000

In 1998, the recession continued, showing no sign of recovery for Thai economy. The SET index at the end of 1998 was almost the same as the SET index in 1997. In 1999, in the aftermath of this crisis, due to growing fear during recession, the Thai government reformed monetary and fiscal policies in order to stimulate recovery.

In March, a value-added tax (VAT) was reduced from 10 to 7%. Then, in August, a package to stimulate private investment, including reductions of taxes and tariffs, capital financing and restructuring of small to medium-sized enterprises (SMEs), and measures to promote recovery of the real estate sector, were launched. The Bank of Thailand (BOT) also helped stimulate the economy by relaxing monetary policy resulting in a decline in interest rates, reducing financing costs for business and facilitating corporate debt restructuring (SET, 2001).

Increases in exports of 7% in terms of U.S. dollars in 1999 also helped in speeding up the recovery and stability. At the end of 1999, the exchange rate was baht 37.5 per U.S. dollar, significantly reduced from Bath 50.24 per U.S. dollar at year-end 1997. All of these factors helped recovery of the market.

The SET index reached 481.92 by the end of 1999, 129.3 % of the SET index of 1996 (SET, 2001).

The 1997 collapse brought with it not only an awakening of need for changing monetary and financial policies, but also set in place a paradigm shift concerning the development and evolution of voluntary measures to improve the quality of disclosure, restoring the trust in, and the reputation of Thai companies in the global community, re-establishing capital investment and achieving lower costs of capital.

Since the 1997 crisis, there has been a fundamental change in the Thai financial market structure. Because of their deficiency problems, at the end of 1998, the BOT closed 56 banks and financial institutions. This situation led to a change in the main source of funding for the Thai economy.

The funds that mainly supply the market as credits have shifted from banks and financial institutions to money markets both in Thailand and from over-seas. This change has stimulated the recognition and the importance of corporate governance, especially, in reference to transparent disclosure. It began to be perceived as more than merely a public relations or advertising program for communicating more fully the picture of the company's past, current, and future performance, and to convince lenders, creditors, and investors to provide capital to the firms (Jelatianranat, 2000). Believing in the benefits of transparent disclosure, ICAAT and SET took steps to improve the disclosure quality of corporate reports in Thailand.

DEMAND AND SUPPLY OF STOCKS

Since the achievement of the capital market is measured by the action on a sufficient demand for and supply of stocks, SET uses 2 tax incentives to increase the demand. These incentives are: (1) capital gains tax exemption, and (2) dividend withholding tax equal to bank deposit withholding tax, with dividends exempt up to a certain amount.

On the demand side, Table 3 shows that the 1999 market situation brought a shift in the aggregate transactions of the major investor groups in the SET. Foreign investors became net buyers for a long period of time and, later on, turned out to be net sellers of stock worth 3.1 billion baht, unlike local investors who were net buyers of 6 billion baht. Local investors were ranked the highest trading value for the year among other investors with the amount of 2.1 trillion baht or around 66% of total trading, while foreign investors' trading value was 946.8 billion baht, almost 30% of the total trading. Other minor investors were local institutions (securities companies and mutual funds) who held the trading value of 157.7 billion baht, or less than 5% of the total trading.

Table 3.   Net Buy Categorized by Customer Type.

Customer Type	1999	1998	1997
Foreign investors (million baht)	−3,134	30,227	55,437
Local institutions (million baht)	−2,872	−3,239	−22,453
Local investors (million baht)	6,006	−26,987	−32,984

Source: The Stock Exchange of Thailand.

There are reasons behind this small portion. Provident fund managers mainly invested in cash deposits and government bonds while insurance houses invested in mostly debentures and bonds, but not in equities due to a strict and complicated set of regulations preventing both improper management of the portfolios and stock speculations. Nevertheless, the Thai government is now interested in having more participation from the provident funds. All of the above indicate that Thai individuals play a major part in overall trading and in the general level of stock ownership within companies.

On the supply side, SET tried to encourage the number of listed companies by providing many benefits such as setting up another board to allow small and newly established companies with promising performance to raise funds through the capital market, and temporarily reducing the annual fees levies on listed companies and unit trusts, etc.

The number of quoted companies before the 1997 crash was 431 which shrunk 3% in 1998 to 418, and to 392 in 1999 because most companies' performances were affected by the 1997 crisis. In 1999, there were no new listed companies. The performance of the existing listed companies was disappointing; 26 companies were delisted (10 voluntary and 16 mandatory delistings) with a total loss for the three quarters of 333 billion baht. Despite all of that, SET believes the number of listed companies will increase due to the lower cost of equity financing compared to the debt financing when listing their stocks with SET.

GAAP, DISCLOSURE REQUIREMENTS, AND THE TRANSPARENCY CONCEPT IN THAILAND

Because of the rise in the significance of trading and the influence of foreign aid, the Institute of Certified Accountants of Thailand was first established in 1948. At times, the influence of the U.S. system via financial aid not only played an important role in the characteristics of the Thai economy, but also on the development of Thai accounting standards. Similar to the U.S. system, the Institute of Certified Accountants of Thailand is responsible for developing the Thai General Accepted Accounting Principles (Thai-GAAP). Most of

Thai-GAAP is based on the U.S. General Accepted Accounting Principle (U.S.-GAAP) (Keynes, 1993).

During the period in which the capital market developed in Thailand, the Thai accounting profession also developed. In 1975, when the significance of the role of certified auditors was well recognized, the institute changed its name to the Institute of Certified Accountants and Auditors of Thailand (ICAAT) (ICCAT, 2001).

During this period, the institute issued 31 Thai accounting standards, most of them based on International Accounting Standards (IAS) and the US – GAAP. They include:

(1) Basic Assumptions on Accounting
(2) Accounting Policies
(3) Extra-ordinary Items
(4) Accounting Changes
(5) Earnings per Share
(6) Revenue Recognition
(7) Leasing – Lessor Side
(8) Long-Term Contract
(9) Accounting for Land, Buildings, and Equipment
(10) Depreciation
(11) Bad Debts and Allowance for Bad Debts
(12) Marketable Securities
(13) Disclosure for Related Companies
(14) Research and Development Costs
(15) Interest Capitalization
(16) Current Assets and Current Liabilities
(17) Accounting for Investments
(18) Accounting for Investments in Subsidiaries and Associations
(19) Consolidated Financial Statements
(20) Accounting for Business Combinations
(21) Contingencies and Events Occurring After Balance Sheet Date
(22) Valuation and Presentation of Inventories in the Context of the Historical Cost
(23) Information to be disclosed in Financial Statements
(24) Reporting Financial Information by Segment
(25) Cash flow Statements
(26) Revenue Recognition for real estate business
(27) Financial disclosure for Bank and Finance institution as well as a like business

(28) Accounting for convertible debt instrument and debt instrument with warrant
(29) Accounting for long-term lease contract
(30) The effect from the changing of Foreign exchange system
(31) Inventory.

According to Priebjrivat (1992), although reported as meeting the standards of the IFC (IFC, 1990), Thai accounting standards for Listed companies are viewed to have inadequate disclosure requirements for providing sufficient information about the operations of the company, profitability, financial health, financial growth and future prospects for investors in determining their investment decisions. As a result the SET requires the following disclosures from all Listed companies:

Type of Information	Time period
1. Quarterly financial statement (unreviewed)	Within 30 days from the end of each quarter
2. Quarterly financial statement re-viewed by the auditor	Within 45 days from the end of each quarter
3. Annual financial statement certified by the auditor. Consolidated statement if the company has invested more than 50% in another company	Within 60 days from the end of the accounting period if the financial statement of the 4th quarter has not been submitted before, and within 3 months if the financial statement of the 4th quarter had been submitted
4. Annual report	Within 4 months from the end of the accounting period.
5. Form for further disclosure of information to the SET (Form 56-1)	Within 3 months from the end of the accounting period
6. Information on operation and financial structure that might affect trading shares and interests of shareholders.	One hour prior to the start of each trading session or after the daily market close for information relating to important events which have or are likely to have an effect on investment decisions, shareholders' interests and securities prices such as capital increases or decreases, payment or non-payments of dividends, mergers or acquisitions of assets. Within 3 working days for information such as changes in the company's board members. Within 14 working days for information such as minutes of ordinary or extraordinary shareholders meetings.

ANNUAL REPORT

The shareholders and SET must have annual reports certified by the authorized auditor of all listed and authorized companies within 4 months after the end of an accounting period. The annual report must have the following information.

(1) Financial statement information according to the Ministerial Regulation No. 2 (1976) and in conformity with accounting standards prescribed by the Institute of Certified Accountants and Auditors of Thailand.

(2) Notes to financial statements describing details of loan collateral, debt covenants, and other company obligations that should affect shareholders' benefits.

(3) If a company has acquired more than 50% of the voting shares of any another company, a consolidated financial statement should also be presented.

(4) A statement of change in financial position.

(5) Two-year comparative financial statements.

(6) If the issue discussed in financial statements is not covered by Thai accounting standard, pronouncements of the International Accounting Standards Committee and the U.S. FASB shall be applied respectively.

(7) Other information:

- Name and location of the company's headquarter;
- Report of the Chairman or the Board;
- Brief information on the company's activities;
- The analytical report concerning the results of the operation and changes
- Important information concerning the parent company, subsidiary and affiliated companies;
- At least five-year comparative statistical data of the operations results and the financial status;
- The company executive's information.

QUARTERLY REPORT

A Listed or an authorized company must submit a quarterly financial statement reviewed by an authorized auditor within a period of 45 days from the end of each quarter. A quarterly financial statement must include the following information:

(1) Most recent quarter income statement; the equivalent calendar quarter of the prior year and year-to-date data for both years.

(2) A balance sheet at the end of the most recent quarter and for the equivalent quarter in the preceding year.

Compared to the annual report the quarterly report requires much fewer items.

ADDITIONAL INFORMATION

A listed or an authorized company is required to disclose further information in a Form 56-1 (required document) to the SET within three months from the end of the accounting period. The required information includes:

(1) Company name, address, amount of listed or authorized securities;
(2) Statement of the business undertaken by the company and its subsidiaries during the year and proposed projects as well as important changes and business developments from the beginning of the fiscal year;
(3) The latest five-year summary of operations for a company or for a company and its subsidiaries;
(4) A short description of the location and general characteristics of land, buildings and other principal facilities of the company and its subsidiaries;
(5) A list or diagram of all subsidiaries and affiliated companies, with the percentage of voting stocks owned in each company;
(6) Legal proceedings;
(7) End-the-year equity shares and debentures information and any changes during the year;
(8) Number of shareholders and the distribution of shareholders;
(9) Detailed information of the company's executive officers and directors, such as names and ages, family relationships among them, date of employment, and business experience;
(10) Principal shareholders and share holding of executive officers;
(11) Direct or indirect interest of executive officers, directors and others involved in any transactions to which the company is a party.

Financial disclosure in Thailand is a recent development when compared with financial disclosure in the U.S. Further, while there have been developments in financial disclosure requirements, there are few specific requirements for non-financial disclosure. However, the SEC, SET, and BOT have shown interested in this area by providing guidelines, instructions, and policies for corporate government and reports.

Similar to the U.S.'s system, The Institute of Certified Accountants and Auditors of Thailand (ICAAT) is the sole professional body responsible for developing Thai-GAAP. Under ICAAT announcement number 010/2540-2542,

"Policy of Setting Thai Accounting Standards", ICAAT has explicitly developed its position supporting international accounting standards (IAS) and US-GAAP by announcing that the Thai GAAP would be based on IAS. If there are no IAS standard for the topic, the ICAAT would set up Thai-GAAP in accordance with U.S.-GAAP. Thus, basically, the Thai-GAAP is a combination of the IAS and the U.S.-GAAP with certain modifications to align with the Thai business environment.

While mandatory measures issued by regulatory bodies such as the SEC, SET, BOT and the Ministry of Commerce are intended to be minimum requirements, the majority of CFO's, accountants and CEO's feel that they represent the maximum standards or a code of best practice. Thus, innovative mandatory measures might be required to improve disclosure quality. To ensure acceptance of any new Thai-GAAP related to disclosure, ICAAT is trying to gain participation from various groups including users of financial statements, private and public companies, and governmental authorities. However, major challenge exists in implementing the disclosure requirements due to different cultural and individual mindsets. Thai culture is not accustomed to formal written disclosure standards. Verbal presentation has long been the main form of communication.

THE AUDIT COMMITTEE, THE BOARD OF DIRECTORS AND THEIR ROLE IN FINANCIAL DISCLOSURE

As required by the SEC since January 2000, every listed company in Thailand, must establish an audit committee, aside from the board of directors, as a body responsible for financial disclosure. Under this requirement, three to five members of such audit committees have to be independent from management (SET, 2000). In this setting, the responsibility for audit, control, and financial disclosure is transferred to the audit committee who acts as architect and engineer to ensure adequate financial and non-financial disclosures. This minimizes the influence of management, which typically represents key "family-members" who are shareholders in publicly traded companies.

Moreover, in the case of such public "family-owned" companies, the market participation of a few key individuals plays an influential role on company business, performance, reputation, and stock valuation. According to these key relationships, shareholders are tied into important family network as well. These related party networks reduce the role and impact of the general published information as a market force per se. Under such a situation, it is difficult for management and the board to understand need and the benefit of increasing the degree of required "public" disclosure. Therefore, the existence of an audit committee in a listed company helps balance influences upon the disclosure behavior of firms, increasing the broader appeal of such firms and making them "open" to more public participation.

Compensation amounts for board members and executives in Asia and in Thailand are typically disclosed in total not in detail. Similarly, corporate governance information is reported in general rather than specific terms. Remuneration packages for both directors and management in Asian companies, including Thai companies, are rarely based on experience and competence. Typically, except for the chairman, most board members receive similar remuneration packages, which yield an executive director several times more compensation than a non-executive director (Jelatianranat, 2000).

In September 1999, the SET issued a Code of Best Practice for Directors of listed companies providing suggestions for listed company board reporting to regulatory entities, shareholders and investors. In addition, in January 2000, a paper containing comments from listed companies over a six-month period was distributed. This paper reflected the efforts of the SET to promote good corporate governance. The report was influenced by the Cadbury Report published in the U.K. and modified to reflect Thai culture and the family-based preferences of listed companies. It offers guidelines for voluntary disclosure. This guidance is presented in six sections; the board, the financial and audit reports, information disclosure and transparency, equitable business conduct, and compliance with the code of best practice (Jelatianranat, 2000).

In the last decade, to encourage listed companies to improve the quality of financial disclosure through annual reports, the SET also initiated an annual report competition involving annual reports amongst listed companies.

The Institute of Internal Auditors of Thailand (IAAT), by endorsing the principle of "transparency," has also played a role in supporting the improvement of the quality of disclosure. IAAT's corporate governance campaign is intended to help stimulate the concept, which is one of the six key principles of good corporate governance advocated by IAAT. A regular TV program – "Transparency 360 degrees" was also launched to provide education about and promote corporate governance. Both the TV program on corporate governance and an annual contest about Best Practices in Corporate Governance have sought to establish a trend for top companies to demonstrate positive values and signal the significance of transparency (Jelatianranat, 2000).

As can be seen from the activities of organizations such as SET and IAAT, after the 1997 crisis, there was a shift into a new way of thinking about Thailand's economy. Attention began being paid to improve disclosure standards in order to restore trust, improve corporate reputations and present companies as being of high quality in the corporate global community. It is expected that all these encouraged activities and promotional campaigns sponsored by professional bodies such as IAAT and SET will help create awareness about the significance of transparent and high quality disclosure, leading to an expectation among business leaders, regulators, the public, and other stakeholders, to support an improved quality of disclosure.

CONCLUSION

Voluntary disclosure is one of the tools allowing firms to communicate their information to investors, strategic allies and others. Information disclosed is intended to help others in valuing the "future" of the firms. To reveal a full picture of the firms, information about governance and non-financial performance measures, which are not mandated to be included in the financial statements, should be provided by voluntary disclosure through means such as messages from the chairman of the board as well as from the CEO. The areas that have been suggested for disclosure include forward looking statements, market share data, other performance measures, dynamics of the business, capital structures, treasury management, future investment or divestment (a three years period), liquidity, corporate governance-framework and practices, business ethics, employment reporting, and environmental reporting.

After the crisis in 1997, Thai financial markets changed from depending mainly on banks and financial institutions to acquiring funds through the money market in Thailand and overseas. When the money market plays a major role in the Thai economy, good corporate governance, transparency, and high quality disclosure affects investment decisions made by lenders, creditors, and investors even more than before. Transparency and quality disclosure are also recognized as beneficial in a global capital market with no practical boundaries.

Emerging Thai disclosure practices following the 1997 crisis are more complex than ever. These reflect family-based management preferences and styles, and the needs of Western-model joint ventures and alliances, as well as practices of a more Asian-model. This new era has brought with it an awakening of appreciation for better disclosure by Thai firms.

REFERENCES

International Finance Corporation (1990). *Emerging Stock Market Factbook 1988–1990.* The Economist Publication.

Jelatianranat, K. (2000). Thailand's Corporate Governance Issues and Development The Role of Disclosure in Strengthening Corporate Governance and Accountability. Paper presented in the 31 May–2 June 2000, The Second Asian Roundtable on Corporate Governnance, Hong Kong, China.

Keynes, M. (Aug. 1993). *Thailand Doing Business: Accounting and Taxation*. Corporate Location.
Muscat, R. J. (1994). *The Fifth Tiger – A Study of Thai Development Policy*. United Nations University Press.
Priebjrivat, A. (1992). Corporate Disclosure – A Case of Securities Exchange of Thailand. Dissertation, New York University.
Skully, M. T. (1984). *Financial Institutions and Markets in Southeast Asia – A study of Brubei, Indonesia, Malaysia, Philippines, Singapore and Thailand*. St. Martin's Press.
The Institute of Certified Accountants and Auditors of Thailand. About The Institute of Certified Accountants and Auditors of Thailand Retrieved March 16, 2001 from World Wide Web: http://www.icaat.or.th
The Stock Exchange of Thailand. *History, Role and Growth Performance*. Retrieved March 11, 2001 from World Wide Web: http://www.set.or.th
The Stock Exchange of Thailand (2000). *Fact Book 2000*. The Stock Exchange of Thailand.
Vichyanond, P. (1994). *Thailand's Financial System: Structure and Liberalization*. The Thailand Development Research Institute.
Warr, P. G. (1999). What Happened to Thailand? *The World Economy, 22*, 631–650.

MANDATORY AUDITOR ROTATION: A CRITIQUE OF THE PANEL ON AUDIT EFFECTIVENESS

Jeffrey R. Casterella, Barry L. Lewis and
Paul L. Walker

ABSTRACT

The Public Oversight Board appointed the Panel on Audit Effectiveness to perform a comprehensive review of how audits are performed and the environment in which audits take place. The purpose of this paper is to provide both a brief summary of the work and recommendations of the Panel and a critique of the approach it employed to evaluate audit effectiveness. We argue that the Panel did not use a coherent framework of auditing that would allow them to identify relevant issues, examine existing evidence related to those issues, or propose additional research. As a result, the Panel apparently ignored the issue of mandatory auditor rotation, despite the fact that both Congress and the SEC have expressed concern about long term auditor-client relationships.

INTRODUCTION

As former Chairman of the SEC the legacy of Arthur Levitt is likely to be defined by his insatiable desire to improve the financial reporting system in

Research in Accounting Regulation, Volume 15, pages 259–268.
ISBN: 0-7623-0841-9

America. One of Mr. Levitt's targets of criticism in his quest to protect investors was the public accounting profession. Mr. Levitt was especially critical of auditors when he said, "the accounting profession, and particularly the AICPA have been almost oblivious to the words public interest" (Dwyer, 2000). Concerned that audits may not be serving the public's interest, Mr. Levitt asked for a full investigation of how audits are performed. On the last day of August 2000, the Public Oversight Board (POB) issued its report on the effectiveness of audits. The 255-page report was the culmination of nearly two years of work by an eight-member panel (hereafter referred to as "the Panel") whose duty was to perform a comprehensive review of how audits are performed and the environment in which audits take place.

The purpose of this paper is to provide both a brief summary of the work and recommendations of the Panel and a critique of the approach it employed to evaluate audit effectiveness. We argue that the Panel did not use a coherent framework of auditing that would allow them to identify relevant issues, examine existing evidence related to those issues, or propose additional research. As a result, the Panel apparently ignored the issue of mandatory auditor rotation, despite the fact that both Congress and the SEC have expressed concern about long term auditor-client relationships.

BACKGROUND

The SEC has become increasingly concerned with the audit profession's ability to protect investors. The concern stems in part from worries about the audit profession itself and from the "new economy" environment in which the profession performs audits. Auditors are required to maintain independence, both in fact and in appearance. While the concept of independence is a reasonably straightforward principle, putting it into action has been difficult. Consider the fact that auditors are hired (and can be fired) and are paid by the client. To make matters worse, auditors are expanding their practices by way of consulting revenues. The SEC strongly believes that auditing and consulting don't mix (McNamee, Dwyer, Schmitt & Lavelle, 2000). Their concern is that certain auditor-client relationships may undermine the independence necessary to perform unbiased financial statement audits. Meanwhile, the economy has experienced unprecedented growth over the past decade, which has created extreme pressure for companies to continually report numbers that will please Wall Street. Large-scale frauds such as Waste Management, Cendant, and Sunbeam suggest that the audit profession might be in trouble. These concerns resulted in the formation of the Panel and a full investigation of the audit process.

THE PANEL'S STRATEGY

The Panel's approach was to critically examine how audits are performed (i.e. the process) and the environment in which audits are performed (i.e. the context). GAAS requires that auditors use a process that is driven largely by the audit risk model. The model is flexible in that it allows for custom-tailored audits that are determined, in large part, by the various risks that are germane to each client. The Panel examined the audit risk model to assess its validity and effectiveness.

From the SEC's perspective, one of the most concerning context-related aspects is the multiple roles that auditors often assume above and beyond auditing financial statements (*Journal of Accountancy*, 1996). With audit revenues relatively flat, public accounting firms have expanded their practices to include consulting, for which revenues are booming (McNamee, Dwyer, Schmitt & Lavelle, 2000).

The Panel used a multi-pronged approach. One of the most significant aspects of its review was a detailed process review of 126 audits performed by the eight largest public accounting firms. 37 of the 126 engagements also involved consulting services. The Panel performed additional review procedures on these engagements to consider the effect of non-audit services on auditor independence. The Panel also investigated the possible audit process causes for audits that had been examined by the SEC. A total of 96 SEC Accounting and Auditing Enforcement Releases (AAERs) were analyzed. The SEC's enforcement division issues AAERs to document their investigations of fraudulent financial reporting.

In addition, the Panel used surveys, focus groups, and hearings to gather information from a wide range of interested parties such as public accounting firms, public and private corporations, academics, attorneys, analysts, and various regulatory groups.

FINDINGS AND RECOMMENDATIONS

The Panel made several major recommendations that were grouped into five areas. The following is a summary taken, in substance, from the Executive Overview section of the Panel's report (POB, 2000).

Conduct of Audits

Overall, the Panel seemed to be reasonably satisfied with the manner in which audits were performed. However they did express concern that auditors were not doing a satisfactory job of detecting material fraud. For example, the AAER review indicated that failed audits were often accompanied by a lack of professional skepticism on the part of the auditors. The Panel suggested that a forensic audit component should be included on every engagement and that auditors should be "driven to a higher plane of behavior" through improved audit methodologies.

Leadership and Practices of Audit Firms

The Panel emphasized the need for professional leadership and a clear understanding of "the tone at the top" of audit firms. The Panel recommended that the firms continue to emphasize the importance of independence and objectivity on behalf of auditors. For example, the Panel called on audit firms to "stimulate their auditors to proudly hold the banner of objectivity, independence, professional skepticism and accountability to the public by performing quality audit work" (POB, 2000, p. xi).

Auditor Independence – Non-audit services

The provision of non-audit services to audit clients has been an on-going concern of the SEC and therefore was a primary issue in the Panel's investigation. In the end, the Panel's conclusions were mixed. Some members of the Panel were in favor of a complete ban on non-audit services provided by auditors, while other members rejected the idea of a ban. One reason for the impasse was disagreement on whether or not consulting services provided ancillary benefits to the performance of a high quality audit.

Governance of the Audit Profession

While the Panel supported a self-governance system, it called for the POB to assume a larger, more formal role as monitor of the audit profession.[1] This expanded role would allow the POB "to serve as the body to whom the SEC, state boards of accountancy, the auditing profession and the public can look for leadership" (POB, 2000, p. xii).

International Perspectives

The Panel decided to relay many of its recommendations to foreign audit firms through the International Federation of Accountants. The primary recommendation was that all countries recognize the importance of strong self-regulatory systems. The Panel also stressed the importance of public oversight, implementation of uniform audit methodologies worldwide, periodic inspection procedures, and progress towards harmonized auditing standards.

Part and parcel to the Panel's recommendations was a dominant theme that an auditor's integrity, honesty and sense of responsibility to society were the most important drivers of quality audits. Despite numerous recommendations and suggestions in the report, the Panel stated that "no amount of guidance, admonitions to do good work, the right 'tone at the top,' or the threat of sanctions will produce a high quality audit unless every individual auditor embraces a high sense of personal responsibility and diligence" (POB, 2000, p. xiv).

A CRITIQUE OF THE PANEL'S EFFORT

It seems clear that the Panel's report represents a significant step toward more effective and efficient audits. The critique that follows is from an academic viewpoint. We acknowledge that our approach may not have been appropriate, or at least may not have seemed appropriate for the Panel to pursue in meeting their charge from the POB.

The Panel examined audit processes and the context in which audits were performed. We believe a more productive approach would have been to view a successful audit as a function of: (1) the auditor's ability to detect errors, irregularities, and fraud, and (2) the auditor's willingness to disclose or report deficiencies. While most academic researchers assume audit technology is sufficient to detect problems, there are many behavioral research studies that have examined and found inherent limitations to auditors' abilities. Such limitations might explain, for example, the fraud detection problem that the Panel mentioned in their report.

The issue of auditor willingness to report, however, could have used a more coherent framework for analysis. Many researchers view the willingness to report as an economic incentives problem (Raghunathan, Lewis & Evans, 1994; Watts & Zimmerman, 1981; Antle, 1984). Such an approach leads to the investigation of relationships that may provide incentives for auditors to overlook problems. While this may include consulting activities (which were considered by the Panel), it would certainly include others such as long term auditor-client relationships (which apparently were not considered by the Panel).

LONG TERM RELATIONSHIPS VS. MANDATORY AUDITOR ROTATION

The concern over long term auditor-client relationships is that audit firms and their personnel may become identified or "aligned" to their clients' interests becoming possibly complacent or less challenging in their attitude and related audit approaches, thereby risking their independence, objectivity and professional skepticism. Over the past 25 years, critics of the accounting profession and regulators have suggested the use of mandatory auditor rotation as a way to manage long standing auditor-client relationships.[2] In 1976, the U.S. Senate recommended mandatory auditor rotation because they believed that competition amongst public accounting firms was lacking, in part, because clients and their auditors were staying together for too many years. The AICPA responded by forming the Commission on Auditors' Responsibilities (the Cohen Commission) to investigate the benefits and costs of mandatory auditor rotation. The Commission concluded that the costs of mandatory auditor rotation were prohibitive. Instead, they recommended rotation of audit teams and partners (Commission on Auditors' Responsibilities, 1978).

In 1985, during the Dingell committee hearings, United States Congressman Shelby asked, "How can an auditing firm remain independent when it has established long term personal and professional relationships with a company by auditing the same company for many years, some 10, 20 or 30 years?" (U.S. House of Representatives, 1985).[3] But, when the Treadway Commission (a private sector group) investigated factors that lead to fraudulent financial reporting, they did not recommend mandatory auditor rotation, but rather the rotation of in-charge audit partners (NCFFR, 1987).

More recently, Chief accountant of the SEC, Lynn Turner, called for research that could help to reduce audit failures and specifically asked, "What is the relationship between the duration of the auditor/client relationship and audit failures?" (Turner & Godwin, 1999, p.295). Mr. Turner's interest in auditor/client relationships indicates that the SEC continues to be concerned about long term auditor-client relationships even though a 1994 SEC staff report on auditor independence confirmed most of the Cohen Commission's findings and seemed to conclude that rotation of in-charge audit partners was sufficient (SEC, 1994).

EVIDENCE ON LONG TERM AUDITOR-CLIENT RELATIONSHIPS

While there have been few, if any, empirical linkages found between audit failures and the provision of consulting services by the auditor, the literature on auditor-client relationships has found at least preliminary evidence that longer relationships are prone to audit failure.

One possible solution is to require publicly held firms to change auditors on some fixed schedule, with five or seven years often suggested.[4] Empirical data show that many companies have auditor-client relationships in excess of seven years. A 1993 survey of 774 companies revealed that the average tenure period is sixteen years. Additionally, 170 companies (22% of those who responded) reported tenure periods of at least twenty-five years and 75 companies (nearly 10%) reported tenure periods of at least forty years (Casterella, Lewis & Walker, 1999).

Early research indicated that both long and short term relationships are prone to failure (Raghunathan, Lewis & Evans, 1994). A subsequent study showed that there are more audit failures associated with long term relationships than with short term relationships (Walker, Lewis & Casterella, 2000). Furthermore, long term relationships that have failed appear to be more costly than short term relationships that have failed. For the years 1980–1991, the average market capitalization loss for companies in failed long term relationships was $138 million, nearly three times the average market capitalization loss for first-year failures. These data seem to suggest that long term relationships are bad and that mandatory rotation is needed. However, a mandatory rotation regime would produce a significant increase in the number of new auditor-client relationships. Is there any evidence that suggests that short term relationships are a panacea?

Walker, Lewis and Casterella (2000) showed that there are more long term failures, in part, because long term relationships are more prevalent than short term relationships. Further analysis found that while the majority of failures involved long term auditor-client relationships, short term relationships had a higher *rate* of failure. The higher failure rate in new audits was attributed to the auditors' lack of knowledge of the client and its business, knowledge that is gained over time. On the other hand, the study also provided evidence suggesting that the failure rate for *involuntary* changers under a mandatory rotation regime is likely to be *lower* than that which we currently observe for voluntary changers.

Consequently, it is difficult to know whether more short term relationships (from mandatory auditor rotation) would help or not. The main problem with both sides of these arguments is the lack of data necessary to support either position. Given how little evidence exists on the key mandatory auditor rotation issues, we believe that additional research is needed to determine the validity of the positions and the value of any proposed changes.

One of the added complexities in understanding long term audits is that they are probably affected not only by auditors' willingness to report (via economic incentives), but also by the ability of auditors to detect problems (Raghunathan, Lewis & Evans, 1994). While longer auditor-client relationships should make the auditor more knowledgeable about its client, research indicates that auditor judgments are often driven by low-grade heuristics rather than by underlying base rate information about the client (Joyce & Biddle, 1981). Other research indicates that auditors are susceptible to evidence confirming strategies and that alternative frames systematically (and adversely) affect auditors' strategies and judgments (Ayers & Kaplan, 1993).

SUMMARY AND CONCLUSIONS

The Public Oversight Board appointed the Panel on Audit Effectiveness to perform a comprehensive review of how audits are performed and the environment in which audits take place. In this paper, we have briefly reviewed the Panel's recommendations and have highlighted the key issues surrounding mandatory auditor rotation.

In mid-November of 2000, Mr. Levitt and the SEC were successful in passing a compromise rule that limits, but does not ban, consulting services to audit clients. The new rule has increased the responsibility of audit committees by forcing them to be more aggressive about monitoring auditors' independence. For example, the new rule requires that audit committees pre-approve any non-audit services before the auditor commences the project. In January of 2001, Mr. Levitt reinforced this responsibility by issuing a letter to the audit committee chairpersons of the top 5,000 publicly traded companies. The letter offered ten guidelines on how to determine the "appropriateness" of a non-audit service. The new rule also required public disclosure of the size of the fees for non-audit services. Academic researchers can use this data to shed some evidential light on the relation between consulting and audit failures.

Given the SEC's interest in auditor rotation now (Turner and Godwin, 1999) and in the past, it is surprising that the Panel did not address rotation as one of its primary research and analysis tasks. It seems that the overriding concern of the Panel was that auditors may not remain independent when consulting fees are at stake. We believe that the Panel's concern over auditor independence should have necessitated an analysis of long term and short term auditor-client relationship failure rates. If auditors don't seem to do well with long standing audits, what does that imply about long standing audits *and* the provision of consulting services? Does the provision of consulting services to audit clients improve or worsen the audit failure rates in long and short term relationships?

There are several other possible research topics related to auditor-client relationships. For example, do audit failures seem to occur because of knowledge deficiencies on the part of the auditor, or are they more likely to occur because of independence and/or bias issues? The accounting profession requires partner rotation on public companies every seven years. Has this requirement reduced the rate of audit failure? Countries abroad have adopted mandatory auditor rotation regimes. Is there any evidence to suggest that audit failure rates have changed as a result of rotation?

NOTES

1. Mr. Levitt expressed his frustration about the cut off of funding for the POB. Mr. Levitt said, "In the midst of enormous public interest in the independence issue and a new chairman being appointed to the POB, the AICPA cuts off funding. Because of that, I believe it is mandatory the POB must change if it's to take on a quasi-regulatory function. It has to have the symbols and the reality of power" (Dwyer, 2000).

2. See Hoyle (1978) for a review of the basic arguments for and against rotation.

3. In 1994 the Senate Commerce Committee considered mandatory rotation for certain telecommunication companies (*Journal of Accountancy*, 1995).

4. Spain and Italy are experimenting with mandatory rotation policies and critics of the accounting profession in Germany and the United Kingdom have called for mandatory rotation of auditors. In the U.K., the McFarlane report recommended five-year appointments. In Germany, Bundesbank decided to rotate auditors in an effort to encourage other German companies to do the same (*European Accountant*, 1996).

REFERENCES

Antle, R. (1984). Auditor independence. *Journal of Accounting Research*, (Spring), 1–20.

Ayers, S., & Kaplan S. E. (1993). An examination of the effect of hypothesis framing on auditors' information choices in an analytical procedure task. *Abacus*, 29(September), 113–130.

Casterella J. R., Lewis B. L., & Walker, P. L. (1999). The effect of auditor specialization and industry concentration on the cost of audit services. Working paper (August), Colorado State University.

Commission on Auditors' Responsibilities (Cohen Commission) (1978). *Report, Conclusions, and Recommendations*. New York: American Institute of Certified Public Accountants.

Dwyer, P. (2000). I want it crystal-clear who's to blame. *Business Week*, (September 25).

European Accountant (1996). Germany: Bundesbank names KPMG as auditor. (May), 4.

Hoyle, J. (1978). Mandatory auditor rotation: the arguments and an alternative. *Journal of Accountancy* 145(May), 69–78.

Journal of Accountancy (1995). News report: Auditing and Accounting, 10.

Joyce, E. J., & Biddle, G. C. (1981). Are Auditors' Judgments Sufficiently Regressive? *Journal of Accounting Research* 19(Autumn), 323–349.

McNamee, M., Dwyer, P., Schmitt, C. H., & Lavelle, L. (2000). Accounting wars. *Business Week*, (September 25).

National Commission on Fraudulent Financial Reporting (Treadway Commission) (NCFFR) (1987). *Report of the national commission on fraudulent financial reporting*. New York: American Institute of Certified Public Accountants.

Public Oversight Board (POB) (2000). *The panel on audit effectiveness report and recommendations*. Stamford, CT: POB.

Raghunathan, B., Lewis, B. L., & Evans, J. H., III. (1994). An empirical investigation of problem audits. *Research in Accounting Regulation*, (8), 33–58.

Securities and Exchange Commission (1994). Staff report on auditor independence (March).

Turner, L. E., & Godwin, J. H. (1999). Auditing, earnings management, and international accounting issues at the Securities and Exchange Commission. *Accounting Horizons*, *13*(September), 281–297.

U.S. House of Representatives (1985). Hearings before the Subcommittee on Oversight and Investigations and the Committee on Energy and Commerce, Ninety-Ninth Congress, First Session, February 20 and March 6. U. S. Government Printing Office.

Walker, P. L., Lewis, B. L., & Casterella, J. R. (2000). Mandatory auditor rotation: arguments and current evidence. Working Paper (November), Colorado State University.

Watts, R., & Zimmerman, J. (1981). The markets for independence and independent auditors. Working paper, University of Rochester.

PART IV:
BOOK REVIEWS

Marquis G. Eaton: A Collection of His Writings.

Edited by Edward N. Coffman and Daniel L. Jensen.
Columbus, OH, The Ohio State University, 2000, 369 pages.
ISBN 1-883356-06-7

Reviewed by Timothy J. Fogarty
Case Western Reserve University.

Since 1993, the Ohio State University has been celebrating the members of the Accounting Hall of Fame with the Thomas J. Burns Series in Accounting History. Volume 5 collects the writings of Marquis Eaton, who, among other professional duties, was AICPA president from 1956 to 1957. This volume collects 37 pieces that were created by Eaton from 1933 to 1957. The editors have classified these pieces into categories that illustrate the considerable range of Eaton's work. The Eaton collection also includes a more complete bibliography of Eaton's works (listing 43 items) and information about the Accounting Hall of Fame. The collection situates Eaton well within the 1950s. Twenty-six of the thirty-seven pieces were created during that decade. However, these materials are well dispersed throughout that decade, reflecting a career of writing not necessarily limited to his period at the helm of the Institute.

The collection comprises many original works that could otherwise prove difficult to access. Many of the pieces are transcriptions of speeches delivered by Eaton and letters written by him. Eaton's Texas roots are clearly visible since many items were originally produced in that jurisdiction.

Those interested in the 20th century history of accounting in the U.S. will find plenty to like about the Eaton compilation. Eaton provides a fresh view on many important events that shaped the profession including the passage of the Securities laws, the early days of systematic standard setting and the post-war expansion of the federal income tax. The book also provides many first-hand insights into the contentious organization of accountants during a pivotal period.

The substance of the materials is organized into seven areas by the editors, a typology that is effective although there are considerable overlaps. These categories demonstrate Eaton's considerable range as a practitioner and professional leader. Eaton seems equally comfortable discussing the pragmatics of practice management, the public interest dimensions of the occupation and the intricacies of the tax law. The categories also show that Eaton operated effectively in the corridors of power and as a "man of the people."

A surprising number of the topics explored in this collection remain timely and relevant for today's reader. Eaton often rails against the public's under-appreciation of accountancy, although he is much more defensive and self-effacing about it than would be fashionable today. The independence concerns created by consulting work was also a palatable issue for Eaton. The penultimate section of the book, given over to relations with the bar, shows that many debates change from over a half-century, but do not disappear. The complexities of the tax code that so bemused Mark Eaton have certainly only intensified over the period since his writings.

On other dimensions, the Eaton compilation demonstrates how far the profes-sion has come over the years. Eaton continuously returns to the poor state of accountant education. He held out much more hope for profession-sponsored continuing education than for university-sponsored degree-producing course-work. The chapters given over to closer examinations of the work done by accountants now appear quaint since they could not anticipate how much would be revolutionized by information technology.

Eaton demonstrates considerable compassion for the problems of small firms and solo practitioners. One theme that repeats itself with some regularity is his belief that these accountants have been underpricing their services. Eaton never passes an opportunity to reiterate the importance of financial viability to practice. He rejects the vogue notions of the day that would contrast professions and businesses, instead insisting that the service is not done until the fee is paid. Although Eaton is unswerving in his belief in the sanctity of accountancy, he also believes in specialization, meeting client demand and limiting oneself to the profitable tasks.

Readers looking for accounting theory will not find it in these pages. Eaton, through his writings, appears more as a politician than a philosopher. Although he usually articulates a case on behalf of specific standards and treatments, he sees his task as selling the standards as being appropriate. His work therefore contributed to modern practice where there is a much more institutionalized acceptance of central authority for the manner in which work is performed. Eaton's efforts also appear to be instrumental in building acceptance for the AICPA as the voice of the profession. Constantly he regales his audiences with evidence that this organization is working on their behalf. At the same time, he acknowledges that it needs to do more.

The readings in this book illustrate the work of a man keenly aware of how professions operate. Modern writings on professionalization are quite consistent with the terrain mapped out by Marquis Eaton. In their totality, we are treated to the difficulties faced at the boundaries by an ascending profession. We are also given plenty to appreciate about the struggles with clientele groups to gain greater access and acceptability.

This book is primarily recommended for readers interested in the history of accounting. Others that might like it are those interested in the evolution of management and the professions that service businesses.

Foundations for the Future: The AICPA from 1980–1995.

By Philip B. Chenok with Adam Snyder.
(Studies in the Development of Accounting Thought. London, England: Elsevier
Science, 2000; ISBN 0-7623-0672-6, $78.50USD).

Reviewed by Kevin Carduff
Case Western Reserve University.

Foundations for the Future details the history of the AICPA from 1980 to 1985
under the leadership of AICPA president, Philip Chenok. Under his period of
leadership the accounting profession endured some of its largest struggles and
faced its biggest challenges. During the 1980s and early 1990s, the business
environment was extremely volatile and exciting with mass merger activity, the
overhaul of the tax codes, Black Monday of 1987, consolidation of the largest
accounting firms, and the call for more relevant financial reporting. Throughout
this period, CPAs were called upon by their clients to continually face all of
these challenges and devise the most innovative and efficient business
solutions. In addition to these new challenges, there were more and more CPAs
entering the profession. From 1980 to 1995, the AICPA membership increased
from 161,000 to 325,000. All of these challenges made this period a very
exciting and important time for the AICPA and it members.

Foundations serves as a form of institutional memory of the developments
made by the AICPA during the period of 1980 to 1995. This is a continuation
of the work started by John Carey in the late 1960s with his two volumes
entitled, *The Rise of the Accounting Profession: "From Technician to
Professional: 1896–1936"* (1969) and *"To Responsibility and Authority:
1937–1969"* (1970). *From Technician to Professional* details the evolution of
accounting and double-entry bookkeeping as effective business tools and crucial
functions of the corporate reporting process to the development of accounting
professionals and professional societies to the establishment of accounting standards and professional accountability and ethics. *To Responsibility and Authority*
discusses the numerous challenges that faced the accounting profession after
the establishment of the Securities and Exchange Commission. During this
period the profession was forced to defend its right to establish accounting standards, develop an official standards board, define new certification requirements,
and continue to develop new ethical standards. This developing record of institutional knowledge was continued by AICPA president Wally Olson to detail
his turbulent years as president from 1969 to 1980 in *The Accounting Profession:*

Years of Trial.

The first two chapters discuss two large issues faced by the AICPA at the beginning of Chenok's tenure: developing a strategic plan and combating the intense amounts of litigation faced by the profession. Two very important issues tackled by the AICPA initially under Chenok were the development of the Future Issues Committee, and from that process the development of a mission statement to guide the Institute and its members. These two developments allowed the AICPA to identify and deal with major issues effecting the profession in coming years, including increased consulting services, competition from non-CPA firms such as American Express, globalization and consolidation of the firms.

Even with all these challenges, the greatest threat to the profession continued to be the constant barrage of litigation faced by the accounting firms. In an ever-litigious social environment, scorned shareholders would look for someone with "deep pockets." In many cases, this became the accounting firms. The rule of joint and several liability hurt the firms most of all because they could be held liable for 100% of the damages regardless of their proportionate fault. Many rulings against the firms after the recession of the 1970s forced their insurers to raise their liability insurance and deductibles. As noted in the book, "insurance for 96% of accounting firms with more than fifty CPAs rose 300% between 1985 and 1992, with deductibles rising nearly sixfold." Many solutions to these problems and threats emerged. The Treadway Commission and the Kirk Report both looked at audit practices and the objectivity of the auditor in the face of rising scrutiny after audit failures. All of these measures forced the profession to improve itself without the assistance of governmental regulation, which was a constant threat.

Ever since the 1930s, the SEC has granted the accounting profession to regulate themselves with only government supervision. The next three chapters are concerned with the varying levels of regulation from state societies to the U.S. Government, the profession's methods for regulating itself, and the increase of the education requirements for certification to be a CPA. Chapter 3 details the different levels of regulation which the CPA profession encounters from SEC oversight on standard setting to the struggles between a national organization and the individual state societies which determine their own certification and CPE rules. One of the largest struggles between the national board and the state societies was the different CPA requirements and exams from state to state. In the hope of establishing a national certification which would be recognized from state to state (much like a driver's license), the Uniform Accountancy Act (UAA) was proposed, and after approximately 10 years of negotiation between the AICPA and the National Association of State Boards of Accountancy resulted in the approval of the UAA in 1992.

In addition to various national and state accountancy societies, the profession was subject to oversight by the federal government in the form of the SEC and the Congress. One of the most interesting section of this book is the detailing of the Congressional oversight committees chaired by Congressmen John Dingell of Michigan. The Dingell hearings were another attack on the accounting profession after some corporate failures, specifically attacking large audit failures and questioning auditor independence. These attacks on the profession forced the firms to begin defensive measures against regulation and to coordinate legislative lobbying efforts in Washington between the firms and the Institute. First, the establishment of a Political Action Committee, which by 1992 had become one of the largest in the nation, enabled the accounting profession to sway influence in Washington. Second, the firms joined together to establish the National Accountant's Coalition to lobby on behalf of the accounting profession for the passage of the Private Securities Litigation Reform Act. These efforts greatly consolidated the presence of the accounting profession within the Beltway.

To further combat Congressional pressures, the profession did take strides to improve its oversight and professional conduct. They recognize that the prestige of the accounting profession lays in its independence and that the validity of the capital market system is based upon the opinions of the independent auditor. The AICPA started a committee headed by George Anderson that came up with three recommendations for improving the accounting profession: better education at the entry level, peer review, and a revised code of professional conduct. These recommendations were well received and given to an implementation committee headed by Marvin Strait to build ground-roots support for the ideas and implementing them. In addition to establishing a new code of conduct, through these efforts the AICPA tackled many difficult issues including opinion shopping, independence, peer review, and, on of the most contentious issues, advertising and contingent fees. This period was a very difficult one for the AICPA; however, it changed many aspects of the accounting profession for the better.

Finally, the issue of increased education requirements had faced the accounting profession since the AICPA officially endorsed a fifth year of college education for CPA certification in 1978. Many people agreed that a fifth year of education was needed to be an effective CPA; however, getting all states to agree and implementing the requirements would be a challenge. The AICPA could not simply legislate across the board certification requirements for all CPAs. Each state board set their own requirements and timelines for these requirements. In addition, to the number of credit hours required to sit for the exam, there were debates over the content of accounting programs and AACSB accreditation standards to consider. In addition to the debate over entry level education and experience requirements, the AICPA began to address continuing professional education requirements and enforcement.

After handling many important issues facing the profession during the turbulent 1980s, the 1990s brought many new challenges to the Institute – most focusing upon a changing profession with regards to its primary role, financial reporting, and the makeup of it constituency. In Chapter 6, Chenok discusses the challenges faced by the FASB over special interest groups, the clamor over a derivatives standard, and the Jenkins Committee report calling for more relevant financial reporting, or "business reporting." Chenok recognizes the fact that the current accounting model is based on an 18th century manufacturing model with property, plants and equipment, while today's business environment is "a postindustrial service, knowledge-based economy" based on intangible assets. The profession is still attempting to resolve many of these issues to bring more relevant financial reporting to the investor community. This is an even greater problem with the proliferation of the Internet, investor relation websites, and streaming financial data to the desktop.

Along with the changing role of financial reporting, the outside perception and the internal demographics of the profession were changing. Several studies looked at the changing make-up of the AICPA membership and looked at the public's perceptions of CPAs with regard to morals and ethics, honesty, reliability and creativity. While the membership of the AICPA doubled over Chenok's tenure the makeup of the members changed drastically. There were more members from corporate practice than professional accounting firms, many members were older or retired, and there was a sharp increase in women CPAs. As to moral characteristics, two groups of people were surveyed: business leaders and the general public. The business leaders found CPAs very ethical and well regarded; however, the general public was more negative or simply was "not sure." To counteract these misperceptions the AICPA began nationwide advertising campaigns stressing the importance of CPAs and describing the roles they perform in society. This was the first time the profession had actively promoted itself to the general public.

Chenok's tenure as President of the AICPA was one of the most tumultuous and important periods for the accounting profession. Under his leadership the AICPA and various constituents tackled difficult issues, faced government scrutiny and change the face and direction of the accounting profession substantially. This book describes this period in detail and gives the reader some personal insights from the man in the middle of all of these issues. It provides an excellent resource to understand what the past issues were and the discussion which centered around them. Often people forget how they got to a certain point and need a reminder of past issues. This book provides a guide for the accounting profession on how to proceed in the future. One fault with the book is that often with collaborations, the single voice of the author gets confused or interchanged with the collaborator. This does occur throughout this book when items are repeated or confused. However, this does not detract from the valuable historical perspective that *Foundations for the Future* provides.

Accounting and the Investment Opportunity Set.

By Ahmed Riahi-Belkaoui.
(Quorum Books, Westport, CT, 2000, ISBN 1-56720-367-1,
216 pages, $69.50)

Reviewed by Reed A. Roig
Case Western Reserve University.

In the preface to the book, the author clearly indicates what he hopes to accomplish:

(1) Explicate the concept of growth opportunities or the investment opportunity set (IOS).
(2) Provide a general model for measurement of IOS.
(3) Show the role of IOS in:
    (a) a general valuation model based on dividend yield and price/earnings ratio;
    (b) the relationship between profitability and multinationality;
    (c) the determination of capital structure;
    (d) a general model of international production;
    (e) a general model of corporate disclosure;
    (f) the relationship between systematic risk and multinationality;
    (g) a model of reputation building;
    (h) earnings management;
    (i) the explanation of relative market value compared to accounting value of a multinational firm;
    (j) differentiation between the usefulness of accrual and cash flow based valuation models.

He devotes a chapter to each of these goals – twelve in all. These are significant and timely issues as we wrestle with our understanding of capital market valuation in this era of "dot com's". In addition, incorporating multinationality as a variable of interest addresses the continuing trend towards globalization in all industries.

Unfortunately, due to a lack of consistency and coherence, data analysis problems and uneven editing, the book fails to achieve most of its intended goals.

CONSISTENCY AND COHERENCE

The first two chapters of the book are meant to lay the groundwork for the remaining analyses. Chapter 1 provides a brief summary of the finance and accounting literature that describe the nature of IOS. The IOS or growth options are defined as "call options whose value depends on the discretionary future investments by the firm" (p. 8). Although other work is cited, this definition is drawn principally from the work of Stuart Myers on corporate borrowing.

He describes fourteen proxies that have been used to measure IOS and divides them into three groups: price-based (7), investment-based (5), and variance-based (2). He also notes the use of composite measures (developed by factor analysis). He concludes by quoting from a paper that tested many of these proxies against realized growth in firms and indicates that market/book measures (such as book to market value of assets or equity, Tobin's Q) and capital investment activity are consistently correlated with realized growth. Other proxies do not appear to exhibit consistent or strong associations with realized growth. He includes the paper, "The Association Between Investment Opportunity Set Proxies and Realized Growth", by Sanjay Kallapur and Mark A. Trombley, *Journal of Business Finance and Accounting* (April, May 1999), pp. 505–519, in an appendix to Chapter 1.

This background forms the basis for his proxy of IOS, a composite of three separate measures – market to book assets (MASS), market to book equity (MQV), and earnings/price ratio (EP) – developed using factor analysis in Chapter 2. He never explains, however, the inclusion of EP in the composite given its inconsistent correlation with growth in the Kallapur and Trombley paper, which figured so prominently in Chapter 1. Using this measure of IOS, he develops and tests a model which defines growth opportunities as a function of its advantages: corporate reputation, multinationality, size, and profitability; and limitations: leverage and systematic risk. While it would be possible to argue that the model should include additional variables (such as industry), using multiple regression, all the independent variables are significant and he achieves a relatively high R^2 of 30.28.

The remainder of the book, however, loses the consistency and coherence of these first two chapters. The next ten chapters give the appearance of ten individual papers included in the book because they examine the same subject matter, but without any effort to blend them into a cohesive "whole". Complete paragraphs are repeated word for word from chapter to chapter, as if this is the first time the reader has seen them. In several chapters, the author refers to himself as "we" (as in "we test", "we agree"), as if several authors wrote the text. Numerous variables, used throughout the book, are measured differently from chapter to chapter, with no explanation for the change. For example, a composite measure for multinationality is developed and used in Chapter 2. This measure is used again in Chapters 4, 5, 8, and 12. However, a totally different measure is used in Chapter 7, and another measure is used in Chapters 9 and 11. There is never any explanation as to why the measure is different than the one used previously, only a statement defining what measure was used. It is as if there is no recognition that the variable was used elsewhere in the book.

In addition, the author is not consistent in his use of variables from chapter to chapter. After he has developed his model of IOS in Chapter 2, he then examines the role of multinationality and profitability of IOS in Chapter 4. As noted above, the model built in Chapter 2 includes both multinationality and profitability as independent variables, and both are found to be significant contributors to the dependent variable – IOS. Why then in Chapter 4 does the author drop reputation, leverage, and beta from the model (all of which were significant in Chapter 2) and add percent change in GNP, percent change in inflation, and an index of business formation as independent variables? If these are important control variables here, shouldn't they have been included in the original model? Again, Chapter 4 is written in such a way that there is no recognition that there ever was a Chapter 2.

Finally, the author is inconsistent in the functional relationships he develops in his models.

- In Chapter 2, IOS is a function of reputation, multinationality, size, profitability, leverage and beta.
- In Chapter 6, multinationality is a function of reputation, leverage, IOS, and several other factors.
- In Chapter 8, beta is a function of reputation, multinationality, size, profitability, leverage, and IOS.
- In Chapter 9, reputation is a function of multinationality, size, and IOS.

The reader is left wondering what the true relationship amongst these variables is – which variables are the cause and which are the effect?

DATA ANALYSIS PROBLEMS

The author uses multiple regression techniques in all of the chapters except one, where he uses MANCOVA. The samples for testing in each chapter are drawn from *Forbes* Most International Manufacturing and Service Firms. The sample years vary from chapter to chapter, again with no explanation for the change. Several of the chapters would have benefited from regression analysis utilizing structural equation modeling techniques, which would allow simultaneous testing of multiple dependent variables or multiple group analysis.

One significant overall data problem that the author has is simply with sample bias. By selecting data from "most international" companies, he has biased his testing of the effects of multinationality, which is a variable in all but two chapters.

A second problem is that he does not always report all the correlation data for the independent variables to allow the reader to look for potential multicollinearity. For example in Chapter 3, IOS and two interaction terms including IOS were not reported in the correlation data. In Chapter 9, there is the same problem, but since he reports the data for the regression before and after the interaction term is added, it is apparent that there is a significant multicollinearity problem that he does not note. The coefficient for one of the variables in the regression goes from 0.42 before the interaction term is added to –5.87 after it is added.

A third problem is with the regression in Chapter 11, where "q-value" is the independent variable and IOS is one of the dependent variables. Q-value is measured as the ratio of "value of the firm to book value of total assets" (p. 177). IOS is measured as a composite of market-to-book assets, market-to-book equity, and earnings/price ratio. This has the effect of putting essentially the same measure on both sides of the regression. Since no correlation data is presented, it is not known what effect, if any, this might have on the analysis.

UNEVEN EDITING

The number of typographic and other editing errors in this book is unacceptable for an author and publisher of this reputation. I noted more than two pages of editing errors and I was not examining the text closely. They begin on the very first page of the book, when Chapter 6 is left out of the description of the contents, and continue to almost the final page when a variable that is not included in the described regression equation shows up in the table of reported results. Many errors are such that it is difficult to determine the integrity of the reported results. One of the worst examples is on pp. 168–169, where the discussion of results states:

> "In addition, the variable of interest, IOS, is significant at the 0.01 level, with a one-tailed test, and *its sign is negative*. Because high growth was coded as 1, the *positive sign* of IOS indicates that discretionary accruals of high growth firms were higher than low growth firms ..." (continuing in the next paragraph) "This growth variable was significant and *negatively signed* ..." (emphasis added).

The exhibit to which this discussion refers has the variable IOS with a positive sign, but the associated *t*-statistic has a negative sign.

SUMMARY

In summary, although the subject matter is of interest and the author's treatment of it begins with promise, the book does not provide a consistent and coherent analysis of the investment opportunity set. As the author notes at the end of Chapter 1, "More work needs to be done to refine both the definition and measurement of growth opportunities or investment opportunity set" (p. 8). In the first two chapters of the book, the author provides a good (but brief) summary of the literature and develops a model that begins to address the definition and measurement issues. Expanding and concentrating on this subject area, instead of performing the additional, multiple analyses utilizing IOS as an explanatory variable would improve the text. If the reader is seeking a "starting point" to examine the issues surrounding the investment opportunity set; this book could provide it. My only caveat relates to the state of its editing.

Frankensteins of Fraud
The 20th Century's Top Ten White-Collar Criminals.

By Joseph T. Wells.
(Obsidian Publishing Company, 800 West Avenue, Austin, Texas; 2000, 386 pages; $29.00. As of May 2001, this book could only be purchased through Obsidian Publishing Company at 800-245-3321).

Reviewed by Larry M. Parker
Case Western Reserve University.

The career of Joseph T. Wells, CFE, CPA, has been largely dedicated to white-collar crime investigation. Mr. Wells has been an independent auditor, and an FBI white-collar crime investigator. He is also the founder of the Association of Certified Fraud Examiners. His main interest in writing this book is to provide insight into why some of the most notorious white-collar criminals chose to "flaunt the law, mock decency, and steal relentlessly and without remorse." (from the Foreword by Dr. Gilbert Geis) The title is designed to provide a parallel between the monster created by Dr. Victor Frankenstein and white-collar criminals. The monster was created by the greed of Dr. Frankenstein. White-collar criminals are monsters created by ". . . the greed of their victims . . ." in the 20th Century (from the Preface by Joseph T. Wells) Mr. Wells believes understanding such criminals is important because reforms designed to stop such criminals have not worked. At the end of the chapter on Stanley Goldblum (of the Equity Funding Corporation scandal) he states, "It appears, almost 30 years later, that the reformers went unanswered. If anything, the financial terrain is worse than ever, teeming with mob-run brokerages, billion-dollar Ponzi schemes, and Internet pickpockets." (p. 168) Mr. Wells believes white-collar monsters are thriving among us, and he has written this book to provide insight into the methods and motives of such criminals.

The book describes ten white-collar criminals and their criminal methods. An Afterword summarizes key aspects of the criminals. The criminals are discussed in chronological order, and the discussions provide a view of an historical trend in white-collar crime. This review will briefly describe the author's discussion of the criminals, and then provide general comments on the book.

The first criminal is the only woman discussed, Cassie Chadwick (1857–1907), the Most Notorious Woman of the Age. Ms. Chadwick had a lisp and was deaf in one ear, causing her to seem a bit retarded. But she was extremely crafty, and from an early age bragged that she would become so rich that she would have to answer only to Queen Victoria (Ms. Chadwick was born in Canada). Although she had little education, she was able to fleece several prominent financiers using a variety of schemes, and became known as the "Queen of Finance." She was imprisoned several times, and died in jail.

Mr. Charles Ponzi (1882–1949) left Parma, Italy, hastily to avoid the Black Hand. Although he was fanatically driven to be rich, he was a failure at virtually everything he attempted. He spent time in several jails, and studied the methods of prominent con men while in the Atlanta penitentiary. In 1920 he worked a postal coupon and money exchange scheme, promising 50% returns in three months, and 100% returns in six months. He would "show them the money" (page 38) by paying investors from money provided by more recent investors. Within a year he had scammed the American public for 20 million dollars. There were never enough postal coupons printed to cover even a small fraction of 20 million dollars. Mr. Ponzi's scheme eventually earned him about twelve years in jail, and then deportation to Italy. He died in a nursing home as an impoverished ward of the State of Brazil.

Mr. Ivar Kreuger (1880–1932), the Swedish Match King, had a most remarkable run of over two decades. His financial empire amassed a huge fortune, built mainly on Krueger's ability to virtually monopolize the world-wide match industry. He appeared on the cover of magazines such as *Time* and *The Saturday Evening Post*, and helped several countries out of financial difficulties (often in exchange for monopoly positions for his matches). But as his empire grew out of control, he began to play a classic shell game with the assets of the companies in his conglomerate. If the books did not balance, he would instruct the accountants to debit the difference to him personally. But the depression of the 1920s began to restrict his ability to acquire more assets to cover his massive shortages. In desperation he printed millions of counterfeit Italian bonds, but even these could not cover his shortages. When his empire began to unravel, Kreuger committed suicide.

Philip Musica, a.k.a. Dr. Frank D. Coster (1884–1938), was the most noto-rious of a family of cons, which, some believe, saved a company named McKesson & Robbins. In 1923 Doctor Coster (fictitious Ph.D. and M.D. from Heidelberg University), with his mother and three brothers, formed a small pharmaceutical company, Girard and Company. The company experienced a remarkable turnaround because Coster and his family used the company's pharmaceutical business to cover a very lucrative bootleg liquor operation during prohibition. Dr. Coster met some of his best customers, such as Dutch

Schultz, while serving time under his real name, Philip Musica. A special government grant allowed Girard and Company to openly produce alcohol, ostensibly for government use. The amount of "shampoo" Girard and Company sold allegedly would have washed every head in the world. This successful company allowed the Coster family to acquire the larger, very established pharmaceutical company, McKesson & Robbins in 1926. The Coster family had an excellent business plan for McKesson & Robbins. The company organized independent pharmacies across the United States and Canada to help them defend against Walgreen's and Liggett's. It also converted its illegal alcohol operations to a legal subsidiary just as prohibition was repealed. However, the Costers set up a dummy subsidiary in Canada for "crude drugs" such as vanilla beans, dragon's blood and ketone musk. The large amount of inventory never existed – the subsidiary was faked to make the company books look better. Some of the inventory was preposterous. The inventory amount of ketone musk, derived from glands of Himalyan musk deer, exceeded the combined lifetime production of all such deer in existence. When the false subsidiary was uncovered, Dr. Coster committed suicide, and the rest of the family was arrested.

Stanley Goldblum (1927–) outlasted four other founding partners of the Equity Funding Corporation, a life insurance and mutual fund investment company. This blend of insurance and investment was innovative, and was credited with revitalizing a struggling life insurance industry. Goldblum was able to wield total control over the business by 1964, which was the first year Equity Funding operated as a public company. Goldblum and his officers employed many illegal techniques to cook the books. A shell company was formed to fund an illegal loan to Goldblum, and future expected revenues were counted in current year numbers when profits did not look satisfactory to Goldblum. The company officers printed $25 million worth of counterfeit bonds from major corporations to use as collateral. But the main fraudulent technique employed was to generate fake policies, then sell these policies, bundled among legitimate policies, to other insurance companies. The dummy policies were counted as revenue for the company, and the resale (reinsurance) of the fake policies generated cash. In addition, Equity Funding would kill off some of the fake policyholders, and receive cash from the insurance company holding the fake policy. A group of young women in a building removed from all other Equity Funding buildings generated thousands of fake policies – over 10,000 fake policies in 1970 alone. This massive fraud required lots of computer work and constant attention by a masterful programmer, and Equity Funding became the first major case of fraud using computer technology. Both the IRS and SEC missed golden opportunities to catch Equity

Funding, and when the independent auditors were provided with evidence of the massive fraud, the auditors turned the evidence over to Goldblum. In 1973 Goldblum and more than twenty other executives were indicted. The auditors, who missed more than 64,000 fake insurance policies, $25 million in fake bonds, and at least $100 million in missing assets, were also indicted. Goldblum spent several years in prison, and has recently been tried for various fraudulent activities as a partner in a string of medical clinics.

Robert Vesco (1935–) dropped out of high school, but was able to pose as an engineer early in his career. He began making deals out of his car, and was eventually able to persuade financiers to back him in acquiring several small companies. In 1971 Vesco was able to use these companies, which he had largely left languishing, to generate enough cash to gain control of a troubled mutual fund company, Fund of Funds. Vesco was able to gain control only after he had employees physically break into a Swiss safe deposit box to obtain additional stock shares to swing the shareholder vote to his side – barely. Vesco immediately began to loot Fund of Funds in every way. The SEC soon accused Vesco of draining $224 million for personal use. Vesco attempted to buy influence in Washington to turn the SEC away. He contributed to president Nixon's campaign, and provided money and helicopters to an organization called CREEP, which funded the activities of G. Gordon Liddy. Vesco hid his loot in various shells throughout the Caribbean. Vesco was never caught to be tried in the U.S. for his fraud. He received protection for many years from the president of Costa Rica. Vesco later moved to his own island in the Caribbean next to, and possibly under the protection of, Carlos Lehder-Rivas, perhaps the worst of the Caribbean cartel drug-lords. Eventually, Vesco moved to Cuba and was granted immunity by Fidel Castro. But in 1996 a Cuban tribunal sentenced him to 13 years in prison for fraudulently promoting a cure for cancer, and he is currently in a Cuban jail.

Eddie "Crazy Eddie" Antar (1947–) was a member of an entire family of crooked retailers. After an initial failure, Eddie Antar, at age 21, opened Crazy Eddie's Ultra Linear Sound Experience in Brooklyn, New York. He hired an actor to portray Crazy Eddie in commercials, and soon began making retail history in electronics. This was a family business, and family members were paid cash "off the books." Eddie and his father skimmed from the business, probably $3 to $4 million a year, putting the money mainly in Israeli banks where it would not be detected by U.S. officials. Eddie became a physically strong, drunken, womanizing thug, and his family could no longer influence him to be reasonable. He decided to take Crazy Eddie's public, and began skimming less each year starting in 1979. Stocks in Crazy Eddie's superstores carried the highest price/earning ratio in the industry. But inventories were inflated by millions, and the Antars had to resort to more and more risky techniques to keep inventory up. They were able to keep sales artificially inflated by pumping in funds through Israeli and Panamanian banks. The auditors never noticed numerous individual checks for retail sales in amounts from $75,000 $150,000. Money was "borrowed" from suppliers – the cash was recorded, but not the debt – at balance sheet dates. Eventually, sales began to stagnate, and the Antars were not able to keep up the fraud schemes they had in place. Eddie was able to sell over $25 million in stock before the share price began to plummet. When a takeover of Crazy Eddie's was organized, the Antars no longer owned enough stock to fight it, and the massive fraud was discovered. Eventually, Eddie served about eight years in jail. Other officers, mostly family members, served lesser jail terms.

John Bennett (1938–) provides an example of a criminal who stole from non-profits. He developed a Ponzi scheme based upon promising non-profit organization that he could help them raise money. Bennett seemed to have no ability to manage money. His first business effort ended in bankruptcy, and his family was living on church charity. But in 1982 Bennett founded Human Services Systems, and later the Center/Foundation of New Era Philanthropy. These organizations were established mainly to help non-profit organizations raise money – a lot more money than the non-profits could hope to raise through their own efforts. The non-profits were kept happy with their contributions to Bennett's organizations, because Bennett paid the non-profits a healthy return using donations/contributions of other non-profits. Bennett became adept at kiting and floating funds between his organizations. Millions of dollars floated into Bennett's pockets. Bennett and close associates owned expensive homes and cars, and took lavish trips. Bennett kept company with top financial, government, social and religious leaders in addition to people at the top of many of the most prominent non-profits. Bennett was able to waylay early questions about lack of investment assets and questionable record keeping (e.g. a "contribution" that was to be repaid with interest was recorded as cash, but no liabilities were recorded) because of his "kingdom focus." He maintained all his work was the name of God, and that God would provide all that was needed. He duped some of the most prominent financial people in the world. By 1995 he was no longer able to address the suspicions of numerous accountants and investors, and his schemes completely collapsed when Prudential filed suit against him. Bennett mounted an insanity defense, claiming he believed he had met with anonymous donors who would provide for his needs. He claimed that when he touched his office doorknob, "The donors appeared." The courts did not buy it, and Bennett was sentenced to twelve years in federal prison with no parole.

Mark Whitacre (1957–) earned a Ph.D. from Cornell. He was an exceptionally dedicated worker, and in 1990 was hired to head the biotechnology division of Archer Daniels Midland. He was hired by Mick Andreas, vice chairman of ADM and son of the CEO and Chairman of ADM, Dwayne Andreas. The Andreas family treated Whitacre as a member of the family. Mick Andreas, designated to become the CEO of ADM upon the retirement of his father, planned to make Whitacre president. The thirty-two year-old golden boy of ADM soon reported that his biotechnology operations had experienced apparent sabotage. A mysterious telephone call to Whitacre from a Mr. Fujiwara seemed to suggest that ADM's Japanese competitors may have been responsible. Mick Andreas and other ADM executives eventually decided to handle this situation as they had on other occasions, by entering into price fixing negotiations with their competitors. Whitacre contacted the FBI, and spied on the price fixing meetings for the FBI. His testimony helped convict Mick Andreas and another ADM official of price fixing, and ADM paid $100 million in fines. Dwayne Andreas had to appoint a nephew as CEO rather than his son. But Whitacre himself was dishonest. For some reason, he told everyone he had been orphaned, and he was adopted. This was not true. He claimed his Ph.D. was in nutritional biochemistry, but it was actually in nutrition. His résumé also stated he had an MBA from Northwestern University, but he never attended that university. Mr. Fujiwara, who basically started the whole ADM price fixing, never existed. Whitacre invented him. And Whitacre embezzled as much as $10 million dollars from ADM. Whitacre ended up being convicted in 1999 as the ringleader of the price fixing scheme, and received the stiffest jail sentence of all the defendants, even though he was the FBI's informant.

Michael Milken (1946–) revolutionized financial institutions with his junk-bond offerings. He began trading junk bonds in 1968 with a small firm named Drexel Ripley Harriman. Milken was instrumental in making Drexel a financial force by 1980, and in 1982 he led Drexel into the merger and acquisition business. His approach drove the M&A wave of the 1980s. The ruthless, arrogant tyrant drove his financial mercenaries mercilessly, and he courted despicable allies like Victor Posner and Ivan Boesky. Milken's arrogance caused him to cross the line of insider trading as a matter of course with no fear of recourse. But in 1989 he was charged with 98 counts of insider trading, and in 1991 he pled guilty to six felony offenses. He served eighteen months of a sentence that was originally ten years. He kept hundreds of millions.

The Afterword, "Why They Were Monsters," discusses the ten criminals. But the author never justifies his contention that these monsters were created by the greed of their victims. There is no reason to assume that investors in the publicly held companies such as those of Ivar Kreugar, Philip Musica, Stanley Goldblum or "Crazy Eddie" Antar were greedy. Greed is avarice, an excessive or rapacious desire for money. The victims were often fooled, perhaps relying too much on regulators or independent auditors. But it is not clear the victims, in general, were driven by an abnormal desire for money. The author does not discuss where we should draw the line between an acceptable desire for money and greed, but it would have been interesting if the author had provided his perspective on this.

There are a couple of weaknesses in the book. It is disappointing that the book does not attempt to better explain the mentality of these felons. It is clear these criminals were possessed by all consuming greed, and all demonstrated incredibly bold cunning. It is instructive to read how the various schemes were executed. But the author does not really provide insight into how these criminals became so driven by the desire for money that they could prey mercilessly on their victims. The author missed an opportunity to help us delve deeply into the human element of fraud. The stories of each of the ten monsters of fraud are very interesting, but they are often hard to follow. Many of the chapters jump back and forth in time, and insufficient dates are provided to help the reader understand exactly where we are in the story. Also, some stories bounce between the financial dealings and the personal lives of the criminals, making the stories seem disjointed. The personal lives are often as interesting as the frauds, and are presumably inserted to provide more complete perspectives of the criminals. But they do not help the reader understand why these criminals became monsters.

I believe auditing professors should examine this book for possible inclusion in coursework. The book is interesting and provides many insights into fraud. But because of the weaknesses mentioned in the preceding paragraph, some professors may decide the book is not appropriate for their course needs.

Delivering the Promise: How to Attract, Manage, and Retain Human Capital.

By Brian Friedman, James Hatch, David M. Walker, all of Arthur Andersen. Simon & Schuster Trade, September 1998, ISBN 0684856581, 225 pages, $26.00.

Reviewed by Julia Grant
Case Western Reserve University.

This book documents an evaluation structure for a firm's processes in managing its human capital, a structure applied, at least when the book was written, by Arthur Andersen LLP in its consulting practice. The coverage is thorough, and provides some interesting insights into how one might encourage a firm to increase its understanding of the importance of this sometimes under-recognized resource.

For the accountant reading the book, surely one of the first things that come to mind is whether the authors will discuss issues around the fact that this important asset, human capital, is not included on balance sheets. The book does mention this point, and promises some discussion of the topic, but it falls short in this area.

Evaluation, strategy, and action steps for managing human capital are all discussed in varying levels of detail. For the human resources manager who is interested in evaluating current programs or, perhaps, trying some new ideas, this could be a useful handbook. It includes not only process descriptions in the body of the book, but also extensive implementation material in appendices. These include worksheets for planning initiatives, incorporating such areas as recruitment, compensation, pensions, and employee communications. There are extensive worksheets for evaluating and managing pension plans from a human resource point of view, though the types of plans and pension cost analysis are also interesting for the accounting perspective.

One brief chapter discusses "Assessing Human Capital Cost." No systematic approaches are offered, though problems with some measures such as revenues "per employee" are discussed briefly, with a nod to full time equivalents. The suggested solution for use in ratios is to calculate a denominator called "human expenses," which includes any costs incurred that provide human services, including both direct employees and adjuncts such as consultants. Another chapter "Assessing Human Capital Value" highlights the questions and difficulties that arise in this endeavor, and talks about measuring value relative to cost. However, the text offers no suggestions for how these measures might affect the accounting function. The measures discussed bring to mind the Business Reporting Model; clearly there are some possibilities for expanding reporting around the use of human resources in the functions of the firm. But this text does not develop that notion.

The book appears to achieve its main goal, the provision of a handbook for human resources professionals. Its discussions of good practices for the management of people provide food for thought when considering the impact of the absence of these "assets" on the balance sheet and when considering what might be included in an expanded Business Reporting Model. However, the authors have not provided specific guidance for the accounting profession in addressing these issues.

Managing Multinationals in the Middle East.

By Wagdy M. Abdallah.
Quorum Books, Westport, Conn. 2000, 288 pages, ISBN 1-56720-267-5, $64.50.

Reviewed by Garen Markarian
Case Western Reserve University.

In his salient exposition of Middle Eastern culture, religion, and financial concerns, Mr. Abdallah has the distinction of providing an in-depth account of the region's promise for multinational corporations. His focus is on five countries that Americans most often associate with the Middle East: Israel for its unique status as a Western-style country in an Arab world, Egypt as the largest and most educated Arab country in Northern Africa, the resource rich Kuwait and Saudi Arabia representing the countries of the gulf region, and Jordan as an emerging market that has contemporaneously started initiatives of openness toward western investment, and itself positioned as a cultural moderate between Egypt and the Gulf countries. Drawing upon the land's rich heritage in trade and import export activity, the author underlies the unique cultural aspects and their effects on accounting and tax issues such as financial reporting, performance evaluation, and transfer pricing. This book is highly recommended to all those interested in having a quick introduction to the region's culture, business traditions, and accounting characteristics. It is also recommended to graduate level international accounting courses, and all business executives dealing in the Middle East.

Mr. Abdallah gives us a concise account of the economic, legal and political characteristics of the five countries. Starting from a historical perspective, he draws the effect of multinational corporations and the need of global financial markets for relevant accounting information; the author outlines four different accounting models that can suit the unique environmental and societal needs of those countries. Models which at the same time hold promise of the necessary flexibility for the influx of foreign capital. Middle Eastern countries having yet to develop their own systems, Mr. Abdallah discusses the unique accounting aspects of each of those countries as being imported from trade with British colonizers and later American influences. He highlights the differences found between those systems and U.S. GAAP and IASC regarding inventories, consolidations, accounting for income taxes, provisions and reserves, asset valuation. There are lengthy sections elucidating the effect of the Islamic culture as manifested through power distances, collectivism, uncertainty avoidance, and masculinity. In this section the author clarifies many ambiguities regarding the Islamic religion and their basic tenets toward trade, women, acceptance of foreigners. He also touches upon basic values such as dignity, honor, and religious values of piety. These sections are especially interesting because they give a candid account on the many misconceptions held about Arabs and their values, the author gives us a first-hand glimpse into the Arab character which is considerably different than stereotypic representations influenced by the region's identification with war, terrorism, masculine dominance, etc.

The latter part of the book discusses purely accounting issues; there is a lengthy section on performance measurement and the evaluation of MNCs and their managers. The author proposes a method where managers are evaluated on a system that doesn't account them for uncontrollable environmental factors such as the efficiency of legal systems, educational variables, economic stability, local skills, etc. Almost a third of the latter part of the book is devoted to the tax systems of those countries, and international pricing issues that depict the unique expertise of Mr. Abdallah in these matters. Each country's tax system is investigated, and the treatment of capital gains, dividends, interest is included. What I found interesting was the author's discussion on special tax treatments and incentives that are available for multinationals in an effort to lure foreign capital and expertise. He draws upon tax holidays, duty free zones, tax relief, low interest loans, etc. Then there is the rather lengthy three-chapter treatment of international transfer pricing issues, and how to minimize exchange rate risk, and how to manage cash flows. I wish this section dealt less with the mechanics of transfer pricing and more with the identification of unique accounting and financial aspects of those countries, dealing with direct opportunities and threats affecting multinationals in the region. The last chapter of the book discusses the future business environment of the region and its effect on the future of accounting development in the region. All in all, this is a captivating account that provides a first hand exposition of the regions unique aspects, the specific accounting treatments, and a highlighting of the issues involved when deciding to invest in the Middle East. Even though somewhat bureaucratic and unstable, the Middle East is a resource-rich area that is untapped, with a wealth of opportunities for all those venturers and those who go the extra mile to attain organizational goals.

Printed and bound by CPI Group (UK) Ltd, Croydon, CR0 4YY

08/05/2025

01864950-0004